SEX IS...

SEX IS...

Memoir of a Woman's Sexuality

Pallavi Barnwal

BLOOMSBURY
NEW DELHI • LONDON • OXFORD • NEW YORK • SYDNEY

BLOOMSBURY INDIA
Bloomsbury Publishing India Pvt. Ltd
Second Floor, LSC Building No. 4, DDA Complex, Pocket C – 6 & 7,
Vasant Kunj, New Delhi 110070

BLOOMSBURY, BLOOMSBURY INDIA and the Diana logo are trademarks of Bloomsbury Publishing Plc

This edition published in 2021

ISBN: PB: 978-93-89165-44-9; eBook: 978-93-89165-46-3

2 4 6 8 10 9 7 5 3 1

Typeset in Manipal Technologies Limited
Printed and bound in India by Sanat Printers, Kundli

CONTENTS

PROLOGUE

This memoir is an intensely personal and brutal account of people and incidents that have shaped my life. Maya Angelou once said, 'Most people simply age, they don't grow.' And I have known both ageing and growing in my three and a half decades of life. I realised that no growth happens without pain. There is a lot of disruption as the sapling erupts from the seed and rises above the ground to become a bough-laden tree. For years, I lay dormant, buried under the spell of indoctrination, obeying traditions and customs. Then one day an opportunity presented itself and I opened my wrought-iron windows wide and smelled the air of freedom. The autumn of my life had passed and I was entering my spring. This spring tasted sweeter because I had braved through storms in the past.

It took a Herculean effort to claim what I truly was destined for and desired. Often our destinies and desires diverge and that results in a deep discontentment. I have seen many people and their families; some families decide the destinies of people, telling them what they can do and what they cannot. I took charge of my destiny from the hands of people whom I had entrusted to safeguard it. I had a string of affairs: simultaneous, sexual, asexual, with younger men, with older men. I underwent a divorce and decided to not ask for alimony: a decision I quickly regretted after I saw a swish, heavily tattooed woman being handed over a 15-lakhs cheque by her terrified husband and father-in-law. I almost contracted an STD twice when the promiscous man I was with insisted on having intercourse without a condom. I have supported two unemployed male partners, consequently going broke myself. I have self-harmed my body as I tried to cope with life's horrible troubles. These scars on my skin are remnants of my pain and suffering, but they also show my will to survive. I turned my attention away from my child's life just so I could focus on my personal and spiritual growth.

Despite all of this, I'm terribly terrified; terrified of men who may molest or rape, terrified of the feelings I develop for men who are nothing but one-night flings, terrified of the innocence of my child who does not know of the evil that exists in the world, terrified of my Baba who always thought I was an illegitimate child, terrified of my brain which has only learnt to mistrust. These fears are difficult to overlook. I both hate and love men; love them with all the intense emotions of my heart, and I hate them for their penises that, unlike vaginas, cannot be penetrated.

But then again, my spirit is indomitable like the mighty Himalayas. I will survive every snowstorm. I'm happy that I have not outlived all my passions, which gives me things to look forward to. I'm happy to have discovered myself, my wants, my agonies and my loathing. I've reinvented my aspirations: from being a nine-to-five worker to becoming an independent sexuality educator.

This is me. Ready for you to read me, uncover me and discover me.

Childhood

Looking back, I think I have had the most enriching childhood among my friends. There was a perfect balance of desolation and hope; just the way a cook balances spices and salt in their cooking, not too high, not too low. Too much desolation could have made me a loner and too much hope would make me an impractical daydreamer. I'm a bit of both. I sometimes resort to an intense emotional response—inward anger, dejection and pessimism—as a coping mechanism in my interpersonal relationships, but I am also an empathetic, intelligent person. One's childhood is the blueprint for one's future. I won't say that one needs a lot of wealth to build a happy future, but a lot of decisions one makes as an adult are based on values, beliefs and attitudes that are founded very early in one's childhood. If I could sum up my childhood in one word, I would say 'unrest'.

As a seven-year-old, I would wake up from my sleep listening to Ma's muffled whimpers. She would sit on the floor near the mat on which Baba slept, rubbing his feet and requesting him to come to bed. He would gently decline her pleas and her wails would turn louder and louder. This happened every night. Our mother would wait for Nishu and me to fall asleep before going to Baba and asking him to come to bed. I pretended to sleep but sneakily watched my mother's tribulations, day in and day out. This memory lodged itself deep in my subconscious mind and kept reappearing for years.

Like my mother, I believed that one had to surrender to one's husband completely to save one's relationship and marriage. I emulated my mother by becoming dependent on my male companions, giving in to their demands even when I didn't have to.

Baba always had an elusive presence in my childhood. He would take us out sometimes: during festivals, when he received promotions or on our birthdays. He was mostly inconspicuous otherwise. He would return late at night, park his car near the garage gate and honk. Inside the house, Ma would wake me up and ask me to go and open the gate. It was usually past midnight when he returned home. I sleepily tottered to the gate and opened it. Like a programmed robot, I used to come back to my room and go back to sleep.

It's weird how memories get imprinted in our minds. What do these memories serve to do? What is their purpose? Sometimes I resent them and sometimes I want to go back in time and live through those times again. The days of our lives are not just days; they are stations on the journey of our lives. Stations where we sit and chart our routes, decide where we want to go. Looking back, it seems like I charted a somewhat haphazard route to contentment and happiness. I had the tools, there was a lot of information, but there is a difference between the information that helps people in their jobs and the information that helps them live their lives. Throughout my life, I strived to earn well because that is what I was taught to aspire for, as a child. I strived to be unconditionally giving because that is what I saw women around me do. No one taught me how to dream or how to find happiness.

I came to terms with the word 'suicide' quite early in my life. It happened near my old house when I was seven. A woman in my neighbourhood, who was in her early 30s, hanged herself. She left behind two small children. I will not name her husband because men always have it easier when such adversities strike. Their parents find them a second partner but the children rarely find another mother who holds them with the same affection as their deceased parent. I remember asking Ma about what happened to her, why she had taken such an extreme step. Ma did not have any answers. She said, '*No one knows why people take such drastic decisions. We had no clue what was going through her mind. She seemed to be doing alright and did not look like she wanted to end her life.*'

I do not know what urges people to end their lives! I have seen poor people, homeless beggars, surviving in the thickest of poverty; people who do not have even a mouthful to eat, people in ragged clothes. I'm yet to come across a thoroughly drafted suicide note. When I find one, perhaps I will be able to understand the reasons that propel a person to take this extreme step. I have a strong feeling that the fundamental reason that drives a person to suicide is fairly common. The reasons vary but the psychological feeling of loss remains. I have been in a similar mental state at least thrice in my life. I survived only because I wasn't focused on taking my own life.

The number of failed suicide attempts is much more than the number of successful ones. I never came to know the reason but I know that Reena Bua, my unmarried aunt, had tried killing herself. She planned it meticulously, which made it seem like she was serious in her intent to end her life. Again, this was a standard case: there were no superficial signs of distress or nervous breakdown. But there were subtle signs and I now know that these are the signs that must be paid attention to rather than ignored. For my aunt, these signs appeared almost three months before she tried taking her life. She used to stay in a hostel and was studying to become a doctor. She was good-looking and was the only sister among her five brothers. Marriage proposals poured in from well-educated, cultured and well-off grooms even before she graduated, pointing to the acute shortage of educated girls in our community. No one could ever imagine someone so popular wanting to take her own life.

But there were signs. She used to visit our home on vacation. Suddenly, the frequency of her visits increased and she came over almost every weekend. Her college was an eight-hour bus ride from where we lived. Baba was naturally puzzled as to why she would waste so much time commuting when she could be studying. He decided not to bring it up because she had always been a brilliant student and had a promising career ahead of her. I, for one, smelled a rat. Her visits were all impromptu and she never carried any clothes and books. She borrowed clothes from me and looked distracted as she spent most of her days indoors, rarely stepping out to meet friends or even go shopping.

And then a few months later, we got to know from a sudden phone call that she had tried taking her life. She consumed poison in the wee hours and was found unconscious in the morning, her body in a pool of her vomit. My father wrapped her immobile body in a bedsheet and rushed to the hospital. The doctor, after hours of keeping her under observation, finally proclaimed that she was out of danger. I was at home, getting to know all about her situation through the gossip of my aunts. Homemakers emerge on such occasions, passing each piece of news with much care. Each news carries the signature hearsay of its carrier. If you hear the same scuttlebutt from different women in the same house, you wouldn't know whom to believe since each version is equally inaccurate.

Some believed that Reena Bua consumed poison because she was pregnant. The women spreading this malicious rumour were arch-rivals of our family and jumped at the opportunity to smear disgrace on us. For some, Reena Bua consumed poison because she had lost all hopes of getting married. As for me, I felt it was a tactic to bring attention to herself. I wonder what sets apart failed attempts from the highly unfortunate successful attempts? Lack of will, lack of experience? I think failed suicidal attempts offer an interesting insight into the convolutions of the human psyche. We do not want to be dead, we just want to pretend that we want to be.

I think our ends are defined by our beginnings. When people say they change, they merely adapt their patterns of coping; the underlying confusion and struggle remain the same. I try to find inferences from my own life and the lives of people around me; we all have learnt to mimic our personalities so perfectly that it is impossible to decipher one's true self. Reena Bua, barring a short spell of marriage, could never come to peace with her life. After losing her husband to swine flu in 2009, she was again left desolate. She had a fleeting affair with a married co-worker, a timid, fearful man who lurched away when my brother and I spotted him with Reena Bua in a flea market. That same night, I secretly went through her mobile phone where she poured her heart out in front of that limp-hearted coward, drawing parallels with the love of the protagonist in *Pakeezah* (a 1972 film starring Meena Kumari that was based on a tale of unrequited love). Bollywood films play a big role in dumbing down our brains. I, for one, have not been able to come out unscathed from the 'happily ever after' dream those films sold to us. I am still chasing my 'happily ever after' but with different people. Such a relentless pursuit love has been!

Reena Bua had met her second husband on a matrimonial site. The search for a life partner is so profitable that there is a marketplace that peddles these profiles in a la carte fashion. You pick some, taste them, show them, try them, fuck them, keep them or discard them. The match was made, she had met her knight in shining armour with a paunch. She got the social approval, vermillion and sarcasm from an embittered woman like me.

Since I developed a sharp intuition very early in life, I sometimes wonder if God had chosen me to be His special child. In the past, out of anger and frustration, I have sworn at idols and photographs of various gods and goddesses. I have smudged His photograph with ash from burnt incense sticks and have spat on idols. I always felt, until two years back, that, God had conspired in a vicious plan against me. And I wanted to defeat him in his Machiavellian plans. I hatched a plot to fool Him so He would finally spare me.

I always thought that I was under God's surveillance, that He was tracking all my happiness and plotting ways of undoing it. To fool God, I decided to wish for things I didn't want. When my board exams were on, I was nervous before my maths exam because I had not studied enough. I fervently prayed to God, asking Him to fail me in the paper, hoping that He would listen to my prayers and grant me the opposite. When the results came in, I had passed by a small margin. My belief that God grants me everything I don't wish for became even stronger. Since then, I have mostly been a pessimist.

Since I was four, Baba has held a grudge against me. I could never understand why he shouted at me for little or no reason, why he never loved me and never bought me presents. All the while, I saw him showering gifts on friends, distant relatives and even strangers. He used to make me wait for a whole hour before he picked me up from my physics tuition. There was a Bengali girl, Antara, who was in class with me. I remember her father picking her up immediately after the class got over. I, on the other hand, kept waiting long after everyone else had left. Though the tutor never complained or asked me to leave her house, I always felt like she was doing me a favour by letting me stay. There were a few rare instances when Baba would be late by only 10 minutes. He would stand outside my class and honk his scooter horn. I would run with joy to the balcony to see if it was him. For some girls, it was normal to see their fathers come to pick them up on time; for me, it was a gift I seldom received.

Baba was promoted in his job when I was eight. We soon moved to a bigger flat in a posh neighbourhood of Bokaro, the town where we lived. I could sense the difference between the kids of that neighbourhood and the ones who lived in our older neighbourhood. We stayed in an industrial town whose neighbourhoods were earmarked for people belonging to specific economic classes. Before moving, we lived in the E-F class neighbourhood that had 500-square-feet one-bedroom houses. These were double-storeyed buildings with four flats on each floor. These quarters were allotted to workers and schoolteachers. The workers belonged to the labour class; they toiled in factories and went on strikes when their demands were not met. Baba joined as a worker and was promoted to being a supervisor. Which is when we moved from E-class to the C-class quarters. Each social stratum was unique in its customs, attire and lifestyles, a difference that was obvious to me even when I was so young.

The kids of the E-F colonies wore plain, tailored dresses. All their store-bought, ready-made clothes were reserved to be worn on special occasions like birthdays, wedding parties and festivals. The tailored dresses were cheaper than the ready-made ones. I remember Ma bringing back rolls of floral printed fabric from our village, which she would use to sew my dresses. All my dresses were identical except for their prints. On my birthdays, Baba would take me to the Ram Mandir market, where he would buy me a ready-made frock, which would always be so much nicer than the ones my mother sewed for me. I would be thrilled and overjoyed every time he took me out to buy me a frock.

There were no elaborate birthday parties thrown in the E-F locality. Kids celebrated their birthdays with their immediate family members. I was never invited to any birthday party and nor did Ma invite other kids to mine. I remember my birthday one year when Baba took me to Ram Mandir to buy me a shiny yellow frock with frills at the bottom. After our trip to the market, he took me to a house that was not ours. There was a beautiful woman in that house and Baba behaved extremely politely with her. Way more than he ever did with Ma or us. I was startled to discover this side of his personality. The woman was neatly dressed in a peach-coloured sari and her hair was braided into two plaits. She was prettier, younger and thinner than Ma. Baba placed a banana walnut loaf cake on a table in the woman's verandah as she proceeded to light the candles. They both then sang the birthday song out loud as I nervously cut the cake with fidgety hands. I was not comfortable in her presence; I was meeting her for the first time and yet was being forced to celebrate my birthday with her. I could not express my discomfort because that would ruffle Baba's temper and I was in no mood for a bashing on my birthday.

In the days and months that followed, our visits to the woman's house increased. Strangely, my mother never accompanied us on those visits. Baba talked at length with the woman but rarely with her husband, who seemed to be a mute spectator just like me. She served us chilled rose-flavoured soft drinks along with delicious home-made snacks. Ma never prepared such delicious things at home, so I ravenously ate them all within five minutes of being served. The woman never brought in a second serving, which made the first serving even more sought after. Those snacks were not the lone reason I liked going to her house. The second reason was the bookshelf that stacked rows of paperbacks. That wooden bookshelf was my paradise. It was my introduction to the alien world of books. Nowhere had I seen anyone spending money to buy books and then storing those books. That world was a refuge from the pain of abandonment I faced in my juvenile years. I started picking some books and took them back home with a promise that I would return them the week after. I never fulfilled that promise unless it was noticed by that aunt's spineless husband who had no qualms letting his wife have a dalliance with a rich man. Why was he even enquiring about the books when he could not question his immoral wife?

One day, Baba took me to her house after she said that she wanted to teach me to play the harmonium. I remember sitting cross-legged with her and practising the seven notes. Her delicate fingers pressed the white and black keys and pumped the bellow of the instrument. We never spoke much. She only talked to Baba. I soon began calling her Rose Aunty. I was instructed to; it made my Baba happier to hear me call her by this name. As a result, he treated me well. He asked me repeatedly as we left her house, 'Isn't Rose Aunty sweet?' I nodded my head not because I agreed but because that was the answer expected of me. I did not have the freedom to say no. When we reached home after the harmonium class, I saw Ma lying on her bed, her body shivering with fever. I cried seeing her in that state. She covered herself with a woollen blanket and feebly smiled at me. I felt a deep sense of guilt when I saw her in this state but I could do nothing. I did not have the money to buy her medicines and neither did she. I cried bitterly as I snuggled against her bosom. Ma kept quiet and held me close and tight. Baba was never quite bothered about her health. By God's grace, her fever came down after a few days.

At 13, it was difficult for me to fathom the sexual attraction between Baba and Rose Aunty but it was clear that he was besotted. I had read in some famous couplet that lovers express their love with their eyes; I could sense a sense of longing in the way Baba gazed at her. Sometimes it felt like I was sitting in a cinema hall, watching a silent romantic film. How naive I was! Then one day, I walked in on Baba kissing her. He had decided to visit her while I was out with him. Parking his car on the road, he went up to her first-floor apartment, asking me to wait in the car. It was 7:30 PM and I had waited for almost half an hour. I was bored and wanted to get home soon. So, I decided to walk up to Rose Aunty's apartment and call Baba. When I reached her door, I saw that it was half-shut. I went inside without knocking and what I saw inside was a scene that I will never be able to shake off my memory.

Baba and Aunty were sitting on adjacent folding chairs in the dining room at the back of the house. Rose Aunty was wearing a cream-coloured salwar kameez with her dupatta strewn around her neck. It flaunted her well-rounded breasts. They were enough to bring any man down on his knees and Baba was no exception.

As Rose Aunty sat braiding her daughter's hair, Baba was kissing Aunty on her face, ears and neck over and over again. She seemed to enjoy it too. I thought Baba would feel guilty once he saw me but he remained unfazed. He stopped kissing her and sat in silence. He probably thought that I was too young to know what was going on but I had already watched the film *Rangeela* and knew how adults kissed. Or maybe, he thought that there was nothing I could do to stop him from cheating on Ma.

Rose Aunty had tried to have children with her husband for 12 long years. Rumour had it that her daughter was born shortly after she met Baba. On his part, he was exceptionally affectionate towards Rose Aunty's daughter. There was no point comparing affection since he had none for my sibling and me.

That same year, when I was 13, our youngest uncle, whom the children fondly called Chhote Papa, came to stay with us for over a month. He had vacated his student accommodation in Patna and needed a place to stay before he joined his new job in Delhi. Chhote Papa had some moderate savings from his earnings as a tutor. Every Sunday, he fasted in observance of his faith in Goddess Durga and then broke his fast with some sweets. He would always take us along in his visits to the sweet shop, which made us very happy. Baba was busy spending all his time with Rose Aunty and barely took us out any more. On one such Sunday, Chhote Papa and I went to the market and both of us had a *rajbhog* each. After he was done paying for the sweets, Chhote Papa and I walked towards the parking lot. To my amazement, I saw a green Maruti 800 parked right in front of me; it looked exactly like Baba's car. I jumped in excitement and told Chhote Papa that I wanted to check the car's licence plate. JHBK88! Yes, it was Baba's car.

I was so happy and waited there to surprise Baba. In those days, theft was uncommon and Baba had left his car unlocked. I opened the door and sat in the front, next to the driver's seat, and waited for Baba to come back. And then I saw him coming out of the market, with Rose Aunty and their four-year-old child. They were walking towards the car. That illegitimate child (calling her this soothes the animosity I have for her in my heart) started stomping her feet and throwing tantrums the moment she saw me sitting next to the driver's seat. Even at that age, I realised that the front seat was not just a seat; it was my right and my inheritance. I refused to listen to Baba as he asked me to step out. After he forced me out of the car, I returned home heartbroken. Since then, I began to believe that the illegitimate has more power than the legitimate; this was true at least in my Baba's case. Years later, I replicated the same pattern in all my relationships. I was the illegitimate woman, the forbidden woman, the seductress. I refused to live the wretched life of someone's wife; for me, being a wife was synonymous with living the painful life that Ma lived. Mistresses always have more power than the legally wedded wife; Baba had taught me that.

I feel very connected to Rose Aunty's memory; she had changed my life. She was beautiful and well-groomed and carried herself well. She cooked delicious dishes, kept her house clean, was joyous and received love and affection from two men. I once saw a bundle of semi-naked photographs of her lying underneath books on the top shelf of Baba's bookshelf. In them, she stood near a stream of water, all wet, her blouse barely managing to hold her abundant bosom; her hands were wrapped around her forearms and she was smiling. Locks of wet hair licked the curve of her sharp brow; she looked like a fountain of erotic pleasure. My throbbing heart stood still for a moment as my sweaty palms tried to hold on to the photographs. I was stunned. Could a wife ever have those pictures taken? And then have them hidden on her husband's bookshelf? I have never considered wives to be sensual; they are always ridden by duties towards their homes and children. At most, one could only see as much as their bare shoulders or their cleavage peeking through their blouses as they washed themselves or their clothes. Near the village well, a lot of women would chatter and giggle with their breasts peeking out of their blouses, but that wasn't half as sensual as Rose Aunty's photos. My dream was clear, I wanted to be a mistress. Secretly, this desire came from a place of pain. I wanted the world to judge me, to berate me so that, in some twisted way, through me, they would also humiliate and berate Rose Aunty.

'See, Rose Aunty. I am just like you and see how they humiliate me. I modelled myself on you and look, how they hate me!'

As I entered my teens, life became more difficult. It was not that the fights between my parents increased but I was finally old enough to discern the complete dysfunctional nature of my family. I could compare my family to the other families who lived around us. I realised that all my clothes were outdated and ill-fitting for my growing body. I desperately wanted to fall in love and escape this drudgery. I wanted a prince to come and save me from the gutter of despair I called home. There were boys in my school, some of whom I developed a crush on. But I could never muster enough courage to approach them and speak to them. You see, I was taught that girls were meant to be wooed; they couldn't make the first move. But no boy looked at me. There were a handful of girls who were outgoing and chirpy, and all the boys pursued them while I sighed at my misfortune. This is when I took to reading and created an imaginary boyfriend.

Reading opened up a new world for me. I read of female protagonists who were unmarried, educated, rebellious and in love. Through them, I could channelise my repressed ambitions and live my dreams. As I read of them, I seemed to imbibe all their energies and I slowly started to rebuild myself. Living within a neglectful household and around nosy, eavesdropping neighbours and relatives was too much for me to take, and it was in those stories that I found myself a blessed escape from my sad reality. It was within those stories that I could finally reclaim my dreams of emancipation. Those books taught me how to dream, how to not surrender oneself to fate. Those books were a rebirth of sorts. I could finally see a sliver of sunlight in my dark and gloomy life.

My mind, unlike my body, was not a prisoner of circumstances. I was a free thinker who imagined a charming prince, who would rescue me from this loveless world. This prince was my boyfriend who loved me to the moon; he showered me with the choicest of expensive gifts. He was very handsome and always called me on the landline when I came back from school. I invented this story so that I could tell my friends about it, so that they would think I am a cool person. He was fictitious but bragging about him brought me comfort. My girlfriends would not pay much attention to my love tales but that did not stop me from bragging. In fact, the more they ignored me, the spicier my stories got. Once, I stole some money from Baba's wallet and bought a beautiful painting from the market. I got it gift-wrapped and hid it in a desolate corner in the school's parking lot. I told my friends that I was expecting a big gift from him on my birthday. Every day, I would check on the gift; I covered it with some dry grass, twigs and leaves so that no one would notice it. After four days, just a day before my birthday, I walked to the corner to take out that gift but it was not there. Someone had stolen the gift. I had a blank look on my face. I was crestfallen! For a whole fortnight, I had been savouring dreams of gifting myself the painting in front of my friends. My illusion of happiness had been shattered. In my vehement attempt to feel acceptable of being worthy of the love of a man, I had resorted to lying, to creating a fake reality; it was one of the early traces of trauma that earmarked my childhood. I began to feel needy of love. The pattern continued.

As I grew up, my fantasies grew larger and larger. I was in my tenth standard, and after a lot of convincing, Ma had got me enrolled in tuition classes because I was an extremely weak student. I was extremely unpopular and that always weighed me down. I always wished that boys would notice me, get attracted to me and then eventually want to marry me. But no one seemed to care. I thought of myself as an ugly, unsocial person who was worthy of no man's love. There was a boy in my class who failed in the annual examination; even he wouldn't look at me. When my self-esteem had completely disappeared, I began to fantasise again; this time about a stalker. A man had followed me home one evening as I cycled back from school. He was tall, about 5'11", and seemed to be in his early twenties. It was a dark winter evening and I was cycling as fast as I could. I turned back and gave him a stern look. This scared him and he went away. I came back home and felt a strange sexual longing for that rowdy man. It did not matter that he was a potential assaulter; he had looked at me in a way that no other boy had. His gaze aroused me and I was yearning to have sex with him. It was like an itch that I could not satisfy. I dreamed of kissing that man as I sat in the backyard of our house. That thought soothed me. It took me three days to come out of that fantasy.

The itch to belong to someone, to be loved by someone was maddening. It followed me everywhere I went. Especially with the onset of my puberty, it was difficult to handle the shame of menstruation and rising sexual urges fanned by Bollywood. I fantasised romancing Shahrukh Khan in a valley laden with tulips, roses and marigolds and about ballroom dancing with my neighbour. The pursuit of a lover did not leave me when I went to my mother's ancestral home. There was a Muslim family who lived in a home overlooking my grandparents'. The eldest son of that family, Rehman, and his younger brother Suleiman were painters and they made the most realistic sketches of people. In those times, clicking a picture in the studio was more expensive than getting a portrait painted. That was their livelihood. I imagined Rehman making a portrait of me, as I stuffed a soiled sanitary napkin deep under the clay roofing tiles of the room of my maternal grandfather.

Pune Junction

It was a warm, midsummer afternoon in July 2007. The train rolled on its wheels on the narrow iron tracks, navigating its way ahead. I had been on that train for more than 12 hours, sitting on the lower berth of a sleeper coach, eating almost every snack that was sold on trains: from cut fruits sprinkled with black salt and *chaat masala* to several *kulhads* of tea with Parle-G biscuits, from crisp and oily *puri*s to sweetened flakes of cube-shaped *soan papdis*. The food was unbelievably cheap and it made me wonder how they were so much tastier than the stuff I ate at fancy restaurants.

The train soon stopped at a station called Bid and I looked out of the window to check it out. It was largely empty except for a few beggars and tea vendors. When no one from the train got off, I heard from a fellow passenger that the station was not a usual stop on people's itineraries. The train offered us stops where we didn't have to embark on a journey but just sit back and deliberate, look at things we wouldn't have noticed otherwise.

The train stopped at Bid for a good 15 minutes before resuming its journey. Bid looked like a village, speckled with mud huts with thatched roofs, where groups of playful kids ran around on barren farm tracts. A lattice of electric and telephone wires spread against the sky. Far away, one could see an overpass and a man on his motorcycle under it. I looked at Baba; he was fast asleep on the middle berth. I pushed my head between two broken rods of the window, only for a short while. I was glad Baba was asleep; he would never let me do this if he were awake.

Outside, it was remarkable! The wind blew hard as the train roared ahead; it was almost 2:00 PM and only the two of us were awake, the wind and me. Sometimes the train joined in on our banter with its wheels rumbling on the tracks and its whistle piercing through the sky. I did not know when sleep caught up. I woke up with a huge jolt. Baba was trying to wake me up; we had reached our destination.

The 28312 superfast Azad Hind train has arrived on platform no. 2.

An announcer's voice boomed through Pune railway station's loudspeakers.

With us, a melee of passengers and their luggage descended from the blue train compartments.

It was an amusing sight. Coolies in their red turbans and navy-blue uniforms stood at the train doors and called out to passengers. Infants tugged at their mothers' waists, frantically crying and wrestling with their tiny hands. Chai-wallahs ran from one window to another, trying to find customers for the steaming ginger tea that they stored in aluminum kettles perched nicely on a burning coal stove. The canteen owner served delicious snacks like *vada pao*, *poha* and *dabheli* to hungry travellers who dropped clinking coins into his brass box. Limbless beggars dragged themselves on their wheeled wooden seats, crooning for some alms.

A newly married couple stood next to me; the wife wore a garish red silk sari with an embroidered *pallu* and glistening gold jewellery. She gently tiptoed behind her husband who walked confidently in his starched cream-coloured shirt and crisp brown trousers. An elderly couple was huffing and puffing while they tried to bring down their luggage from their coach; the coolies were asking for too much.

There were so many people one could see at a railway station, more than anywhere else. Different shades, colours, fortunes and lives unfold at a railway station and make us realise that the world indeed is truly rich and diverse.

I was looking at all of this with amazement. I had been to railway stations before but none of them were as big as the Pune railway station. I was there to study, make a name and earn a living, all on my own. I loved Pune but Mumbai always remained the city of my dreams. Every time I thought of Mumbai, my eyes brightened up. I always dreamed of belonging to the glittery world of cinema and glamour, like most 23-year-olds from anonymous small towns.

Standing on the railway station platform, I felt like I had woken up from a deep sleep and was standing on a mountaintop, with the vast expanse of the sky opening up in front of me. I looked at my shoulders and imagined a pair of fluttering wings on them. I was all set to fly. It was a new phase of my life. I was one among the hundred-odd students who got admission to the management studies course at Symbiosis.

The early twenties are always a strange period in a person's life. Officially you are a grown-up, you can vote, you can marry the person of your choice and are held accountable for all the decisions you take in your personal and professional life. For your parents, though, you are still not an adult; something of an 'adult-kid' suspended between childhood and adulthood who still needs their unsolicited, unwavering support to deal with the newer realities of life. It's like your hands are tied but legs are set free. There is a little freedom but not complete independence. How amazing it must be to be independent, I thought back then, but much later in life, I came to realise that financial freedom is the first step towards attaining complete freedom.

Baba had come along to help me settle down in this new and unfamiliar city. Through my childhood, I had always been closer to my uncles than to him. It was them I would always run to and flaunt my grades. On the other hand, my conversations with Baba were limited to the bare minimum. This was the first time I was travelling alone with him.

Finally, we made our way through the maddening hustle and bustle of the railway station and walked towards the exit. Just where the gates ended, an array of autorickshaw-wallahs assembled and honked loudly to attract the attention of hundreds of potential passengers. Baba negotiated the rates with a few of them and finally settled to go with the cheapest one. We tossed our luggage behind the back seat, hopped onto the three-wheeler and rode towards the town.

As I sat inside the autorickshaw, I breathed in a whiff of fresh air. The warm, moist breeze surrounded me with a dew-like freshness. It patted me on my cheeks and left them warm in its afterglow. A smile appeared on my lips and I felt intoxicated. Was the air here different from in other cities, or was it the same everywhere? Sometimes it stood still as a stone and at other times it flowed uninterrupted like a river. I could smell distant flowers in the wind that lashed against my face, and I felt a deep sense of happiness.

Nature is universal and yet so different in its ways and manifestations: so many colours, so many variations and so many different things and beings. Just like humans. We are so alike but all our thought processes and emotional mechanisms differ from person to person. We all feel pain and joy, yet we remain at loggerheads. If feelings remained the same across the whole human race, the world would be a much better place.

At a funeral, mourners comfort each other while they grieve. When we share the pain, it lessens in its intensity. Similarly, at a wedding, people dancing in a procession amplify the happiness of the occasion.

In half an hour, we reached Shivajinagar, which was close to my college. We got off the autorickshaw and walked to the hotel. I hated staying in hotels for they seemed so hollow despite their cleanliness and meticulousness and the comfort of room service. I always preferred to stay at a relative's place while travelling. It may not have been as comfortable, but there was always the promise of warm, home-cooked food amidst magical conversations. But there was no one we knew in Pune who would host us.

Finding our way to the hotel was an adventure in itself, as we tried finding our way through a maze of unknown zigzag streets, one leading to another. In those days, there were no Google Maps, and the only way to get to a place was by asking strangers. We asked for directions and walked on. In a couple of minutes, we finally reached our hotel. It was a small hotel located in the city centre but overshadowed by a big under-construction mall. That was probably why the rates were not very high, despite its location and great service.

In the evening, we walked to a nearby market to buy some things that I would need in college: a couple of saris, utensils, bedding and stationery items. Ma had already packed everything else I might have needed: from needles, a torch and a few hangers to clothes pegs, paracetamol tablets, home-made snacks and sanitary napkins. After all, a girl living on her own in a big city was no small feat.

Once Baba and I were done with our purchases, he took to scouting for local food outlets. He was a foodie; even at home, he would always bring in packets of different snacks, jars of fruit preserves and pickles of different flavours. He would introduce us to exotic foods like sweetened bamboo shoot preserve. He often overspent in his efforts to acquaint our family with different kinds of food. Just behind the headboard of the bed he slept in, there was a large wooden shelf with multiple racks; they were all stocked with various jars and containers, which he would often gaze at. When we had guests, he would often bring them out and serve them these rare delicacies.

Baba finally settled for a semi-luxurious restaurant. There were other restaurants in that area and I wondered why he chose this specific one. They offered a thali at a great price and the manager was a friendly guy and a food connoisseur. He made an effort to tell us about local recipes and advised us on good restaurants. This was a time when one could eat at a restaurant to one's heart's content without worrying about the bill. I was happy!

Those two days of Baba's stay in Pune were predictably relaxed, away from all his worldly troubles. Lunch was one meal that I always looked forward to; we would leave our hotel room and enjoy delicious lunches. After lunch, we walked to the railway station and drank chilled sugarcane juice served in little glasses. Baba would always bargain with street vendors and buy some local sweets. We ended our evening with a visit to the S.B. Road cybercafé so that we could read up on all the updates from my new college.

Those two days brought me closer to Baba. We had casual conversations and shared some hearty laughs. I realised that when two people are left alone to themselves, they always find ways to communicate. Back home, there were too many distractions and responsibilities that always kept Baba away from me. In Pune, there were none of those responsibilities to handle, so we bonded. There was a mild discomfort in the night as there was one large double bed and we had to sleep on the same bed. Though there was ample space between us, I was still ill at ease. It is unfortunate how gender roles make it difficult even for a daughter to be close to her father.

It was soon time for Baba to go back home. I felt extremely sad but could not quite understand why. Back home, I often loathed his guarding presence and could not wait to be by myself and start attending college, and now, I was sad he was leaving. Looking back, I marvel at the nature of human relationships: how do they work, what binds them? Why does it happen that someone seems significant only when we fear their loss or departure? It is a basic human instinct to take things for granted when they become our own; we assume they are ours forever. Why are our emotions driven by fear rather than by love? Why do we always remember God when faced with woes but not when we are happy?

Before leaving, Baba found me a paying guest accommodation. It was a duplex with a giant turquoise-coloured gate; the lower floor had been converted in to a shared accommodation while the landlady and her family lived on the upper floor. The room I leased was basically a kitchen converted into a makeshift bedroom. I was on a paper-thin budget and this was all I could afford. At least, I would not have to share my tiny room with anyone.

As I sank in my 6 x 4 bed for the first time, I felt a sharp pang of loneliness; I stared at the light blue walls and then at the iron rods of the window, which barely let a ray of sunshine into the room. It was a gloomy room and keeping my spirits up in that room looked like an uphill task. The deep meditative silence was interrupted by a murmur. It came from the adjoining room. I got up and walked towards the room, wanting to meet my neighbour.

I knocked gently on the door before it opened with a screech. There she was...tall, slender, pixie haircut. She wore a pair of shorts and a vest. Her room was pulsating with loud music, by Rihanna, as she looked at me, puzzled at seeing an uninvited stranger. One look at her and I found her whole presence annoying, so I decided to introduce myself and be done with the pleasantries.

Her name was Latika, though her looks and attitude did no justice to her mythological name.

A short customary question-and-answer session followed and I soon came back to my room. With nothing else left to do in my gloomy room, I decided to go to the nearest cybercafé. I logged in to my Orkut account. Before I reached Pune, I had sent out messages to a few seniors of my college, asking for their help in finding a place to stay and other college-related matters.

One of them was Harsh. He had replied to my message. I decided to check his profile.

Harsh was three years my senior in college and had just graduated. Hence, it was highly unlikely that our paths would ever cross in college. Nevertheless, I noted down the number he sent me in that message. I decided to call him.

It was still 2:00 PM and I had loads of time in my hand. We had decided to meet. I was rummaging through my almirah looking for something to wear. To my dismay, I discovered that my entire wardrobe was full of oversized salwar suits, all stitched by the tailor back in my hometown. I did not want to come across as a small-town bumpkin and decided to wear a formal shirt and a pair of trousers, the only western outfit I owned. It was too hot to wear those trousers but I had no other option. I put on a brave face and a fake smile and left my room.

I always felt shy when meeting people for the first time and struggled to find the right words to say after the first hi. It usually took a garrulous stranger to have a 10-minute-long conversation with me. I would usually just answer whatever questions this person would ask me. Harsh and I mostly talked about academic stuff the first time we met.

I came back home somewhat dejected. Here I thought that I was about to meet my Prince Charming, that we would have great conversations, sip coffee together at Om Supermarket and live happily ever after. All these dreams died a slow, painful death.

'Girl, you deserve much better!' I told myself as I did after every unrequited crush. Harsh was a bespectacled nerd and I did not ever want to date a nerd. I said this to myself over and over again.

I heard a sound coming from Latika's room. It was strange since she barely ever stayed in her room during the day. Intrigued, I tried to peep in through her door. I saw a demure, young girl unpacking her stuff from a big carton. She was Latika's new roommate and looked completely her opposite. She wore a plain salwar-kameez, her hair was tied into two braids and she wore heavy-rimmed glasses.

I felt a kind of affection towards her when I heard a male voice and the voice of another woman. Probably her relatives, I thought. I went back to my room and waited for them to leave. After some time, when things went back to being quiet, I walked into her room and saw her arranging her books on the study table.

I sat down to speak to her and after spending some time exchanging pleasantries, I was back in my room. Her name was Bhavya and she was not very talkative.

She was someone who minded her own business, which was a huge relief given how so many women my age would always gossip. Somewhere, she was very similar to me.

There was still a week remaining for the college to open. Days went by and Bhavya and I became good friends. In my universe that spanned my one room and kitchen, Bhavya was the only person I talked to. We discussed our careers, ambitions, studies, past lives and struggles. I always lent an ear to her queries and this made her open up to me. I discovered that she liked a Telugu song called '*Aa ante amlapuram...*' I did not know what the words meant but the song had a nice rhythm. As the song played on her tape recorder, we both danced with our dupattas flying all around. There was very little space in that room but we somehow managed to dance.

Meanwhile, our respective colleges opened and we got busy with our classes. All our days were spent in classrooms, evenings were spent with college friends and then most of the nights were spent studying. Bhavya and I often ate dinner together. We had not yet found a tiffin delivery service and every night, we walked to the nearest restaurant. We mostly ate *daal khichdi* and occasionally treated ourselves to tandoori roti and *malai kofta*. Bhavya was not a picky eater and ate whatever I ordered. I was astonished. I did not understand how anyone could not have food preferences. Food, after all, is an art, a passion.

College was a refreshing change for me. Having studied in an all-girls' school, coming to a co-ed college was a new and rewarding experience! All the escalating sexual tension accumulating from the start of adolescence could finally be released and relieved!

I could not wait to start dating. The prospect of being wooed was intoxicating. While outwardly, I was a recluse, having rarely interacted with boys, I was waiting for someone to break that shell.

There was an array of management classes on offer and it was daunting to try and assimilate all the information. I was determined to make the most of my years at college and so I ended up not studying at all and resorting to cramming everything I could days before my exams. I had tasted the deadly combination of freedom and easy success and I would not turn my back.

Among all my classmates, I was close to one person. His name was Viplav. We met at our orientation where we were sitting next to one another. As it turned out, we were both from Bokaro. Naturally, we had a lot to talk about and share. He spoke very good English and was very affectionate.

One day, classes got over earlier than usual and I was back in my room before lunch. After having my lunch, I sat staring at my walls again, trying to deal with my loneliness. I thought it would be a good idea to call Viplav. He picked up the phone and after talking for a few minutes, I got to the point where I asked him out to meet at a cosy little coffee shop that also boasted of an impressive menu of European desserts. He agreed. After a while, I stepped out of my room and walked into the parking space. I pushed open the rusting iron gate that always made a squeaky sound when being unlatched.

It was drizzling. I was wearing a pink collared t-shirt and a pair of body-hugging, flared blue jeans. I did not have an umbrella but did not mind it; I had always liked getting wet in the rain. It wasn't raining hard. I realise only now that the bliss of getting wet in the rain was an experience I would reserve only for myself. It was a happiness that I could not share with anyone. While I stood enjoying the rain, I almost forgot that I had to meet Viplav. It was a moment of crystallised time. It was only when he called on my phone that I remembered that I had to meet him.

'Where are you? I have reached.'

The hoarse voice on the other side of the phone said.

I looked at my leather-belted watch and realised that I was late. I walked fast on the pavement to quickly reach the café. As I approached the café, I saw Viplav from the tinted-glass window screen; he was seated at a corner table. I was nervous and blushing; how could I have asked a guy out? Then I comforted myself, I had just asked him to meet me and enjoy an evening together. That was it. It was not a big deal. In about five minutes, we were facing each other. Unlike me, he was carrying an umbrella that leaned on the armrest of the chair he was sitting on. He was wearing a light-grey t-shirt with a pair of chinos. His eyes were framed by thick spectacles. A typical nerd, I thought and sighed.

I skimmed through the menu and ordered a hot latte for myself and a cold espresso for Viplav. He had to pay the bill being a man, hence I did not order a lot. I decided to come back to this café a second time and splurge on the yummiest desserts. For a minute or two, there was silence. Then he kicked off the conversation.

It lasted till the last sip of our coffees. We then left the place and walked our ways. I was lost in his thoughts, in that evening, in that feeling. It was a wonderful feeling. Love was alive! Love happened at first sight.

I think my determination to make this a date and this man mine made the conversation easier. Since I was an introvert, I had memorised and rehearsed the topics of conversation I would have with him. I knew about his school but did not know much about his time there, his teachers, his friends. These things could seem mundane but fill up awkward silences. I would ask him about his subject streams in the MBA, his hobbies, his stay in Pune. I had also calculated the time in my head and was relieved when I realised that it would take us a good 15 minutes to talk on those topics. In school, most men never approached me because of my stone-cold silence and circled around chatty girls instead. I was determined to break that curse this time. It was unnerving to find out later that Viplav did not utter a word in that hour-long date. In half an hour, my tongue was tired and I almost yearned to drop my face straight on the white tablecloth adorned with embroidered lilac flowers. Nevertheless, I coped with the garrulous stretch and my perseverance did not go unrewarded. As the sun proceeded to set, inviting the night, I gestured to leave.

We walked together, huddled under his umbrella that rainy evening. As our bodies huddled closer, I felt happy inside; I was enjoying his company, his being. We were not holding hands but we were speaking very softly to one another. The first signs of a brewing attraction between two strangers are intoxicating. It's almost as if the whole world had come to a standstill and nothing else mattered. The only thing that mattered was the deep connection developing between the two strangers.

The situation reminded me of the famous rain song from the film *Shree 420... 'Pyaar hua ikraa hua...'* I wasn't in love with him yet but I was aware of my budding soft feelings for him. Was I in a hurry to fall in love at the first opportunity? Meeting Viplav made my days more enjoyable; I looked forward to meeting him and talking with him. I did not feel lonely any more. I was happy but what I missed noticing, however, was that I had stopped enjoying being with myself.

As time passed, we started knowing more about each other: our initial struggles, our backgrounds, our choices, our dreams. But these conversations only scratched the surface of my soul; Viplav wasn't able to dig deep. On the other hand, the physical need for intimacy was increasing. We contented ourselves with momentary, occasional and furtive gestures like holding hands, kissing and exchanging hugs.

I was a completely different person in the class—my classmates had no idea that I was a sociable and fashionable person. I usually attended classes in a pair of faded jeans and a kurti. But all the impressions my classmates had of me changed forever after the freshers' party.

We got to know that our seniors had planned a freshers' party just three days before the party, so there was not much time to plan outfits. We were new to college and it was too early to form a rapport with our seniors. In class, my friends Grishma and Palak and I talked about what we would wear for the party. Like me, Grishma and Palak wore simple clothes and did not socialise much. That's probably one of the reasons why we were good friends.

'Listen, where can we go shopping?' Palak asked.

'Laxmi Road,' I suggested.

'That's too far, can't we go to F.C. Road?' Grishma intervened.

'F.C. Road is quite expensive. Stuff in Laxmi Road is cheap.'

We all agreed upon Laxmi Road. After our classes, the three of us took an auto there. The market was extremely busy and teeming with shoppers. Scores of matchbox-like shops with slanting asbestos roofs crowded both sides of the narrow road. The shops sold everything—from junk jewellery and dresses to footwear, bags and belts. All sold at throwaway prices. There were shoppers all around us: families, women with their children, wholesalers, college students like us.

In the shops selling clothes, the clothes were hung outside on the shop verandah on rotating hangers and were piled on congested racks within the store. The shoe stalls all had a large table where hordes of footwear were piled up. The food stalls were all surrounded by the delicious aroma of freshly fried *pakoras* and sugary *roshogollas*. Some stalls sold spicy *golgappas* and sweet-and-sour *chuskis*. A few people looked like walking shops themselves as they carried several shopping bags on their slender shoulders. Some people sold leather bags, belts and picture frames. Everyone in that market had something to offer. India is famous for its art of bargaining and the ability of its people to strike up innocuous conversations with passers-by. The shopkeepers looked like anxious suitors asking for the hand of the shoppers, luring them with their best possessions and sugar-coated conversations.

We wandered deep into the market in search of the best merchandise to be bought at the smallest possible price. There was some method to the madness in this market but it was beyond the reach of our comprehension. But everything worked at a perfect pace in this market.

After bargaining at a few shops, we settled for a shop that seemed to have an expansive collection and was manned by a courteous shopkeeper. I bought a kaftan and a wrap-around skirt, while Grishma bought a pair of jeans and a t-shirt. Puja picked up a pair of cotton kurtis and a pair of leggings. We had spent almost all of our meagre savings but we were happy to have struck a great bargain. Smiles flashed on our faces as we boarded the autorickshaw back to our respective homes.

On the day of the freshers' party I was happy as a clam. This was my moment of fame, and I resolved to make the most of it. I was going to look my best as it had already been a month and my intelligence had not cast any magic on the potential suitors. By that time, a few girls and boys had complimented me on my towering height and I knew that I had to walk with my head held high. I was going to beat every girl in the oomph and confidence department. I decided to not wear the kaftan and skirt and resorted to borrowing clothes from my friends.

I left my hair loose and wore a black t-shirt with a red short skirt. As I left home and walked on the footpath, I felt a bit shy seeing my bare legs. I almost felt like going back and changing into something more modest, but there was barely any time. Passersby were staring at my legs. I hurriedly walked to Grishma's flat and then we both went to the Koregaon Park pub, where the party was being held.

This was the first time I had ever set foot inside a pub. The atmosphere was intoxicating, and everything was reverberating with the throbbing music. The alcohol counter had bartenders making quick drinks. Some of our classmates had already arrived by the time we reached. A few of them were tapping their feet to the music played by the DJ and a few were seated with their girlfriends and boyfriends. I could see some of them already queuing up at the bar. For a moment, I felt like a recluse; I neither drank and nor had a boyfriend. On top of that, I was too shy to dance. I was relieved when I saw Viplav. He was standing alone and I quickly started walking towards him. The music was so loud that we could barely hear what the other said, but it was fun speaking loudly to each other. We kept bursting into laughter.

The whole pub looked like an elaborate erotic set-up. Revolving lights in red, blue, yellow, purple; rings of smoke emanating from the burning edges of cigarettes; clinking glasses and bottles of beer, wine and vodka; girls gyrating in revealing clothes which gave bystanders a sneak peek of their round buttocks and bountiful breasts. I felt like hooking up with Viplav. Nobody would even notice. In that pub, everyone was granted their little world of privacy under the dim lights as an air of nonchalance enveloped everyone. I started tapping my feet and moving my arms, the closest to dancing I'd ever get.

Soon Viplav also started grooving to the music and we occasionally held hands and smiled at each other.

That was the real icebreaker; we were getting closer beyond the standard boundaries of friendship. I loved that closeness. In my heart, I desired to be held close, to be hugged and to be kissed. Like a dormant volcano suddenly erupting, I felt this urge for physical intimacy engulf me. I guess the same was happening to Viplav. From what I had heard, guys have a harder time restraining themselves. I was feeling restless but wanted him to make the first move. I made my desire evident through my inviting glances; I was ready to take him in and reciprocate. We moved in a bit closer and on an impulse, he rubbed his lips against mine, and we kissed. It was nice and warm and a lovely indication of things to come. My lips felt moist and I wanted to kiss him again. We quickly kissed again, which left me wanting for even more. But I soon managed to get back to my senses; I was afraid someone would see us. We did not want to become the talk of the town. I was amazed at my restraining capability. In our country, in our society, our fears always cordon our desires. I looked at Viplav and pursed my lips as a sign of the satisfaction that he had given me.

'Let me go and meet my friends,' I told him.

'Alright, I'll be here,' he said.

We both wanted to detach just to affirm that we were not together and that nothing had happened between us.

I moved to the wider area of the pub and there I saw Vijay. The charming, flamboyant college heart-throb. He wore a black shirt, with sleeves rolled up to his elbow, and a low-waist, striped pair of jeans. He had tied a red bandana around his forehead, which made him look sexier and even more appealing. That night, I was free to feel anything I liked. I was aware that I was looking hot and was aware of the passing, furtive glances that boys around me were throwing at me.

My towering height made me look sexier than the other girls in my class. I felt confident in my attraction to Vijay. I was already comparing Viplav to Vijay.

Vijay's candidness surpassed Viplav's tepidness.

Viplav was not as stylish as Vijay.

Viplav was not adored by everyone as Vijay was.

Vijay, Vijay, Vijay. My heart was racing and the memory of the kisses I shared with Viplav was lost in afterthought.

I knew Vijay liked me and I liked him too. A lot. We started dancing. An adrenaline rush took over me and I couldn't stop dancing with him; I tilted to my left, he tilted to his right, so on and so forth. I was over the moon and had forgotten about everyone else present in that room, including Viplav.

We danced passionately for around five minutes. The urge to kiss him became stronger as I stared deep into his dark brown eyes. Those eyes looked inebriated under the influence of alcohol and I could not make out if there was any attraction towards me in them. I felt clueless but enjoyed the moment, the intimacy and the building desire.

After some time, I remembered that Viplav was waiting for me. Unwillingly, I paused my dancing.

I was on cloud nine. Here I was, the centre of attention of two guys, one of whom was the heart-throb of the entire class. Though nothing more happened with Vijay, I was the only girl with whom he danced at that party. I was contented with that privilege, although I strongly and truly believed that I deserved it.

'Vijay, I must go now,' I said.

'Sure,' he smiled.

When I turned to meet Viplav, my feet felt heavy. All my passion for Viplav had fizzled out. I realised that Viplav was only the consolation prize and Vijay was the grand reward. I also felt bad about harbouring feelings for two guys. One was my need and other was my desire. But I always stood by my decisions and never regretted them. I never aspired to be a Sati Savitri; I was human and I had every right to change my mind in the pursuit of my happiness. But I also had a weakness: I often put my loved ones ahead of me. Viplav was not the dream guy for me but he gave me a sense of comfort, a feeling of love and companionship, which helped me sail through the turbulence of my college life.

I gathered my wandering thoughts and put an immediate stop to them. I walked towards Viplav. We spent the rest of the night eating from the delectable spread. We sat on the red cushions and took a lot of photographs.

The next day, I woke up late in the afternoon. My head was still heavy from all the loud music, although I had not drunk. I bathed, got ready and transformed back to my shy, mundane avatar; I wore a cotton kurta and faded jeans. I headed straight to the library. There, in the library, was a broad wooden desk overlooking the window; it could sit around 10 people. A few of my batch mates, Supratik, Sunny and my friend Grishma were sitting there and reading. I walked towards them and sat facing Supratik. We were having our usual friendly banter when Supratik remarked, 'You were looking hot yesterday.'

Sunny joined in, 'Yeah, she was looking like a babe.'

I was both amazed and flummoxed by this generous dose of compliments. It was the second month of college, and I had spent almost all this time looking like a nerd. The compliments soothed my aching heart. I was elated but succeeded in concealing my happiness.

'Really!' I said, expecting a repeat of all the compliments.

'Yeah, you outdid everyone else.'

'Where were you hidden all this time?'

'Everyone was talking about you.'

Appreciations started pouring in. I realised that we are all secretly hungry for validations. Appreciations satiate this enormous hunger.

Since I was too shy to reciprocate their praise, I stuck to simply thanking them. They gradually got back to reading and gossiping amongst themselves. I could never take part in these conversations; I was more into soul-fulfilling, deep, intimate conversations, the ones you can have with only one person. I did have those conversations with a few of my friends in college and they had a lasting impact on me. The best I could do in a group was to be a good listener who listened with rapt attention but never had much to say.

Since that party, I had a growing desire to be with Vijay. While I just wanted to strike a friendship, my subconscious mind wanted something deeper. Vijay always behaved warmly with me and was always cordial.

Lovemaking Debut

Being the lazy bum that I was, I would always get to class mere seconds before it would start. Even though I stayed very close to the college. Vijay would always save a seat for me beside him. He wouldn't let any other girl take that seat. That was his way of conveying that I was special.

I was happy. I had attended an all-girls' school, and now I was in a co-ed college where I was the centre of the attention of the class heart-throb and a nerd. My hands were full. Indeed, the progress had been bewitching!

Today, when I look back, I'm not sure what defined the passion between me and Viplav. For me it was an attraction for someone of the opposite sex with some emotions and common passions. What true love is I still do not know. For me, any love must comprise physical attraction and intimacy, and I fear that often overshadows the eternal and soulful connection. In the Indian society, we are raised to consider sex as a taboo subject. We cannot express our carnal desires openly. While sexual maturity hits us in our teens, we are taught to restrain and suppress it silently. Naturally, we take to masturbation or imagining wild sexual scenarios with people we are attracted to. It is this suppression that guides our feelings of love; when we meet someone we like, our feelings are driven more by physical appeal than the mental connect.

Do we think that we would still express love in the same way if the society had allowed us to have open and free sex, if people were more open in expressing and flaunting their desires? Why does sex have to be portrayed as a necessary evil? Sex is a vital necessity of the human body, a medium for us to satisfy ourselves internally and externally. It relieves us of anxiety, and it can have far-reaching positive consequences in the way this society behaves and in the way we behave with each other.

Coming back to Viplav. The larger part of my attraction towards him was solely sexual. This was evident in the way we spent time with each other. Most often, we looked for secluded places where we could relieve our sexual tension. Pune, back then, had a fortunate number of such places.

I still faintly remember how we discovered our favourite spot.

It was after class; Viplav and I stepped out of college and strolled towards the road leading to a Sai Baba temple. He was deeply religious and often visited the temple to offer prayers. I would often accompany him even though I wasn't fond of visiting temples.

The Sai Baba temple was a beautiful white structure built with chiselled marble. White is symbolic of peace and I always felt tranquil when I entered the temple. There were intricate hand-carved designs on its walls and surrounding the central shrine were a group of smaller temples dedicated to Durga, Kali, Shiva and Vishnu. There was a lush mango tree in the courtyard, beneath whose green shade was an iron bench. While Viplav spent hours worshipping, I sat on the bench with my legs stretched out. I would sit and admire the beauty of that place. That time was 'me time'. The temple was usually secluded at that hour and I enjoyed the solitude.

I guess it was the only time I felt at complete peace with myself. I was enjoying my own company amidst the resting trees, soft grass, tinkling golden bells and chirping birds. Solitude is so empowering and pacifying at the same time. I realised that I wanted to be with Viplav as loneliness scared me. The sweet interlude lasted for about 15 minutes and then someone patted my shoulders again. It was Viplav. The addiction to companionship rushed through my veins again!

One day after attending a seminar, Viplav and I walked towards our respective homes. He instructed me to walk behind him. Our closeness was attracting too many eyeballs and he wanted to avoid the mushrooming rumours and murmurs. I diligently followed him, tiptoeing in my flowing sari. After walking for a bit, when he was assured that no one was watching us, he turned back and signalled me to join him. I increased my pace and soon we were walking together, hand in hand, heart with heart.

We longed to pursue our newly found passion, looking out for unexplored places hidden in the cityscape. Yes, that was an interesting pastime for us. Pune's landscape was dotted with hills, open expanses and lush green spaces. Urbanisation had still not killed the natural beauty of this small town. There was a neighbourhood called Khidki, which was then a huge, wide, open expanse. After walking for a bit, we spotted a path leading to a wired fence surrounding paddy fields. I was ecstatic! It was a spot of calm, furtively nestled inside the maddening rush of Khidki.

The path was 100 metres long, dusty and narrow. The soil was soggy, and while we walked, we left behind our footprints, which we endearingly kept looking back at. There were many green bushes lying scattered. Those bountiful bushes were the perfect examples of the fundamental truth of life: that we should let all life forms take their own shapes. Everything finds its own course eventually.

Amongst the foliage of bushes lay a small marble temple with a deity inside. The temple's roof was so low that one could barely sit inside it. I guess that was done on purpose, to teach us the importance of humility in our lives. There was no priest inside the temple, only a *Shiva linga*. I walked inside, my head bent. I folded my hands together and whispered some prayers. I shared my insecurities and my wishes with the Almighty. I prayed for the long life of our love and for Viplav. I then walked around the *Shiva linga* and poured holy water on it from a *lota*. After finishing the rituals, I walked out and Viplav entered. Being the steadfast worshipper that he was, I was expecting him to be inside for at least 15 minutes and decided to take a stroll while he finished his rituals.

Outside, a cool breeze blew and played with my hair. The air was pure and the sky was clear blue, dotted with scant, dispersing clouds that looked like little plumes of smoke. The sky seemed to stretch for an eternity. The farm had just been ploughed, as was evident from the undulated ground. Suddenly, I felt like walking into the fields and touching the mud but the fence was too high. I contented myself by kneeling down and reaching inside the fence. I touched the ground and the feeling was ethereal. The softness of mud, its warmth and its rawness caressed my palms. I clenched the mud tight in my fist and started rubbing it between my fingers. We build up piles of emotions within ourselves and clog our hearts like the mud in my hand. If we can just release those thoughts stuffed inside us, it would create more space for love and other positive emotions.

I felt lighter. Nature had such a profound impact on my thoughts and state of mind! That place had liberated me; I was lost in my solitude, oblivious of everything around me. The peace was captivating, away from the noise and maddening hustle bustle of the town. I felt a hand on my shoulder. It was Viplav. He had completed his prayers and had come back looking for me.

'Isn't this place just like heaven?' I exclaimed with childlike excitement.

'Yes, it is indeed. I told you to come take a walk with me. You were the one not agreeing to it.'

'I know, I was wrong. I am happy we came here. That's all that matters,' I said.

We walked together, hand in hand. We were both in our early twenties and our youth, along with our new love, led us to a state of trance. We had not been physically intimate after the freshers' party because we had not found a private space. The urge to find new places was driven by the urge to find some privacy in this not-so-private city.

To the left of the temple was a narrow alley with a building surrounded by high walls. The walls were stained with fungus and were almost 20 feet high. Just beyond the alley lay some deep bushes. That was it! We had found our secret place, our little place of love. We were sure that the place was uninhabited and we did not see any other person around us. We embraced each other; my arms were around his neck and his were around my waist. For a moment we stood still and then locked our lips in a wild, passionate kiss. All the floodgates were broken. Our lips kept looking for the other's lips hungrily. It was not a gentle kiss, as I now recall. We went on for around five minutes indulging our amoral, carnal desires. Love seemed to have taken a backseat for lust to rule over our bodies.

In some time, the fever subsided and we detached our bodies. I noticed that Viplav was not wearing his spectacles, and his face looked very different in their absence. He was smiling and looking lovingly at my face. I was feeling a myriad of emotions—puzzled at the unanticipated turn of events. All my life, I ran away from men; their proximity made me tremble. I sighed looking at other girls who could easily make friends with the opposite sex. I never thought I could ask a man for his friendship, be friends with him. And here I was all unrestrained and amorous. I thought it would be a sluggish, soft kiss. But as it turned out, it was a breathless kiss, his teeth grazing my lower lip and mine nibbling his upper. I was sheepish at letting a man access my modesty but was enlivened with the feeling of being loved for the first time in my life. I looked up at him and then we again started to kiss each other wildly. I wished it would never end. While kissing, sometimes I took a break and just let Viplav kiss me. At other times, I took charge and kissed him vigorously. Our lips were trying very hard to release the sexual tension pent up inside our bodies. It was not just love but something beyond that. A thirst which lay unfulfilled. This time, the kiss lasted slightly more than five minutes.

After this, I got more confident. I understood that it was perfectly normal to kiss. I was trying to act modest but in reality, I was only acting. I was not content and wanted much more. I wanted to have sex but could not reveal my intentions. I wanted Viplav to take a lead and would happily let him in. Our defences were lowered, and we understood each other's desires without needing to say them out loud.

Viplav stroked my midriff and moved my sari aside. He wrapped his hands around my waist and squeezed it repeatedly. I felt a pang of lust and held onto his back tightly. He was gentle and slowly felt up the entire area between my blouse and the petticoat. In between, he kissed me on my lips. He then moved his hands up and started unhooking my blouse. I whimpered, 'Don't do this. Someone might come.'

'No one will. This place is abandoned,' he assured me.

He undid all the hooks on my blouse one by one and my upper body lay bare in front of him, covered only by the veil of the sari. He then felt my plump breasts and squeezed them, gently at first and then harder. I stood still, enjoying it all to the hilt and holding him, letting him do the work. He then tried to move my bra up, but it was hooked. He moved his hand to my back, wanting to unhook my bra. I resisted unwillingly.

'That's too much.'

'It's nothing,' he smiled mischievously.

'Do you want me to stop?' he asked.

'No,' I replied.

He then unhooked my bra and let my breasts loose. He moved his hands inside my now-unhooked bra and clasped both my breasts. He started pressing and stroking them ferociously. My heart was beating fast with excitement and anxiety. The fear of someone seeing us and the sexual arousal were too much for my inexperienced heart to hold.

After kneading my ample breasts for a while, Viplav lowered his mouth to suck the protruding nipples which were now hard and erect. I was feeling ecstatic and was completely comfortable letting him do what he wanted. After all, this was what we both wanted. It was pure erotic bliss!

He opened his mouth and took my left breast in and started sucking it. His mouth was full and eyes were shut. His hands were busy squeezing the other breast. I was enthralled by the emotions that took over me as I watched him suck my breast. I lovingly caressed his hair with my fingers, encouraging him to suck harder. He did not disappoint me.

I realise now that the average Indian woman is suppressed by her outward modesty; she withholds her lust but she, in fact, is very wild. I was witnessing and experiencing my wild side at that time. Though I did not initiate it, in all my capacity and eagerness, I was letting Viplav do what he wanted.

He sucked my breasts one by one, at times trying to suck both of them together. For the first time, I said something, 'Do it one by one. It gives me more pleasure.'

He looked at me, his tiny eyes met my large eyes.

'Sure,' he said.

He then proceeded to suck my right breast passionately and then the left.

Right, left, right, left....

We caressed, touched, kissed and discovered more of each other. Due to the lack of space, we could not lie down but were sitting beneath the shade of a tree, out in the open. The only cover we had on us was the deep sky and the fleeting light of the dusk. In a moment of ecstasy, under the dimming light, I wanted him to enter me but how could I ask? Viplav was a novice in lovemaking, just like me. He actually needed my nod before proceeding with every gesture. The kissing, hugging and cuddling was all good but sexual intercourse? He could not have imagined having sex! I tried some old-fashioned coquetry and asked him to step forward. Being a shy girl, I felt it was considered inappropriate for me to be upfront about my sexual desire.

My lips moved a little bit and I murmured, asking him to touch me down there. He was quick to jump on the cue and unzip his trousers. It was difficult for me to lift my petticoat, my hands rendered immobile by age-old ideas around morality. I made it seem that I was not too interested in sex and was rather abiding by the irrational, carnal desires of my lover. Now that I look back on that incident, I feel weird about having behaved like that. I could have easily been accepting of my sexual urges but I felt that doing so would defile me. Viplav gently brushed his penis against my stomach. Then he ruffled my untrimmed pubic hair, sending little sparks of excitement inside my vagina. I squealed with pleasure for a few seconds but was suddenly alarmed as pregnancy fears came to the fore. I shoved him away and started fretting about pregnancy. Viplav was stupefied! He couldn't deal with my histrionics and tried to assure me that nothing had happened yet. But I was not ready to listen. I kept repeating like a chant, 'I can get pregnant!' To assure me, he started vigorously jerking off till he came.

'Look! All the semen came out. You are not pregnant!'

I tried to believe him and diverted my attention to the moment we just spent together. We started putting our dishevelled clothes in order. I hooked my blouse and tied back the loosened string of my petticoat, fastened everything with safety pins. He buttoned his shirt and zipped his trousers. I noticed, in exultation, that a part of my sari was torn. I glanced at it lovingly as a symbol and expression of our love. Emotions take precedence over money, for me. We left the place together. I realised that I actually wanted to stay back and talk to him, but that didn't happen.

When I reached my room, I looked at myself in the mirror and gazed at myself. My lips were swollen from the kisses. Though they were dark pink in colour, in that moment, they looked dark red, as if the circulation of blood had increased due to frequent rubbing. I decided to stay in my room for the rest of the night, not even stepping out to meet Bhavya. Soon the pregnancy fear caught up with me again. What if a few drops of semen from the tip of Viplav's penis had entered me? The very thought made me nervous. I was appalled at the prospect of a pregnancy. It is so much easier for men to have sex and get away with it, while a woman needs to take all the blame. Indeed, patriarchy is alive and kicking. I was resilient enough to take measures to ward off this disaster. I wondered whom to speak to and could think only of Bhavya; I knew no one else in the city. Viplav would probably think me to be an idiot if I brought this up again. I knew Bhavya would judge me immensely if I told her but I wanted to get rid of my fear. I felt alone!

I went to Bhavya's room but it was locked. I had saved her number but could not gain enough courage to call her. Anxious, I paced up and down the deserted corridor. Half an hour passed and I heard someone's footsteps from a distance. It was her! Without wasting a second, I blurted it all out. I told her that Viplav had brushed his penis against the opening of my vagina and I was scared that I might get pregnant. Bhavya was stunned! She lashed out at me, scolding me for my immaturity. She was angry at Viplav too! In that state of helplessness, all logic was beyond my comprehension. How can desiring sex make one a pervert? Yes, of course, he was immature and irresponsible. He should have stayed back and listened to my fears. But how could I expect him to be mature? He was all of 22 and also equally fearful of social shame.

Seeing me panic, Bhavya agreed to come with me to the hospital. We took an auto and after a few kilometres, spotted a hospital. It wasn't full of people and I was relieved to know that there wouldn't be too many witnesses to my confession of having indulged in premarital sex. I plodded into the cabin and burst into tears as I described my ill fate to the young female doctor. She was empathetic and assured me that nothing would happen. She also told me that at an early stage of pregnancy, the foetus could be aborted with a pill and that no surgery was needed. I was so relieved to know this. As I left the doctor's cabin with Bhavya, I grew more confident in having premarital sex.

Viplav and my secret excursions continued after that episode. The doctor had dispelled all the myths that could have stopped me from having sex. I, however, decided to not have penile-vaginal intercourse. It had become a routine for us to scout for deserted spaces, where we would undress, kiss and make out. Our limitations had imposed on us a lifestyle that we relished wholesomely amidst towering fears of someone spotting us. Each day, we strolled further, navigating our way through dense bushes and shrubs, to hand-pick places for our carnal union. It was during one of those adventurous trips that we stumbled upon a high-walled building. It was an old institute that seemed to have been built in the pre-independence period, as was evident from its colonial architectural style.

But what interested me more was that the entire place looked like a savanna jungle; the tall, imposing walls seemed like baobab trees whose canopies would cover all our actions. My eyes glimmered with the excitement of finding a secret haven to unleash our carnal urges, fearless of being caught by anyone. Finally! We could indulge in making out for as long as possible. Endless lovemaking right in the lap of nature! I didn't delay any further and gestured Viplav to sit on the grassy ground. I sat beside him and in one swift move, lifted my top and helped him unbutton his shirt. It was dusk, and darkness camouflaged our bare upper bodies. I started kissing him thirstily and made him suck my breasts in an animal-like frenzy. Our naked upper bodies rubbed against each other; trembling and shaking from the electric spark of eroticism. I had lost awareness of Viplav as my lover. Instead, my hunger for sex was so high that at that moment, he only seemed to be a medium to release my long-suppressed desires. It's strange how a suppressed urge can make you objectify the body of a living being. At that time love had ceased to exist; I was blinded by the lust for the person whom I loved. Lust coexists with love, sometimes replacing it. It is as much an authentic and natural human emotion as love is.

The impatient exploration and explosion of our bodies continued along with the kissing. Our lips stuck to each other's like green moss on an old brick wall. We were no longer children, we had grown older and this moss of lust might look dirty and sticky but it was quenching our long-dried souls and bodies. We kissed each other all over the lips and face, inching towards other parts of each other's skins and then finding each other's lips and tongues all over again. We never had a plan to do things a certain way, it was all in that moment. That moment became our guide. So much so that we forgot that we were not inside a house but on an open patch of land, at the mercy of bushes and trees to hide our modesty. The society could not allow the unbridled demonstration of passion on open streets and here we were, all naked. We created our small tribe of two tribespeople in the heart of an upscale town. I think this daring had made our sexual encounters even more interesting. Deep inside, we were rebels at heart, erupting at the slightest chance.

A yellow flash of light splintered our wild reverie. Like cats who get alarmed by the appearance of dogs, we became alert and stooped further to the ground. I was startled! Who could it be? It was a two-wheeler that soon sped off, and we were relaxed. Our lust still had some more time to quench itself. We got back, with bated breath, to fondling each other. Our hands were all over our bodies, trying to grab and squeeze as much as possible. It seemed like there had been a long famine and now we had chanced upon an abandoned warehouse full of wheat, rice and pulses. We were like rats in that warehouse, nibbling, with our chipped teeth, everything we could get hold of on that amazing night. But we were interrupted again!

The same two-wheeler had returned after taking a U-turn and this time it stopped a foot's distance away from us. The rider took off his helmet and peered sideways, as if searching for someone. We were frightened and tried to hide ourselves by huddling behind those scant bushes and descending further onto the slimy ground. In that moment, I turned into a religious person, murmuring silent prayers to save us from the ignominy that we would face if that man spotted us. The man had a torch and flashed it in our direction, waving it left and right. The light came nearer and nearer as the man stepped closer to us. He spotted us. We were stung with shame! I didn't have enough time to wear my top so I just wrapped it around my bra. The man was staring at us now. A hoarse voice cut through the serenity of that place, 'Don't you have any shame? This act is to be done at home and not on the road, near an academic institution. Wait! Let me inform the officials and the police. They will come and put you behind the bars for this obscene act.'

I tried to protest and to let him know that we were not perverts but committed lovers who studied in a reputed institution. This revelation made little difference to him as he was adamant.

'Do well-behaved people do this?'

I knew I stood no chance in this argument. I was distraught with the fear of my parents getting to know about this. I knew that Baba would put an end to my studies. I would again be relegated to that dungeon, that hell where my self-worth would get violated by his nasty remarks. My dismal future shook me and I wailed in pain, howling until my eyes became swollen. That mellowed the man a little bit and he quickly began to sermonise. He gave us a strict warning, saying that if we were seen like this again, he would inform everyone around, including the locals, academy officials and our parents. I had just escaped a brutal massacre of my honour by this man's impulsive pardon. I did not know what would have happened to Viplav if his parents came to know. Maybe he would've been scolded but I was sure that no one would put an end to his studies. I realised that having a penis in India went a long way.

As we walked out of that lush green terrain, our hands were clenched together, our heads stooped in shame. I decided to break the deafening silence. I suggested we have a croissant to celebrate our escape. Food had, in the past, comforted my worries and I was hoping it would work this time as well. I wanted to divert my attention from the moral stripping we just had. There was a small roadside bakery near us. Everything about it looked mystical, the red brick walls and the freshly baked treats that lined the wooden shelves on the wall. I went in and ordered a cinnamon hazelnut coffee for myself and a croissant for Viplav.

Money does help in overcoming humiliation, and maybe one wouldn't mind being humiliated as long as one has a loaded wallet. I smirked thinking that the scooter rider did not have as much money as I had. He could not afford to have a Rs 600 cinnamon hazelnut coffee whenever someone insulted him; he had to probably make do with a Rs 10 *kulhad* chai or a ginger tea made by his ever-nagging fat wife. By the time I had three sips of my coffee, I was out of that nightmare. I told Viplav that from then on, we had to be more careful but we could not deny ourselves of that ecstatic pleasure!

As I returned to my PG, I was apprehensive. If someone saw me, what would they think? The signs of lovemaking were vivid on my swollen lips. I had biscuits with milk and cornflakes in my room and did not step out of my room that night. The next day, as I woke up, I rushed towards the mirror and looked at my lips. They looked normal again. I heaved a sigh of relief. I bathed, put on my clothes, combed my hair, patted some talcum powder on my face, applied *kajal* and left for college. In class, Vijay was waiting for me as usual, having reserved a seat for me. There was someone who waited for me, saved me a seat every day. I didn't want anything more. I wanted to stand at the door and endearingly look at the vacant seat on which Vijay had kept his bag so that no one else would take that seat. That little black leather bag and its strap grazing the ground clumsily serving its purpose of sealing the love between two friends. My rainbow of imagination was snapped by his voice.

'Hey, you disappeared suddenly yesterday. Where have you been?'

I knew he had a soft corner for me and in that moment, I almost felt as though I was cheating on him. I also knew he had a feeling that Viplav and I were an item. It was like that truth which is often unsaid but everyone is aware of. Viplav and my relationship was that truth which we tried to keep under wraps. Similarly, the profound fondness Vijay and I had for each other was kept hidden due to the existence of the former truth. I could clearly see that Vijay was trying to woo me in his simple, natural ways. This attracted me to him even more. He was from a prosperous family, which was evident from his clothes, his bike and his spendthrift ways. But I prided myself on being a loyal person and hence brushed aside my feelings for him. I had been doing this for the past two months, reveling secretly in Vijay's company and yet sticking to my love for Viplav. But fate clearly had other plans.

The sheer enormity of bodily needs put me in grave embarrassment twice. First, when that middle-aged man on a scooter caught us behind the bushes and second, when I had to hide my bubbling attraction for Vijay. I do not think I was at fault in the former case, especially because as an unmarried couple, Viplav and I did not have a house of our own to have socially sanctioned sex. But we were both young and had hormones raging in our bodies ever since we hit puberty, ever since we started watching romantic films and ever since we read in textbooks that sexual intercourse happens between a man and a woman. Did the textbooks ever mention that sex needed a man and a woman to be married first?

The lack of a home and the lack of experience, coupled with raging hormones, propelled us to bring out our carnal frustrations in the open. After that sexual debut, we continued touching and caressing each other in empty parks, behind the high walls of our college, in lifts, under trees in deserted roads at night. Public spaces became our arena of lovemaking. Since Viplav had a roommate and I stayed in a girls' PG, it was impossible for us to bring our companion home. I remember the day when I broke the rule. That day, my lock was jammed and I struggled to open it with my key. After trying to unlock it for half an hour, I tried to break the lock. But I wasn't strong enough. I went to my landlord and explained the situation to him and asked him if I could ask a male friend to break the lock. He said yes and I was ebullient. Not because the door could now be opened but because I finally had a chance to sneak Viplav into my room. I called him home and it took us 20–25 minutes to break the lock. Once inside, I shut the door and we jumped into the bed, indulging in wet kisses.

Love has its own seasons. This is not a cliché. I experienced it in my affair. In college, when we had semester examinations, Viplav's roommate attended extra classes and hence he would not be home before 7:00 PM. Viplav told me about that and sensing the opportunity, we both decided to move our carnal trysts to his room. During the exams, this became a routine. I went to his place on the pretext of having lunch. There was a local mess behind his room that served hot, home-made tiffin at a very reasonable price. Viplav insisted that I try their special omelette but being a vegetarian, I turned down his offer each time. But love prevailed and one day, upon his insistence, I ate the omelette. Post lunch, we strolled towards his room, while we kept an eye out to ensure that no one was following us. As we reached his room, Viplav latched the door and I lay on his bed. He lay down next to me and then we indulged in kisses. We took our tops off and made out. We never undressed completely, I was quite cautious to not lose my virginity. Each time he insisted on going further, I said, 'Let's save something for marriage.' It irked him a lot but he never made it apparent.

Our semester tests continued for a month and there was ample time for us to indulge in our amorous pleasures. One day when I went to Viplav's place, as we were deep in our carnal sojourn, someone knocked on the door. To say that I was scared is an understatement. I panicked and sat on the bed. Viplav, on the other hand, was calmer and called out to the visitor. It was Pramod, his roommate.

'How could he come at this time? Did you know about this?' I looked at Viplav in suspicion and asked him in a trembling voice. He did not. What would we do now? Our clothes were all strewn on the floor and across the edges of the bed. There was hardly any time to get dressed. The knocks grew louder. It almost seemed like Pramod thought there was a thief in his room. We both got up from the bed in a frenzy and started dressing up as quickly as we could. It was easier for Viplav to pull up his pants and button his shirt, but I had to hook my bra, drape a sari and use safety pins to put the pleats in place. I panicked and that made it even more difficult for me to tie the sari. Pramod had lost his patience and started calling out from outside the door. To calm him, Viplav replied, 'Yes, I'm opening the door.'

The room was small, approximately 10 x 8 feet in size, and it would take a maximum of 20 seconds for someone to leave the bed and walk up to the door to open it. Here it had been more than three minutes. What must he be thinking? I managed to wrap my sari around and clip the safety pin on my shoulder. The other pins were not fastened. Viplav opened the door. Pramod came in but I could not look him in the eye. I was filled with extreme shame. I sat in a corner and tried to talk to him about my exams but noticed that he was not looking back at me. It was strange! Pramod was a decent person. He never misbehaved with me and now he was ignoring my presence in the room. I felt that something must seem awkward to him and I looked at my sari. Oh god! In the rush to drape my sari, my *pallu* had completely dislodged. The pleats stuck together and looked weird. On top of that, they made the curve of my left breast visible. From where Pramod sat, he could clearly see that my left breast was not covered by the *pallu*. Realising that the *pallu* had gone awry, I nervously pulled it over my left breast. I met with half-success and in this tussle, my safety pin tore the sari.

In retrospect, when I recollect that incident, I am surprised at how embarrassed I was! Why was sex so looked down upon? Something to be ashamed of? Sex is the reason we are here on this earth. Our parents had sex! They had sex while we were growing up. In fact, children are made to stop sleeping in their parents' room only so the parents can have some privacy for lovemaking. As an adult, I only carried forward a natural, biological act that my parents and many others practised. Wouldn't it be good if we were sexually empowered and informed and did not consider sex a taboo? On that fateful day, when Pramod came into the room, wouldn't it have been much simpler if Viplav had told him the truth and said, 'Pramod, can you wait outside for a while? Pallavi is dressing up.'

The entire room was a mess as Pramod waited outside. I was scared out of my wits as I tried to arrange the sari back on my body. My sari was all over the bed; some part of it was wrapped around the bedsheet and some lay near the foot of the bed and some was entangled around the pillow against which Viplav undressed me. It took me a few minutes just to assemble the entire garment, let alone the time it took me to drape it around me. Viplav was ready in his shirt and trousers and was brushing his hair. My hair was dishevelled and I couldn't find my earrings. What was Pramod thinking? Why could he not just leave the place and come back afterwards? My anxious mind tried to create excuses that put the onus of this soon-to-be-discovered mishap on Viplav. I grabbed hold of the sari and wore it in the shortest possible time. I combed my hair with my fingers and sat in a corner of the bed as Viplav opened the door. It had taken us almost 10 minutes to open the door. Could Pramod have guessed that we were making love? The thought made me red-faced and I curled my big toe in shame.

Something did not feel right then. I tried to shrug off the concerns as I thought I was overthinking but my intuition would not let me rest. I could not pick on the signals that made me feel something was amiss in that room. Pramod was sitting on the bed in front of me and talking to Viplav. Everything seemed alright except Pramod had not faced me ever since he had walked into the room. I felt offended! He probably thought that I was a promiscuous woman, but he was a nice, well-behaved guy. He did not have a girlfriend and treated girls with a lot of respect. As I tilted my head down to look at the sari, I was appalled. In that haste, I had forgotten to wrap my left breast with the pleats and my protruding, aroused nipples could be seen from under the blouse. On top of that, the hooks had been fastened unsteadily and some of them remained open. It was a complete breakdown of my dignity and modesty. Pramod was trying to save me from disgrace by not looking at me. How I wished in that moment that he were my boyfriend.

Viplav insisted on making love every day after we finished our classes. And while I liked our amorous sojourns sometimes, at other times I was simply too fatigued, not in the mood or just bored to do the act. But now I had no other choice but to acquiesce to him because I had made that choice. I never knew that you can also say no in an intimate relationship. All my life, I was never encouraged to say no in my house, or in my school; how could I learn this now all of a sudden? What I secretly desired was that Viplav would guess my inhibitions and lack of interest and would step back on his own. But that never happened. On that fateful day, when I saw the sober, chivalrous side of Pramod, I almost wanted this man who seemed to be not hungry for a woman's flesh. He could have leered at me, ogled at me, could have stolen glances but he did none of that. His calm detachment from the carnal realm of love elevated him in my eyes.

The Financial Parasite

It was during those days that I came to know that Viplav was not from a well-to-do family. Though he never spoke about his humble background, it was evident in his spartan lifestyle. Having said that, he did a good job of making a good life out of limited resources. His clothes were always neatly washed and ironed and he was very meticulous at keeping his things in order. He was a typical man next door. He neither drank nor smoked and was deeply religious. All in all, complete marriage material.

But there were subtle signs that were hard to ignore. He would repeat his pair of light brown trousers often and all his shirts were tailor-made and not bought ready-made from malls. His shoes were well-worn on the sides and the laces were fraying. I often reminded him to buy a new pair but he always got the old ones repaired instead. This was unusual in our college where everyone came from affluent families and always showed off their new clothes and accessories.

I often saw Viplav repeating his pair of five-pocket corduroys, his t-shirts and a pair of faded blue jeans. I realised that those were not his favourite clothes as he claimed they were but were actually the only clothes he owned. He told me once that his father was a clerk, which meant that his salary would be no more than a paltry sum of Rs 18,000–20,000 a month, which he used to pay the tuition fees for his two sons and support his family. I felt empathetic for Viplav, for his humble background. I guess my love for Viplav was triggered by a combination of my desperation and loneliness and his qualification despite his humble background.

Baba transferred generous amounts of money to my bank account, most of which remained unused. He had paid my rent for a whole year in advance and since I lived very close to the college, I spent nothing on transportation. It had been six months since I moved to Pune, and the monthly allowance kept piling up in my bank. It took me some time to adjust to the sudden onrush of money in my account. All my life I was made to starve for the little luxuries of life: books, dresses, shoes, and now that I had money, I could not dare spend it recklessly on my own. I had never learnt self-indulgence, so it was difficult, but it became easier with time.

I always felt bad for Viplav, especially when I saw his shoes, and wanted to do something for him. I was developing new tastes in fashion and often took him along for shopping. I felt bad that while I stuffed my shopping basket, Viplav just stared at the clothes in the men's section. Seeing his all-too-austere lifestyle, I decided to use my money to help him live a better life. It made me feel happy. After carefully scrutinising the entire shopping district of Pune, I selected the Brand Factory outlet located in Aundh. It was a factory outlet and one could buy branded clothes for very little. I then asked him to accompany me for shopping, indicating that I had to buy some clothes for myself.

We soon reached the mall and walked through the basement parking and exchanged a few kisses inside the lift. Once in that store, I started to look around for clothes; I could not let Viplav know the real purpose of the visit. The women's section was on the ground floor and the men's was on the first. After picking up a top, I suggested that he check out the men's section as there were deep discounts. He was not very keen on this suggestion. After 15 minutes, I picked up a pink salwar kameez set. I liked the fabric and it had a *bandh gala*. Viplav approved of my choice. I bought a pair of tank tops and then asked Viplav if he had picked something for himself. As anticipated, he had not. I told him that now that we had come all this way and that there was a sale, he had to buy something.

We walked to the men's section where an array of items was on display. Racks and hangers displayed shirts, trousers, shoes, belts and other accessories. A big cart held a lot of clothes, all of them being sold at throwaway prices. I was brimming with excitement which I tried hard to conceal. I was very happy because I was doing something for him. I knew I had inherited this trait of giving from Baba. Like him, I liked to be a giver rather than a taker. That was the first time I had purchased something for someone, though not with my own money. Viplav walked up to a shoe counter where shoes of different types from different brands were neatly stocked on steel racks. He picked a few of them, turned them around to check their firmness, checked the quality of the leather and then the price tag. He was particularly interested in a pair of black shoes and he looked at them again and again. But he kept them back after holding them in his hands for a while.

I followed him and slyly looked at the price tag. It cost around Rs 1,000 and I felt mildly uncomfortable looking at the price tag. I was perplexed since I realised that I wanted the contentment of giving without really shelling out money. Human nature's complexities, I thought. It's difficult to part with money when one is not spending it on oneself.

But seeing Viplav's dejected face, I decided that I would buy that pair of shoes for him. It did not occur to me that, like him, I too was practically penniless without the support of my rich father. This was a hard realisation I came to when I had to earn for myself. Earning money is definitely difficult but sustaining a consistent income is even harder, especially when you are no Tata, Birla or Ambani.

I looked at the shoes that Viplav liked, picked them and furtively carried them to the counter. I asked the salesman to pack those shoes and then hurriedly walked to the payment counter. Viplav still was not aware of my plan; we would unpack the shoes once we got back to his house. We took an autorickshaw back to his place. It was easier to go to his house in the afternoon as his roommate Pramod was in college. His classes finished at 4:00 PM whereas ours ended at 2:00 PM. As we opened the door, I could not contain my excitement and spilled the secret. I showed him the pair of shoes. He was stupefied! I expected a scolding but he did not shout. Instead, he asked in a feeble tone, 'Why did you do this?' The reaction was far subdued than what I had expected. I thought he was bound by gender norms to not accept an expensive gift from a girl. He was grateful, surprised and happy.

I eventually started supporting Viplav by paying for things like our meals, our shopping trips, the films we watched and the auto fare. It began slowly but quickly became very frequent. I had become the eternal giver and he the relentless taker. In the beginning, he was reticent and hesitant but with time, he became quite vocal about his financial needs.

Over the next few months, his hesitation crumbled as I pushed him to indulge in luxuries that my bank account could afford and his could not. I continued to entertain his requests; we dined in expensive restaurants often and took autorickshaws everywhere we went. I bought him expensive clothes and also lent him money for his other expenses. The double financial burden started bogging me down. I became fearful that Baba would notice my expenses and ask me for an explanation. This financial burden soon put a strain on the relationship and I transitioned from being buoyant in love to being despondent in love. Nonetheless, I was carrying this baggage with aplomb and without complaining.

Viplav had become a financial parasite. When I first met him, he appeared self-respecting and unostentatious. He had a modest life and wore simple clothes. He was frugal and non-materialistic. I survived on the money Baba sent me. Thankfully, he had got very generous after I started studying for my MBA. That was so strange! I had always been his daughter but he became more loving and appreciative after I cleared my exams. I decided back then that I would never discriminate against my child the way he did with me.

Viplav never forced me to pay for things. He would often, quite innocently, ask me to the pay the bill when we went shopping or dining together. I don't know why but I could never say no. All my life, I was never allowed to say no. How could I start so late in life?

Around the same time, when my patience with Viplav's expenses began waning, I fumbled upon another bitter truth. Like Viplav, his elder brother too was being supported by his girlfriend. In fact, she was paying his rent. I confronted Viplav. I was very irritated; in my pursuit to become the ever-gracious, ever-sacrificing mother of Jesus, I had ignored that I had competition. I expected unanimous and unmoving admiration for my generous doles for Viplav. It would not happen now.

Of course, I resented the fact that both the brothers were dependent on their female partners. Initially, I felt it was justified for Viplav as he was the younger one. Plus, his elder brother had a whole apartment to himself; sharing it with flatmates could have lessened the rental cost. Viplav told me that Sonali Di, his brother's girlfriend, often spent the night at the apartment. I could see that both the brothers were content living off their girlfriends. But then I had already committed myself to Viplav. What did I do next? I waited patiently at a bus stop till a biker pulled up and gave me a lift. I had subconsciously started planning my exit from the relationship and I did not have to wait for long.

Viplav had lured me into this relationship with the promise of marriage. I came from a broken home, conspicuously marked with fights, unrest, hostility and lack of love. I started insisting on a commitment to marriage and I wept and stomped my feet when he refused. I did not give in and persisted till he finally agreed. I had assessed my relative gain and took a decision where I stood to gain more happiness. The profits of the relationship were Viplav's constant company, companionship and, of course, sexual gratification. These were qualitative gains. The losses were quantitative, that is, always financial.

I think we all make such choices in life, and compromises, adjustments, sacrifices and flexibility are some of the fancy words we have created to justify how we coerce ourselves to make these choices.

I was reprimanded for not having been able to get good grades. I was compared with other kids in the neighbourhood who always fared extremely well. The benefit of this harshness was that I had grown into a resilient and tolerant adult. But the downside was that a part of me had stopped reasoning and had learnt to follow orders. I had grown comfortable with imposing choices on myself which would not appeal to my heart. It is true that our parents act in our best interests, but it is also important to cultivate the freedom of choice, of individuality, of unhindered thinking in a child.

I could see that I was blindly giving in to Viplav's demands and could sense that I was not happy in this relationship. The recent chain of events had led me to question if Viplav really was the right person to be with.

Viplav always disapproved of my friendship with Vijay. Either he was insecure or he was a sincere well-wisher: he used to warn me often saying that Vijay was not a good man and that I should stay away from him. But I could not see any signs of disrespectful behaviour from Vijay, which would have led me to believe Viplav's theories. I did not stop talking to Vijay.

I remember one day. It was around 8:00 PM. I was in my PG, lazing on my bed. Suddenly my phone rang. It was Vijay. I was happy to see his call and immediately answered.

'Pallo!'

'Yeah?' I was trying hard to contain the excitement in my voice.

'Pallo, India has won the match against Pakistan and we are celebrating and dancing at Om Supermarket. I am missing you so much and I wish you were here at this moment. I wanted to dance with you, Pallo.'

This serendipitous outpour of affection startled me and got me thinking why he would say something like that. I knew he had a circle of friends and that he admired me. But to miss someone when you are already surrounded by a horde of people...wasn't that a sign of love? Or was I overthinking again?

I was older than Viplav by a year and half and I had hidden this fact from him. I had lied to him about my age. That the woman in a relationship had to be younger than the man was nothing but a silly patriarchal rule but this fact was so firmly ingrained in my mind back then that I felt the need to hide my age from Viplav. Since I was a deeply honest and virtuous person, this lie played in my mind every time I met him or talked to him. Even in his absence, I kept thinking about this. At times, our talks veered to topics that led to the discussion of our ages, which served as a repeated reminder of my guilt. At other times, I had to hide some of my personal belongings from him: my student ID card, PAN card and bank passbook as they all mentioned my date of birth. I did not let him touch my bag.

Not being able to bear the burden of this lie any more, I decided to reveal this to him and started seeking the right time and opportunity to speak to him about this. What better place for confession than a temple where people from across the state came to wash off their sins? Viplav and I often went for early-morning walks to Chatursshringi temple. We used to meet at an intersection point, equidistant from our homes, and then walk to the temple. The temple was perched on the mountain slope and was frequented by hundreds of devotees every day. One had to climb almost 100 steps to get to the temple; the stairs were two identical rows of steep rock slabs carved out of the mountainside. They were guarded by yellow, slim iron handrails on both the sides. The stairs turned hot in the noon due to continued exposure to the scorching sun, making it even more difficult for someone to climb barefoot.

To an outsider, or a first-time visitor, it might seem like a daunting task, but the place was so serene and enchanting in the morning that climbing the stairs actually was a fun activity for us. I enjoyed climbing stairs for many reasons. One, I had Viplav by my side. Two, I had to conquer this to be able to reach the hill. I always liked challenges and the feeling of jubilation in overcoming them. Three, I was filled with energy seeing the fellow devotees climbing up the stairs undeterred.

The devotees were an eclectic mix of people from different backgrounds, age groups and financial status. It was evident from their gestures, their clothes, their accessories and their behaviours. There were married couples, families with a kid or two in tow, elderly couples, young lovers, friends, single men. They all carried plates filled with flowers, incense sticks, garland, camphor, turmeric and sweets. A few touched the first step of the stairs before embarking on the uphill journey. This included me.

It was then when I realised the power of groups. Any activity would not seem difficult if performed in groups. Why? One, we tend to downplay our suffering when we see others facing the same. Two, we get strength from the struggles of others. At times, unity is premeditated where people consciously come together for a cause. At other times, unity is incidental. People get thrown into circumstances or have a chance meeting with someone who shares similar feelings, suffering, injustice or an event. It is important to mobilise this power of groups, and it can only be done by sharing wisdom, learnings and mistakes. I was in a phase where I depended on one man for all my happiness, security and comfort and I still felt empty from within. There were signs all over. I was feeling guilty for being older than him, something that was not even my fault. We were physically intimate and yet I felt this age gap would prove a hindrance in our alliance. Being alone only increases your vulnerabilities. I yearned to be among those groups of devotees, happily chanting, clapping, singing and forgetting all my woes in this relationship.

We soon reached the precincts of the temple, prayed to the goddess and then left the place. It was early morning, around 7:30 AM. We walked together on the pavement adjoining S.B. Road. Flanking the road were some Bengali sweet shops that also served lassi and chai. The sky was clear and the morning sun was shining with a demure brightness and spreading warmth all around. Pigeons were flying in V-shaped flocks and very few vehicles were plying on the road; there was no trace of smoke. I could feel the warm sunshine and soothing morning air filling my heart with positive energy. I finally mustered the courage to say the truth but was reticent. It was like my lips moved but I could not speak. It was when Viplav was bidding bye to me that I finally broke my silence.

'Hang on! I need to tell you something. I actually wanted to confide something,' I said it like I was about to confess a crime, 'I'm not 1984-born. I was born in 1983. So, I'm older than you.'

He stayed mum for a while and then spoke, 'So, we have a huge age difference.'

My heart sank on hearing this. I knew from the very beginning that Viplav would not do well with this revelation.

He continued, 'See, you have spoken about our marriage in the past. But given our age difference, do you know how difficult that will be? It will be difficult for me to convince my parents. You know how our societies operate. I thought you were only six months older, so I had some dim hopes for our marriage but now it seems implausible.'

He had declared his decision! I was, for a moment, confounded. I knew in my heart that an age difference was not as big an issue as it was made out to be. Love knows no boundaries, no limitations and no differences. I had always believed that. Furthermore, I was far more attractive, intelligent and even more affluent than Viplav. Despite these differences, I loved him unconditionally. Yet, I was the one who was being shunned. There was a war of logic and blind love going on in my heart. Love seemed to be emerging victorious over logic.

'So, you have made up your mind that nothing can happen between us?' I questioned him again.

'Yes, what can I do? You never told me about this in the beginning. In fact, you lied to me. I had a little hope for us but now nothing is possible. We can never get married,' Viplav concluded.

He seemed to be a cold-hearted person. I wondered, where had all the love gone? All the sacrifices, duties, intimacy...everything that I had given to him so painstakingly seemed to have left no impression on his heart. I drew a blank expression, turned my back on him and started walking back to my home. That walk seemed to be the longest walk of my life. My feet turned heavy and happiness vanished from my face. I felt directionless. Since the time I had been with him, he had become an integral part of my life, my dreams, my desires. With him gone out of my life, I had to weave a new life, which seemed so difficult at that moment.

Now that I look back and introspect on what had happened, I realise that there were very clear signals that I had chosen to not pay heed to. These signals come from vibes, actions, behaviours of the people we are in relationships with. In my relationship, too, there were always signals that Viplav was not interested in a committed relationship but I chose to overlook them.

I found it difficult to accept rejection or even face it. I liked someone, fell in love with him, now I wanted him for myself, period! I became so obsessed with this desire that I didn't stop to consider if he was even worth all the effort. Whether he cared for me in a way I should be cared for, whether he respected and valued me as a person. All of that now seemed to hold very little concern for me; I was obsessed with him and stubborn enough to still cling on to him. I could not take rejection even if it meant losing so much self-respect for that.

I was hurting myself by being with a man who didn't care, love and respect me in the way I deserved. I let myself accept abuse and yet did not walk away. As if enduring all that torment would make me a stronger woman. I knew I was unhappy inside, yet on the surface, I appeared satisfied because for me, the idea of being with him overrode all other desires. I wonder now why I behaved like that.

Of course, I was ill-equipped to handle rejection. In the process of coping with Viplav's rejection, I started rejecting my self-worth and my whole identity. Viplav's rejection was not the only one I faced in my life; my parents had rejected my dreams and aspirations when I couldn't meet their expectations, there were friends who had rejected my company.

We often define ourselves not by the person we are but by our relationships, achievements, recognition, circumstances and everything equally transient. Rejection is a matter of perception. Over the years, I'd like to believe that my capacity to accept rejection has improved. I have become more conscious of my abilities and of my worth as a person. I respect myself much more than I used to.

I had been and am still a giver. I pride myself in keeping a check on my desires for the benefit of others.

This behaviour is typical of women who grow up within a strict patriarchal set-up where men are always given priority over women. Due to the early collapse of my parents' marriage, I was always scared of losing someone dear to me and hence I started valuing relationships more. As a result, I always went out of my way to appease people whom I deemed important in my life.

I now believe that the way we spend our childhood leaves an everlasting impression on our characters. As time progresses, our circumstances change, people in our lives change but a part of our character always remains the same. It is important that we understand this and be more accepting of our flaws and strengths. It is painful, no doubt, when we are let down by someone we love, especially for no fault of our own. But we all learn from our mistakes. It is important to be in relationships where our partners accept us with our mistakes and choose to forgive them. Punishment is too evil a concept for me. Life is too short. Instead of punishment, if we are bestowed with forgiveness, we all live in peace.

I was crying as I walked back to my PG after Viplav rejected the idea of our marriage. My gentle heart was broken, my mind was numb and I couldn't think of anything to make it better. I was disappointed with my luck and with myself. I felt like a victim at the hands of luck for I knew that I had not done anything wrong. The age difference could have been overcome by the love, sincerity and loyalty that I offered to him.

I reached my PG and sat on the bed with a heavy heart. It was time to get ready for class but I refused to pull myself together. I sat still for a whole hour and kept checking my phone in the hope that Viplav would call or text. He didn't. Soon it was lunch time but I kept sitting on my bed. And then, in a sudden second, I realised that my endless pondering and repenting would not change the outcome and that I had to start learning to live with the truth. I had to carry on with life, for life would not stop.

I looked at my mobile phone again. It was 1:00 PM and I wondered if I should skip the next class or attend it. After 10 minutes of contemplation, I decided to go for the class. I felt at the least, it would distract me for some time. However, I knew that it would be a while before my mind could process the pain of this break-up. Viplav sounded firm in his decision and there was no way he was going to reconsider.

For the next few days, I carried on with the routine of sobbing and lying listlessly on my bed and dragging myself to class. I had stopped socialising with my classmates. I was walking back to my PG one day when I heard Viplav's voice. I should have felt delighted upon hearing it but I did not. The last few days had taught me to accept his absence and I had grown immune to everything concerning him. Nonetheless, I stopped and he came up to me.

'I was missing you,' he said.

I stared at him. A week back, I would have died to hear those words, but my heart and mind had shut down completely. Maybe I had moved on, maybe I had put the past behind. Viplav shook my arm.

'Are you listening? I said I'm missing you. I want you back,' his voice was louder this time.

'Back for?'

I was still not able to comprehend what he was trying to say. Sometime back, he had said he did not want me, now he was saying he wanted me.

'I told you I miss you. I want us back. Like we were before,' he summed it up for me.

I was neutral. But now I was able to understand that he wanted to make amends and get back together. Inside, I felt a bag of mixed emotions: of quandary, victory, contentment, inertness. I stitched together pieces of my emotions and my mind and announced a brief response:

'I want some time.'

'What!' he exclaimed with astonishment. He interrogated me.

'Why? You wanted me not to break up and now you don't want me back?'

I knew it was not him but his bruised ego speaking.

'What about our marriage?' I popped the decisive question.

He looked at me in a way someone looks at an obstinate kid standing in a shop and throwing a tantrum.

'Why are you stuck on this topic? I told you, let's be together. That is most important.'

'What would I do with this togetherness, when there is no assurance that you and I will be together in the future? What would I do if you leave me tomorrow? We have been physically intimate and do you even realise how difficult it is for me to get over that? How would you feel if you stood naked in front of someone and then learnt that you were just a passing phase for them?'

I blurted out a series of questions and accusations. He went away in silence. I remained there watching him drift away from my life. I did not feel a twist in my heart, unlike in past instances. I managed to hold my pieces together and stand there. I was immobile for a moment, my heart turned rigid; a trace of sympathy for him could make me go weak in my knees again. He was soon out of sight.

The next day as I walked towards my classroom, I saw Viplav's brother standing at a distance. I was perplexed. He studied in a different college and had no business being there. Was that happenstance or had he come to meet me? My feeble heart was not ready for another drama. He walked towards me and mumbled, 'Viplav cannot bear this separation and is leaving to go home for a month. He might not come back as he says he cannot study at a place where he will see you every day.'

The disclosure shook me. I was shivering with guilt. Here was a man who would ruin his career for me. No doubt he loved me, I thought. It is strange that we often associate love with obsession, possession and destruction, thanks to the melodrama doled out by films. I had no other model of reference except for what I had seen in films and it broke my heart to imagine letting go of a man who had developed self-destructive tendencies because of my absence. I immediately changed my mind, burst into tears and rushed to meet him. I misconstrued his possessiveness as his love.

The Red Scars of Love

It was a day before Holi. I was fond of cooking and decided to cook something for Viplav, perhaps out of my sense of guilt. I still remember how I struggled to learn to cook when I was young. I was all of 11 when Ma asked me to come to the kitchen to make chapatis. I was acutely disinterested and always tried to say no to her demands till one day she refused to cook for the family if I didn't accompany her in the kitchen.

'It is important for girls to learn to cook. After all, when you get married and go to a new home, you will have to cook for your in-laws and husband,' she said.

Cooking was another thing that my brother, who was just a year younger than me, was never asked to do. I refused to listen to my mother and my resolution lasted for almost two hours, till I got hungry and walked to the kitchen reluctantly. My first tryst with cooking was a horrifying tale as all my chapatis were misshapen. I must commend my mother's patience because she wouldn't stop correcting my ways till I could make perfect chapatis.

I was thinking about what I could make for Viplav. I had been pretty traditional in the ways I pampered my boyfriend; cooking was one of those ways in which I showered my love on him. This time, I thought of making a dessert; it would be the perfect festive treat. I had a single stove and a handful of utensils. I often ate outside and hence the groceries at hand were limited.

Since it was almost Holi, I did not want to step out for the fear of being molested by drunk local boys roaming the streets.

I looked around in my kitchen: there were a few plastic containers filled with rice, pulses, sugar, salt, spices and oil. On the left-corner wall, I had drilled a nail from which a bag of potatoes hung. I started thinking about the possible dishes in my mind. I looked at my supplies and decided to make kheer.

I started making it with undivided attention, complete dedication and precision. I call it meditative cooking. I made a rice and milk mixture and kept cooking it on low heat. I started to get ready while it cooked. I bathed and shampooed my hair and picked a pink salwar suit to wear. I left my long, voluminous hair loose, applied light *kajal* on my eyes and was all set. At that time, I was in a complete bliss: cooking for my beloved, getting ready for him and waiting to meet him. He was the centre of all my attention. I was so happy in that moment that I became completely oblivious of the fact that I had digressed into a state where my happiness was dictated by Viplav's happiness.

The milk had thickened and turned brown. A coat of thick cream enveloped the softened rice on the top. I added sugar and chopped almonds and covered the pan with a plate. I was anxiously walking around in my tiny room.

After waiting for half an hour, I touched the pan. It had cooled down. I took out a tiffin box and poured the kheer into it. I put the box in my bag, wore my sandals and left my room. Viplav lived a kilometre away from my house. I had been to his place so many times that I could probably walk there blindfolded.

The road leading to his place was straight, with two turns in between, one left and one right. Like all of Pune, it was flanked by lush green foliage on either side. On my way, I saw groups of men coming from the opposite side; their faces were painted and clothes were stained with the garish colours of Holi: black, green, red and metallic silver. They looked unrecognisable and frightening. I pretended to be unaffected but shivered inside as I crossed that group. Once that group was far away, I took a sigh of relief and started walking faster.

I pause to think. The mere sight of that group had sent chills down my spine but they did not seem to have any malintentions. I guess, our mind always jumps to the worst consequences. It looks out for cues, traits and other physical evidences to draw a hasty conclusion. Trust and hate are the two far ends of the behavioural spectrum, with the majority of emotions lying somewhere between these two ends.

I reached Viplav's room and knocked on the door. I had informed him when I was on my way. He called me from inside his room and told me that the door was only ajar. I pushed the half-shut door with my right hand and walked in. The room was neat and tidy as usual, a far cry from my clumsy room, I thought. It had two beds, one for him and one for his roommate Pramod, two study tables with vertical piles of books on them. There was a stack of racks that held their clothes. Viplav lead an ascetic life compared to the flamboyant standards of our collegemates.

Of late, physical attraction had taken dominance and precedence over emotional connect for us. I could hardly resist myself in those moments of intimacy and privacy when we found ourselves alone in his room. Our repeated sexual encounters had made me more uninhibited and it was me who now made the first move. I raced towards Viplav and hugged him; it was followed by a long passionate kiss. At 25, I was still wary of sex and so we could never progress to that point. I made it clear to him that sex had to wait and he obediently agreed.

After the passion settled down, I took out the tiffin box from my bag and opened its lid. The aroma of cardamom powder filled the room. I fished out a plate, poured some kheer on it and offered it to him. He gladly ate it, making appeasing sounds. After we both finished our desserts, we lay together on the bed, facing each other, our arms wrapped around each other's necks. I gazed at him lovingly and said, 'I want to make this kheer for you for my entire life.'

I looked into his eyes as I said this, and this statement served dual purpose: one, it was a wish and two, it was an indirect way of probing him to commit to marriage and commitment. As expected, he stayed quiet. I was anxious. I knew from his silence where this conversation would veer. Still I decided to pursue the conversation.

'You didn't say anything.'

'I've told you so many times to not discuss this topic but you still find a way to ask the same question, to which I have no answer,' he snapped.

'What did I say?' I was confused at his anger.

'I have said this, I do not know anything about commitment.'

'You need to tell me,' I was firm and needed an answer from him.

'I said there is no prospect of marriage at present. I do not know.'

I felt heartbroken. It all seemed so strange. Everything was perfect; it was a holiday, I was with him, we made out, ate together, we had each other for company. His words seemed like an aberration in that perfect set-up of things. I remembered when I was travelling to Goa, I had packed a bag full of things: new clothes, books, wallet, purse, tickets and other travel essentials but had forgotten to take my charger. The flight got delayed and my mobile phone's battery drained out. To top my woes, the zip on my bag broke and it seemed like everything inside my bag would fall out. It all looked like a nightmare even in the perfect setting of a vacation. I felt the same way about Viplav's response.

I tried to remain stoic but inside I was filled with despair and agitation. I eventually walked back to my room. It was all dark inside; I slumped into my bed and rested my head on the pillow. In my heart, I knew how this would end. Viplav always averted queries about marriage.

The agitation was becoming too intense for my tender heart to bear. I wanted to lash out and inflict my fury and my pain on someone, but whom? There was no one around, no friend, not even my hapless mother. I saw the kitchen knife lying in a corner of the kitchen slab. I walked up to that corner and held the knife in my right hand. In a moment, I made a few gashes on my left wrist. I count them now as I write this. There seem to be five cuts but they have all faded into one another. I keep looking at these scars now. Sleek, two-inches-long trails of forlorn love. I'm proud of my scars.

The tendency towards self-harm comes from a space of provocation. I had self-harmed on more than one occasion. The means were different, sometimes they were extreme like hitting my head against a wall, slapping my cheeks, smashing my phone. At other times, the self-harm was subtle: giving up on a wish, hurting someone, tolerating ill behaviour, brooding over the past, letting someone else take decisions for me, being critical about someone. Many youngsters cut themselves to self-harm. In my experience, self-harm eases the pain of the troubles which engulf us.

I slept for the remainder of the day and did not step out of my room. I missed my class and stayed hungry. I was punishing myself, but why? I had lied to him about my age, maybe I was punishing myself for doing that.

It was four in the afternoon and I was still lying on the bed, ruminating over what had happened. Unable to take it any more, I stepped out of my room and walked out of the PG. I wanted to talk to someone, and that someone was Vijay. There was no balance on my phone and hence I went to Om Supermarket to call him from a PCO. In that state of bewilderment, agony and self-hatred, I was still looking attractive. I was wearing a faded blue, high-waisted jeans and a body-hugging hooded black jacket. My hair was let loose and slightly messy. My eyes were red from all the crying.

I opened the screeching glass door and entered the PCO. I picked up the telephone receiver, dropped a one-rupee coin in the box and dialled Vijay's number. I waited for him to pick up the phone.

'Hello!'

'Hi Vijay, Pallavi,' I managed to speak only this much and then burst into tears.

'Hello, yeah Pallavi. Pallavi... Pallavi!'

He kept repeating my name, unable to get a response from my side. I controlled my sobbing and spoke with a heavy heart.

'Vijay, I want to meet you.'

'What happened? Why are you crying?' he got concerned.

'Just come to the supermarket, Vijay.'

'OK, give me 15 minutes.'

He came after half an hour. I was feeling miserable and he was the only one whom I could talk to. I was standing at the pavement outside Om Supermarket when Vijay arrived on his bike. He had been riding it since he was in tenth grade, he had told me once. The mighty two-wheeler was gifted by his father. He loved it like his own child and could not think of selling it to buy a new one. It is amazing how people attach deep emotions to lifeless things, but then how is it so difficult to feel deeply for real human beings?

Our eyes met. He smiled, I reciprocated with a feeble smile. In that moment, I felt enormously light. A few minutes back, my world had come crashing down and now just his presence alleviated my woes. I noticed he was looking handsome as usual. He had curly, short, unkempt, black hair, a few strands of which hung on his forehead.

He had a round face, high cheekbones, piercing grey eyes, sharp nose, thin lips, sly smile and an athletic body. He was wearing a pair of low-waist, striped and faded blue Levi's jeans and a black t-shirt. I had never looked at him so closely before. Maybe I was so besotted with Viplav that I had ensconced myself away from the rest of the world. That day that veil from my eyes was lifted and I could see the world and its people in a new light.

Vijay gestured me to sit on the backseat of his bike. I reached to the side of the bike and sat behind him. I felt a little awkward with our physical proximity.

With this ride, the second phase of my love life started.

He rode for about 10 minutes before stopping at a bistro in the neighbourhood market. He parked his bike and we got off. We stepped into the bistro and I looked around. The restaurant was not air-conditioned but looked cosy.

There were around seven steel tables and plastic chairs in sets of four around each table. At that hour, there were very few visitors in that restaurant, giving us our much-desired solitude in that public place. We both looked around and found a table in the remote corner. Vijay broke the silence.

'Tell me. What happened?'

It seemed like I was a dormant volcano waiting to erupt. I started blabbering, unmindful of whether he would be interested in knowing it all. I went on and on for about 20 minutes, speaking about my life. That emptying had a cathartic effect on me. I felt lighter and relieved. He was yet to speak but even having him listen was a healing experience.

I guess that is the problem with most of us; we try to speak but are not ready to listen. We become so deeply engaged, obsessed and engrossed with our own thoughts and issues that we stop paying attention to other people's problems. And hence we should be grateful to a listener, who hears us without interrupting. I now feel that most of the sorrows of this world can be healed if we become better listeners. The world needs more listeners!

Vijay comforted me by gently placing his right hand on my left shoulder; he kept looking intently at me. I was sobbing all this while and was wiping my face and running nose with a napkin. I could feel that he adored me in that moment and with him by my side, I was gradually moving away from the melancholic state I was in.

I could not remember what we talked about, but I do remember that he spoke about his unrequited love: a girl he loved passionately and truly, who left him for another man. He told me that he fought against all odds, travelled miles, spent his pocket money and persuaded his parents to accept her into their family. But all those efforts were in vain as the girl finally broke his heart. I was taken aback with this disclosure. On the surface, he looked so effervescent, flamboyant and playful. But deep inside, he had hidden a suffering, away from the eyes of the world. I guess, with his revelation, I was able to forget my miseries and attend to his pain. I had been a strong girl, having braved many obstacles in the past, but this setback took a toll on me, not because I was weak but because I was vulnerable. I think there is nothing wrong in being vulnerable. Being vulnerable means being human, being able to feel, which objects cannot do. Talking to Vijay helped put me at ease, partly because he had made himself vulnerable too.

Melancholy is like being stranded on an island with no food and water. The only way one can survive is by swimming out of the island. I didn't know how to swim, but here I was talking to someone who had swam out of this island. I got help in that moment of need because I asked for it. We Indians are a lot more hesitant and reticent when it comes to divulging our weaknesses, miseries, pains and insecurities. There is no life which has not been stung by these pricks but we rarely talk about it. All we talk about, instead, are our achievements, our moments of happiness. Imagine the immense courage it would take for us to share our deepest insecurities but wouldn't we feel relieved? Why do we need a trusted confidante to share it? Doesn't the mere fact that each one of us has our own secret unhappiness and failures make us worthy of being each other's trusted confidante?

Talking my heart out to him, I realised that there was nothing that could replace the comfort of a physical meeting, a face-to-face interaction. I realised the need for people to come together and talk. I realised the need to talk openly about not just our merriment but also our woes, our disappointments, our struggles, our emotional upheavals. That requires courage and a nakedness of the soul. But like the clothes we wear, we have covered our souls with layers. If we feel hot, we should shed those layers, for the heat might burn our souls. But we do not, for we see others' souls covered with layers and so we keep ours.

Vijay shared a lot with me, and I realised that Viplav and I had not shared even a fraction of the intimacy Vijay had shared with his former girlfriend. Vijay made me realise what true love is, it should be selfless; he travelled for two days by train to meet that girl just because she called him out of the blue and expressed her desire to meet him. He taught me that there should be respect for one's partner. I think in hindsight, my mind was quickly processing this new-found information to declutter itself of the destructive thoughts. I was slowly restoring my usual self, replenishing my confidence. As Vijay finished talking and looked at me, I was a changed person, very different from the one he met an hour earlier.

He continued to talk; I think he forgot that I was the one who was supposed to talk. He too had travelled back into his own past. He told me that there was a girl in his life who loved him immensely but now he had lost the right to proclaim his love in front of his parents because he believed that he had let them down with his previous relationship. I had not even told my mom about my relationship with Viplav.

By the time Vijay finished speaking, he was successful in conquering my heart. We had a long history of mutual admiration. Suddenly he said, 'I like you a lot, I can love you but I cannot marry you. I have lost that right. I'll marry whomever they want me to marry.'

I was so love-starved that this decision was easy for me to make. I wanted his proximity, his companionship, his support. Marriage discussions could happen later, I quickly thought.

I said, 'It doesn't matter. I want to be with you. That's all that matters to me.'

Not much was said between the two of us and nothing was promised, yet a faint hope flickered in my heart. I could trace some signs of a future companionship with Vijay, which would bail me out of my current situation. What I did not know then was, I was looking for an anchor in the form of a new relationship to save me from drowning in the current relationship. I did not want to learn how to swim out of it, rather, I was looking for a coach. I was and still am vulnerable. I still need relationships as much as I needed them back then but I have spent half a decade of my life trying to lessen the harm I would inflict on myself. For instance, I now know how to destroy memories and march ahead, rather than destroying a part of myself.

I came back home and slept peacefully that night for the first time in weeks. I now had no fear that stopped me from meeting Vijay and I could talk to him as much as I wanted. Our evening dates were sheer bliss. With him as my partner, I explored newer aspects of life. In the evenings, we went on long bike rides, sometimes as far as Wakad. There were large tracts of uninhabited land all around. We got down from the bike and sat on the pavement and gazed at the dotted skyline for hours. We did not talk much and our first kiss was still due!

Money spices up sex appeal and the eventual sexual experience. I realised that with Vijay. He belonged to an upper-middle-class family and wore expensive clothes. He also got a hefty pocket money from his father that he lavishly spent on parties, drinks, dining and shopping. In those days, students rarely had camera phones but

Vijay had one. It was not just his looks and his friendship but also his wallet that attracted me to him. Having grown up in a society where women marry men who are richer than them, I was happy to be with Vijay. I was so underconfident in those days that I found myself fortunate that Vijay was heaping his attention on me, much to the dismay of other girls in college. It had been two weeks since we had got together and Vijay and I had eaten out every night since then. For me it was a welcome break from the usual monotonous PG food. I started drifting away from the memories of Viplav but hadn't yet told him that I had moved on.

I think all relationships follow a pattern; it started on a high with Vijay but reached a plateau soon afterwards. Maybe the loaded wallet had started emptying out. We often spent nights in his friend's flat in Indiranagar. His friend stayed with three other boys in a two-bedroom flat and would always vacate one bedroom for us. The four of them would adjust among themselves and sleep on the couch. I always felt a deep sense of shame.

Walking into that room, my head drooped in embarrassment because I knew that the rest of the boys knew that Vijay and I would be having sex. I am sure that they also liked to imagine the act. They would imagine how Vijay would undress me, enter me, thrust inside me and how I moaned and so on. It made me uncomfortable to think that this private act no longer remained a private act. I tried to bury that shame by immersing myself into Vijay's manly, hairy chest and his heavyset body. Indeed, lust is the antidote of shame. I lusted to get over my shame. It got nearly impossible for me to have sex with him in the presence of four strangers pretending to sleep in the other room. They were probably gossiping, discussing imaginary lurid details, violating my modesty with their sleazy remarks; unbearable! I smothered my dignity by transmuting my genuine affection and love into lust. What I ignored was that on Vijay's part, it was always just about lust.

I was too influenced by films where consummation of love is always shown as an act of love replete with dramatic elements: slow motion, gentle caress, the shy girl, the approaching man, light kissing on the eyes. Things in real bedrooms were the opposite of that! I dropped a tear as Vijay entered me for the first time. It rolled down from the corner of my eye, quietly, unnoticed by him as he gently thrust inside me. It was the first time for him too and he seemed anxious.

My life was back on track. From one relationship I had moved to the next without a breather. I had become addicted and reliant on the presence of a man in my life. Until Vijay came, I clung to Viplav like lichen on tree bark. But I didn't care much for him, not after he abandoned me. But Viplav had started becoming uneasy about the break-up even though it was he who had initiated it. Strange, self-centred fools we humans are. He did not predict my departure so soon and was now longing for my presence and more importantly, my wallet. He started pursuing me, and I have no qualms admitting that I was swinging back and forth between these two men.

Though Vijay was in my life, he barely ever had time for me. Initially, I wanted just his presence but I realised that I also wanted his time. I felt lonely again. Viplav, for all his financial dependence, stuck by my side all day. It was a perfect deal, a perfect exchange of money and time. He had the time and I had the money. Vijay did not work that way. When I complained to him, he said that he wasn't the sort to spend all his waking hours with his girlfriend. He liked his independence and could not remain tied to a girl.

Being pursued and pursuing is how I would describe my state of mind in those days. That was my first brush with polyandry. Could I manage two men in my life? It was hugely strenuous and mentally exhausting. I felt like I was left with no time to myself. Monogamy then seemed like a matter of practical convenience. But life and relationships are not so easy. Vijay was closer to me in terms of who I was—rich, smart, outgoing—but I was clearly not a priority for him. Viplav did not match my sensibilities at all but was eager to be a constant companion. I realised through my situation that most of us often settle for a less deserving partner in exchange for a cure for our loneliness. I could finally see through the pragmatic aspect of love; love is not just a saccharine dream, it must allow us to thrive through the harsh realities of life. Therefore, love had to be mixed with other practical aspects of life.

I dreaded loneliness. Viplav was all too happy to get back into my life but he was unaware of my dilemma. I told Vijay that I could not be with him because I needed him to devote more time to the relationship but I also did not want to lose the erotic longing I had for him. I would often sneak into his house for a quick making-out session; sometimes we would go to his friend's flat and have sex. Viplav did not know about

Vijay but Vijay knew about Viplav. He didn't seem to mind but the bitter part of the deal was that I had to keep offering my body to Viplav to keep him assured that I was his. When with Vijay, I cautioned him not to leave bite marks on my neck. It hurt his ego but he had no other choice. Then once Viplav caught me in this triad when he went through my phone. The mobile phone was my possession but it allowed others to infringe upon my personal space, entitled them to know about my whereabouts anytime. My life ceased to be mine; it was put on public scrutiny.

A huge fight ensued between us, followed by a torrent of tears, obviously from me. I grabbed hold of him as he moved away from me, fearing I will again become a victim to loneliness. I squeezed his arm as he tried to sever my hold on him. It took some time for the tussle to settle down, and at the end of it, we were both exhausted and quiet. I tightly held his forearm and walked with him. There was a flicker of despair in my heart as I knew that I had reached a compromise: exchanging my money and my body to deal with the loneliness, but my agile mind, sharpened by impeccable education, managed to stifle that groan!

Viplav took me to the temple to seek blessings of the deity, praying that no more fights occur between us and no other man come between us. It was certain that he was not looking to marry me but he was looking for a commitment that would last two years, till we graduated. As we reached the temple on the hilltop, a warm tender breeze fanned my hair. It was surreal! The lush green canopies swayed in the breeze, the fragrance of rain-drenched mud filled the air, clouds floated like little boats in the dusky skyline; all this gave me a trance-like happiness. Nature had abundant healing powers. It filled me with an abundance of peace and joy. In that serene moment, lust blinded Viplav. He came near me and started kissing me vigorously. I was taken aback. I stood against a derelict wall as he reigned over me. It was a terrible experience; I wanted to say no and walk off but my own compulsions made me silent! I tried to feebly object.

Viplav started opening the buttons of my kurta. My vagina was wet with dread and it started palpitating in fear. Little electric currents of protest ran through my veins but popped. Viplav scooped out one breast from the tight-fitting kurta and took it to his mouth. He started sucking it as if he had been thirsty for ages. My desperate mind started thinking of ways to stop him. I shook him.

'We are in a temple and you believe in God, don't you? Then why are you contaminating the sacredness of this temple with your lust?' I blurted all of this in one quick breath and gaining further sense, I tried to push him away. But he was stubborn. Lust had blinded his better sense. He had become a beast and I was like a living corpse. In his fervour, he didn't notice that I was not participating. Sexual pleasure can be one-sided; what a travesty of love that is! Since that incident, it became routine for me to share my body between those two men. I relied on one for the fierce chemistry and on the other for averting boredom. The common deal between the two men was the body. I came to think that it was impossible for a woman to have a man support her unless he had access to her body. But then one day the bargain turned into an ordeal.

I went to Vijay's friend's flat. I earnestly admit that our sexual chemistry failed to fade after countless rounds of lovemaking. I liked everything about him. His flesh, his rugged skin, his thick neck, his hoarse voice, the way he held me with masculine force made my feminine body surrender to him. Though our kisses lasted a few minutes, in hindsight, it felt as though we had kissed for hours. His touch was like a magnet pulling me towards him. Whenever I went to meet him, no words were exchanged between us. We quickly took to our carnal roles with fervour, kissing, touching and exploring each other. How could someone say no to such a soul-gratifying, body tingling experience? I justified that bargain quite easily in my own head, unknown to both these men.

I could not explain the rationale to my lovers, so I astutely managed schedules and places, coordinated lies, cooked up excuses. I had been able to use my management skills in keeping the two men from locking heads. But still I could not conquer technology. When I was at Vijay's house, my phone rang. It was Viplav. How could he call me again? I had just met him an hour back. I was stupefied! I ignored the calls but they would not stop. What do I do? My mind started kicking. It would take me half an hour to reach his place and he would ask me where I had been all this time. I knew I was a bad liar but a fabulous withholder. To lie is not the same as to not disclose.

I stood up and hurriedly got dressed. Seeing my anxiety, Vijay could sense that I had to get back to the other man. He was at unease with the sudden wrapping up, especially when it was being done for some other man. But when he saw me fretting, he lost his cool. He dropped me near Viplav's home and Viplav saw us. I went berserk trying to imagine the evil outcome that would push back my life into an abyss of loneliness. In a jiffy, I followed him to his house and bolted the door as soon as he and I were inside. And then quickly, I unbuttoned my shirt and scooped out my left breast from under my bra and with another hand pulled his mouth to suck it. He was dismayed at this sudden move, I was fiery and tumultuous. He tried to stop me and said it made him feel guilty. But I was so swamped by the threat of being caught that I wanted to put all his concerns to rest by immersing him in a pool of lust.

After three months of oscillating between those two men, I decided to stop. Of course, neither of them was going to marry me. With a morose heart, I thought maybe in the remaining one year, Vijay would get addicted to me, so much so that it would become impossible for him to leave me. But I was wrong and I started getting clear signals in the last semester of college; he stopped paying me any attention. Something weird happened around the same time; strangely, Viplav started begging for my presence in his life. I still remember how, when after everyone had left after class, he came to me and pleaded, 'It is impossible for me to stay alone in this campus. No boy of my class is ready to share his room with me. I'm all alone. To be with you, I left all my friends and now all of them are making fun of me. Please be with me just for this year. You can also continue your relationship with Vijay. I have no objections. But at least be a good friend. It is impossible to be alone.'

The loneliness bug had bitten him too. But I had no intention to keep his hopes up. He had betrayed me on a lot of occasions, he had violated my body and had never agreed to commit to marriage. That year, he ended up sharing his room with a junior; his grades dropped and he did not find a job through the campus recruitments. A woman had ravaged his life! I had no ill will for him but I was not sad for his dismal state either. I was content! But his ill fortune could not heal my woes. In my six months of togetherness with Vijay, I tried everything to make him fall in love with me but to no avail. In our last month, when it was clear that he had no intentions to sanctify our relationship, I suffered a heartbreak. I cut my wrist again. I was clear that I was not giving up life over this broken affair simply because I could not bear the pain. In that respect I must say that people who have taken their own lives have had supreme courage to bear the tormenting pain they inflicted on their infirm bodies.

It took me three months, a job, lots of music and Rohan to bridle the pain of abandonment by Vijay. It was our last month in campus and job offers had dried up. I had started applying on job forums but lacked skills to write a proper mail to the job poster. Most of the times I frequented job sites of companies and uploaded my resume. But nothing happened. I was losing hope; the 2009 recession had sabotaged my dreams of a stellar career and fat pay cheques. I was morose. A month passed by and nothing happened. I tried my level best to clear job interviews, dressing impeccably, smiling vivaciously, reading and revising all course material provided to us, but the fact that I was not an engineer spoiled my chances at these interviews. In my disillusionment, I started applying to minor white-collar jobs of receptionist, typewriter or anything else that came my way. Viplav was unemployed as was Vijay. There were more than 30 students who were jobless. Our glorious days were behind us. Reality is far more threatening. I did not want to face the ignominy of going back home and tolerating my father's wrath again!

There was a notice displayed on the notice board outside our classroom. It advertised a job interview with an emerging IT services start-up based in Pune. I immediately applied for it and was overjoyed when I got the interview call. Technology had always been my step-sibling. I shared a love-hate relationship with it. I could never grasp technology but getting a job required a grip on technology and so I had to force myself to like it. On the day of the interview, I walked inside the office, filled a questionnaire and a tedious form about my personal details. A few more rounds of interview followed and after a gruelling day I was selected. I was on cloud nine. I immediately called Vijay and informed him about my selection. He did not apply for this job as it was a small company. I wanted to embrace him and shout out to the world that I was employed. That was the moment I could see how one's professional worthiness could make or break one. I could have had the easy life of becoming a homemaker, tolerating my husband's taunts, surviving the drudgery but Baba did not let me become that archaic version of Indian womanhood. I was glad he did that. I was soaring high, I had a job! Yay. Vijay came after an hour of waiting as he had to take me back to the PG. When I saw him, I flung my body in the air, hugging him as his friend and my classmate Ritul watched us. His body felt like a safe enclosure where I could sneak in. All the past pain of betrayal was forgotten. Victory expunges the scariest of memories from our heart and mind. I remembered this lesson for the rest of my life.

Krawler, my new workplace, was a welcome break and a new beginning to a host of things in my life. I learnt to be financially independent much to the chagrin of Baba who couldn't make peace with the fact that his daughter was no longer dependent on him. This was the first time I saw his vulnerable facet where he insisted that I continue taking money from him. I resolutely refused it, but not because I hated him. I could never bring myself to hate him, despite all the adversities he inflicted on me. He was still my father. I think Baba took so much pride in being the sole caregiver of the family that he forgot that one day his children would grow up and fly to their respective havens. I did not earn a lot but it was enough to manage my monthly expenses. I did make some positive changes in my lifestyle, from staying in a hostel or a PG, I switched to a fully furnished flat with my college friend Grishma.

Personally, life was great! Vijay was still unemployed and wanted to talk to me more than ever to kill his time. His friends had been placed and had left the campus and there were only three students remaining in the entire campus. In my entire year of college, that was the sole brief period where he was lonely and I was occupied. Though I tried not to revel at the change in power positions, I was satiated nonetheless. A void inside me had filled, with sweet revenge!

I was relishing this new phase of my life to the core. I was new to the workplace and hence was quite ebullient in performing the tasks expected of my role. In between there were minor skirmishes between Grishma and me. I came to know that she had enquired for a 2 BHK flat with our other roommate without telling me, which meant that I would be the only one left in our current apartment. I felt repugnant towards her because of her betrayal but did not make it obvious. It had become a pattern in my life: people leaving me, and I struggled to reject this truth of my life but failed. I think somewhere this had made me rigid in matters of love and I stopped looking for a partner for a while. Things happen when you least expect them. On one moonlit evening, I was having dinner with Grishma at a nearby restaurant when my phone rang. It was an unknown number. I picked it up half-uncertain. Pat came the reply, 'Pallavi, I am Rohan. I have shifted to Mumbai.'

Was this a pleasant turn of fate? I started becoming hopeful again in that moment. It was no sheer coincidence that he had moved from Delhi to Mumbai, a city very close to where I lived. Did destiny want us to reunite? I cupped my frail heart with compassion, a heart that had bled enough in the past from a series of letdowns from undeserving men. This time, I felt the man truly valued me. He was seeking my presence. There was finally someone seeking me.

But this time it was different. I had turned more cautious and did not want to commit to this man, whom I had met on a matrimony portal a year back. I had heard that once one becomes content with their life, life unfolds with miraculous opportunities. There was a time when I was running behind a man, offering my body, my emotions, my money and yet I was left starving, and here a man was showering his undivided attention on me and I was not ready to take it. My aloofness irked him but he remained steadfast. He told me that he wanted to have me as his life partner but my body evoked no response. He was well-groomed, well-behaved, well-educated and worked in a reputed company at an influential position, drawing a handsome salary. But I had no intention of getting into a relationship. I told him softly, 'I like you as a friend, as a person but I just came out of a relationship and I don't want to get into one so soon.'

Three days had passed and he had not called me. It started to bother me. Talking to him had become an after-office, evening ritual and it averted boredom. There is something about the constant, continuous presence of a man in one's life. It can be due to the couple-driven culture where each person is expected to have a partner. Rohan, at that time, was not my significant other but somewhere, my unconscious mind treated him as a potential other half. Hope keeps people afloat in a culture ridden with expectations. Now with him gone, I had lost hope again. It was a quagmire. I knew if I had to get him back, I had to give in to the pressure of marriage. Eventually, loneliness got the better of me and I called him. It is surprising how our relationships are driven by the threats than the positives. If you deconstruct relationships, behind the distempered surface, you will find deep insecurities that bind us together, most prominent of them being the fear of living alone. How can fear drive you to take better decisions?

Rohan picked up the call and I asked him why he had not been calling me. It was because I was not responding to his feelings. He had felt it was better to keep his distance. It shook me. Now it was a do-or-die situation. I had to decide right then if I wanted to marry this man. I said, 'I do like you. I just need some time. But if you snap all connections, how can I even decide?'

I was forced to consider him and soon enough, I yielded to the pressure and said yes to a relationship. He was over the moon. The following week, he called up to check if I had a passport. I asked him why and he said that he wanted to plan a foreign tour for our honeymoon. I was a bit taken aback at the hastened pace with which things were rolling but nevertheless, I was happy imagining a life together, a life of commitment, social sanction, status, financial increment. All these potential benefits outweighed my incertitude. I pacified my anxious, once bitten twice shy heart and with an open and generous heart welcomed Rohan into my life. He soon planned on visiting Pune to meet me. On the appointed date, I took a lot of time to get ready and looked my best. In the excitement of meeting my 'committed' lover I forgot to notice that my roommate had been fired from her first job in a span of just one month. My romantic rendezvous made me indifferent to her pain. Her mother had come to be with her but I knew that my joy and radiance would have severely hurt her.

I wanted to surprise Rohan as he was meeting me for the first time. I knew I was beautiful and the grooming had added sparkle to my aura. To hide my face, I wrapped a scarf around it. I was also nervous to meet a complete stranger for the first time and did not want to make it evident. From behind the scarf, I could gauge his presence, his energy and once I became comfortable with his presence, I would uncover my face. It is weird, the extent we go to only to hide our anxieties. Better pretend than be vulnerable.

As I took off my scarf, his jaw hit the floor. He was amazed by my charm; I felt my confidence skyrocketing in that small restaurant. All the effort to look good, the make-up, the new dress, had worked and I now had his undivided attention. It seemed my biggest achievement to make him not regret the decision to come meet me. He said, 'When I was coming to meet you, I had a little apprehension about how you would be; but now after meeting you, all my doubts have been put to eternal rest. I'm confident that my decision is right.'

What struck him in those five minutes? At that time I was all too happy listening to him and receiving his compliments, all of which centred on my looks and not my intelligence. It is so sad and unfortunate that women are so conditioned to receive compliments based on their looks as if, ultimately, all that matters to us is whether we are able to captivate a man with our beauty. Yes, it mattered to me that I looked beautiful in front of him. It became so much of a habit that every time Rohan visited Pune, I went shopping to buy new dresses. With my meagre earnings, I saved nothing thanks to this compulsive habit of shopping. I ate only home-made food but looking good and buying new clothes had become an addiction.

Rohan did not know that I was not a virgin. Though he knew that I was in love with another man, he chose to not discuss the specifics of the relationship and probably just assumed that I was a virgin. I was unsure how he would react if I had told him the truth. I was scared that he would find out when we eventually had sex. I had heard countless jokes about a woman's vagina getting stretched from too much sex. What if Rohan felt that my vagina was loose and stretchy? He could easily make out that I was not a virgin. I felt like a criminal.

On the night we had sex, I was very scared! It is strange that fear makes us irrational and we lose our capacity to think logically. I dreaded the impending disclosure, so once he undressed me and himself fully, I pushed him aside and panicked. He assumed this was the first-time discomfort and slid away. But we eventually had sex that night. The next day, I got my period. I had a proof to show him that I had lost my virginity to him. I merrily tiptoed on the stairs and told him that the intercourse had made me bleed. As sexually ill-informed as he was, like me, he believed me. Maybe it didn't matter to him but to me it was important that I remained a virgin wife for him.

Months passed, and slowly and gradually, our relationship declined in passion. He did not pamper me like he used to. The talks of marriage also became infrequent. It was my turn to keep the relationship alive and I was trying my best.

I was then working at a start-up run by four young entrepreneurs. They were young boys in their late twenties and toiled hard to keep the company afloat. I took a liking to one of them. He was the chairman of the company and mostly sat in his cabin. He was tall, fair, had jet black hair, almond-shaped black eyes and a thin moustache. He was one of those rare men who could carry off a moustache. Not just that, he always took a special interest in correcting my faults. It embarrassed me, I was a public-school-educated girl with a masters in management and here he was correcting my mistakes! For every email I sent him came back an email highlighting the mistakes. It made me reluctant to even send emails to him and I tried bypassing the hierarchy by seeking approvals from the manager instead. I worked on my vocabulary and started using difficult words but I again ended up becoming a subject of mockery when he pointed out my near-Victorian English. It was strange! Desire works in the most unpredictable manner. I was very attracted to him but it became hard for me to accept that because I was in a committed relationship and I cherished my loyalty. I could not be disloyal. But your mind, heart, and body are not always in alignment and do not always speak the same language. My mind, my social conditioning, my ingrained values pushed me to stick to my partner despite his negligence but my heart implored me to pursue the unknown, the forbidden! That's why marriage needs a legal certificate—so that people can continue the relationship even when their hearts detach from each other.

At my end, I tried everything to keep the extinguishing flame alive. Rohan had stopped visiting Pune on the pretext of back-breaking work deadlines. I would eagerly wait for the weekends only to hear him say, 'I have to go to office today.'

The drought lasted until I decided to do something about it. I decided to go and meet him in Mumbai. I had a six-day-work week and it was tiring! Sundays were the only days I had to myself. I hopped on to a bus to Mumbai and called Rohan to inform him that I was on my way to see him. I met a girl on the same bus. She was travelling alone to her home in Mumbai. She and I bonded marvellously during the ride. We talked about everything under the sun. I was genuinely happy with her presence. It did not occur to me that you don't always need a man to feel happy if you are able to build enriching connections with others. But my obsession with my man had no recourse. It is strange when love becomes an obsession, an ego drive. Your worth as a human being is defined by your love and when it is not reciprocated you are left gasping for breath.

After some great conversation, I bid goodbye to her. She said she really liked meeting me. Her candid admission startled me. Could I really make a difference to someone's day? Could someone feel grateful that they met me? It is unfortunate that our self-worth plummets in our quest of love. I was held hostage, always standing on my toes to get that one lingering gaze from Rohan. And here was someone, soaking me in a fountain of appreciation. When I reached Mumbai, Rohan was at the bus stand. He was beaming to see me. After a long time, I felt that our old love was back. He took me to a corner, mischievously pulled a packet from his pocket and said, 'I have a surprise for you.'

He said this and opened his palm. It was a condom. I was dismayed! But I could not comprehend the meaning of the shock. I realised that I was only a sex object, an outlet for his release. Rohan was too eager to take me home but I was hungry. I had only eaten a *chikki* on the bus. He took me to a small mess where I had a plate of idli. I asked him to join but he said that he had just had his lunch. Even if he had taken a small bite from my plate, it would have made me very happy. It was awkward for me to finish the full plate as he sat there looking around. Rohan took me to his flat and as he bolted the door, he quickly turned off the tubelight. He did not even let me rest for a moment before thrusting himself on me.

It was an assault on my soul. I was committed to him, I had come all the way to meet him, I was in love with him, I wanted to marry him, but this complete lack of respect for consent really bothered me. I understood what people meant when they said marital rape. Rohan stripped me and without much foreplay, entered me. I lay there motionless, unable to react. I was taking solace in the fact that at least he was still interested in my body. After he came out, he slipped on his trousers, rolled over and fell asleep. It was 9:00 PM and he was not hungry. The last time I had visited him, we had heated some ready-to-eat food. He was still trying to woo me then but now it was all so different.

Finally came a day when I ended up cheating on Rohan. It is naive to believe that you can conquer your desires. Our desires are invincible. 'Don't go near the road,' I would hear mothers yell at their children and yet the children would walk to the road teeming with fast cars, bicycles, hawkers and hurried pedestrians. It starts from there. Whatever we are asked not to do, our mind wants to try it, to explore it.

I was in office, working a late shift. A meeting had gone on till 11:00 PM and I had to stay back to type up the minutes. It was thundering and raining outside. My boss Sanjeeb came near me and looked over my shoulder. That night only the two of us were in the office. I looked at him and picked up my bag to leave with him since he had said he'd drop me home. The rain was roaring and it would take just over a minute for someone to get drenched. He rushed to the garage and swerved his white Toyota in my direction. He opened the door and I quickly got into the front seat. He drove towards my house asking me for the directions. We made small talk but something far more intense was happening inside me. I felt something tingling inside me; his breath, his cologne, his pale white shirt with the sleeves casually rolled up to his forearm, it was all intoxicating. Something my heart had secretly desired for so long was now within my reach. My senses were awakened. I desired him but had no courage to lean towards him and kiss him on his mouth. I secretly wished that he would take the lead but it was a lost dream. Soon he dropped me home and I lay on my bed. I fell asleep thinking about the lost opportunity.

The next morning, I woke up when my phone rang. It was Rohan. I had not called him the previous night. I always called him to wish goodnight. At that point, it was just me holding on to the fragile thread of that relationship. He said as I answered the phone, 'You did not call me today.'

I looked at the time; it was 10:00 AM. I moved the curtain a little; outside, it was a gleaming day. I had slept late. Was Rohan's heightened concern some kind of a karmic retribution for my desires the previous night? I felt like I could not hide it any more. In my head, although nothing had happened, I had transgressed, I had cheated.

Soon enough, I resolved to crush all my attraction for Sanjeeb. My moral tussles helped me reach my goal sooner and I became a loyal woman once again, in body, mind and spirit. But the deterioration of our relationship happened faster than my return to loyalty. Rohan broke up with me and he did it very smartly. I had this habit of saying 'I will break up with you' whenever there was a bitter fight between us. I never meant that in principle but said that to scare him. The threats had worked in the past. I remember once I had asked him to call my mother and he did not do it for three days. This triggered my old insecurities about abandonment and I texted him that I was breaking up with him. It unnerved him and he literally begged for forgiveness. He was so exasperated that he wanted to meet me the next morning for breakfast. This was when he stayed in a different city, which meant that he had to travel six hours to meet me.

That was how things used to be. I soon became accustomed to using this threat as a magic wand to turn his attention towards me. I had started threatening him nearly every day. While he no longer came down to Pune to apologise, he would at least call to pacify me. I threatened to leave him only to make him stick to me more and he took advantage of this weak spot to end the relationship. In one of my fits of anger during a fight, I threatened to leave him and he nodded on the other side of the phone and disconnected the call.

I was waiting for him to call me back as he usually did but this time, he did not. My pulse was rising and

I started becoming impatient. I decided to call him and shout at him. I was jolted out of my cosy trust when he said, 'I respect your decision. It's over for me too.'

I spent the next two weeks pleading, sobbing and wailing on phone, while sitting in my office cubicle and on my way back home, but he did not relent. Rohan did not pick my calls for most of the time and when he did, he just kept saying that he was obeying my wishes. I was stunned! 'I never intended it,' I told him but he did not listen. He kept repeating the same thing like a parrot. It took me a long time to realise that he was piling all the guilt on me so he could have a blame-free exit from this relationship. I feel now that he had carefully planned his exit from my life by bringing me to the tipping point.

Soon enough, it was three months since our break-up but I was not ready to give up. I decided to stop hounding Rohan for a while as he clearly had begun to ignore my calls. After 15 days, with much courage, I called him from a different number and he spoke to me. I was delighted that he was talking to me and had not disconnected the call. In that haste, I made a last attempt to lure him back in, 'No one is at home today. Why don't you come over? I want to talk to you and mend things.'

This made him cheer up. He said that he would come by 9:00 PM. His ready acceptance put me in a fix. My mother was visiting me and I didn't know what to tell her. I would have to request her to spend the night at the neighbour's hpouse. She had seen me suffer my heartbreak and would readily agree, I thought. My heart swelled with joy. I started dreaming about all the intimacy and lovemaking with Rohan. I was sure he would tell me, as the night thickened, that he could not live without me. My sacrifice and long wait would be suitably and abundantly rewarded. Ma's exit was essential to realise that fading dream.

'Ma, Rohan is coming home today. Can you stay at the neighbour's place?'

She was stunned! She barely knew my neighbours. I pleaded with her, my face grim with pain and desolation. I confess that I never treated my mother the right way. That night she eventually agreed to stay over at the neighbour's house, hoping that it would salvage my pride and my relationship. We told the neighbours that some of my co-workers were coming over and I did not want them to disturb my mother. I had a bath, changed into a sultry little black dress and called him. He quickly picked up the phone and said, 'Listen! I'm on my way and I'm getting my favourite gift for you.'

I was genuinely surprised. I asked him what the gift was and he said, 'Flavoured condom.'

I was stunned, unable to react. My love or rather my obsession for him was so high that I had forgotten that he saw me only as a sex object. 'You don't need to come any more. It's over,' I told him.

I think that was a rare night when I slept well without any lingering, haunting thoughts of Rohan's absence in my life. I was content though not joyous. In hindsight, I often think why it took me so long to realise that Rohan was abusing me. Part of it could be because I was addicted to companionship. I was so afraid of loneliness that I withstood anything to fill that void in my life. I believe couples should be co-dependent. But the word dependence itself is so derogatory, I would rather love someone and grow with that love. That love can never become an ennui. But such love can only be attainable when a couple doesn't stay together.

For the next three months, I found bliss in my singledom. I moved to Mumbai to seek a change. Changing places often helps in erasing the old memories. I appeared for a job interview just a day after reaching the city. I reached that office half an hour before the appointed time. I eventually got selected for the job and after a lull of the six months of my separation from Rohan, I got a new beginning of life. New place, new premise, new people, new work. There was so much unknown to keep me intrigued and involved. I was quite shy, which made it difficult for me to make friends. It was much later that I realised that my shyness was more a result of my feeling of unworthiness.

Soon enough, I started seeing people around me getting married. E-cards, packets of sweets and invitations crowded my worldview. The glitz of weddings started haunting me again. It made me feel inadequate again. I had no boyfriend, no husband. I got envious of my married colleagues. It all looked like a dream and no one even had a clue about what went on behind the glitz; the temperamental issues, the fights, the interfering in-laws and so on. I again became desperate to get married.

The Great Indian Illusion

My obsession with marriage started as I entered my adolescent years. Baba rarely took us for outings but watching *Dilwale Dulhaniya Le Jayenge* was an exception. I was 12 years old when the film released and I remember that all my classmates were excited about the film and the lead pair's romance. In my imitation of Kajol, I would tie my shoulder-length hair in a high bun. I was sold on the idea of love the film peddled; I had a naive belief that I would find my heartthrob in that film theatre. As I watched the film inside the dark theatre, I started believing in a happily ever after. I believed that you could get happiness only when you had eternal love. A real soulmate was someone who followed you across the world, protected you from all dangers and observed a fast for you. I started believing in love and wanting a soulmate for myself. That pursuit continues till today.

In class picnics I would don my best floral printed frock and would timidly walk up and speak to hordes of boys at the picnic lunch. Our teacher would spread a mat on the ground so that everyone could lay their lunches on it. I would ravenously look at the variety of food: *chole bhature*, *dosa*, *uthappam*, sandwiches, fried rice. The delicacies were in abundance. But my hungry eyes always searched for a companion, a soulmate who could make this class picnic memorable. On our return, they would play some music in the bus and some girls and boys had no qualms grooving to the music. The rest of us, the shy lot, contented ourselves with clapping our hands, singing along with the chorus or playing *antakshari*. In that bus, I looked around at all the boys, seeking someone who was most compatible, someone who might also be looking at me, and always, I was left disappointed. But the year I watched *DDLJ*, something changed in my pursuit. I decided to come clean and make it clear whom I liked. I realised that boys get attracted to beautiful girls and so I decided to groom myself. I took a keen interest in make-up and at 12, I would secretly visit a nearby beauty parlour to get my eyebrows shaped. I did not have money, so I often stole from Baba's wallet when he was asleep.

I felt liberated by the handful of money I had when I walked into the make-up shop. I bought a small make-up kit, some rouge and eyeshadows. There was a small mirror in it. At home, a single tube of Fair and Lovely cream was all the make-up my mother owned, along with a small case of *kajal* made from the soot of a lamp and a single pack of Shilpa sticker bindis. I had never seen anyone have a make-up kit like mine. I sneaked it into my school bag and then hid it in my cupboard. I started wearing make-up to school every day. I thought this would tempt the boys towards me. Any boy would do; even Durbil and Durgesh, the short, squint-eyed twins who failed in most subjects.

When I was about to appear for my board exams, my aunt was getting married. In small towns like ours, everybody knew everyone and one got invited to all functions and get-togethers. My aunt invited me to her home a few days before the wedding so that I could help out with the arrangements. Those days in her house were blissful and a lot of fun. On one of the nights, just before I was about to leave for home, I felt the gaze of the bride's elder brother on me. Brown-skinned, beady eyes, with curly hair. He was in his late twenties. Suitable age for marriage in Indian middle-class households. I stealthily scanned him to check his eligibility as a potential suitor; my benchmark was not too high. Once satisfied, I turned my head to see that he was looking at me quietly. His gaze felt like a cool breeze. I had been leered at, jibed at by strangers many a times before but this was different. No words were exchanged between us but his gaze said it all. It was deep, brief and poignant.

He was a respectable person and I knew that he did not have any bad intent. His stare was not piercing, it was very soothing. My cravings for adolescent love were fulfilled by his stare. When I returned home, I was full of disappointment, of not having been able to reciprocate the imagined love of that man. I was quiet, pensive and kept to myself. Sensing something amiss, my mother asked me, 'What happened?'

I could not muster the courage to tell her the reason. What would I tell her? That I was in love? All hell would break loose if she came to know the reason. But what else could I do? It was difficult to keep a secret for long. I relieved myself in one quick go, leaving Ma in a shock of a lifetime! How could she react to the fact that her daughter was just 17 and was hell-bent on getting married. Her reaction was unexpected. She seethed with anger at my stupidity and naivety and said, 'Are you in your senses? This is the time for studies, to make a career and establish yourself professionally and financially. You are blessed to get this opportunity to study. I did not. What will you do if you get married to that man? Become a housewife? Wash utensils and cook in the kitchen? Toil all day to for your in-laws and still receive their bashing?'

Her response jolted me from the comfort zone I had created for myself. It was a hard dose of reality. The women in my family sweated in their small kitchens all day. No, I didn't want to do that ever. Thus, I said goodbye to my first urge of marriage. My mother was right to say that girls needed to be independent before they got married. But she missed one point. Marriage doesn't need only financial empowerment, it also needs self-respect and self-love.

As I inched closer to financial independence, by securing a seat in a prestigious management college with a promise of 100% placement, I decided that it was now fair to ask for marriage. Why was I so hell-bent on getting married? I suppose it promised me a fairy tale-like escape from the travails and struggles of my paternal home. Seeing Baba's nonchalance at arranging my wedding, even when I was 25, I started pestering and reminding him. I would force Ma to tell Baba to start looking for an alliance for me. My poor Ma, nothing was in her hands since her separation from my father in the late 90s. She had a limpid existence in the house but I had no one else to reach out to. My inexperienced mind convinced me that she was an elder in the house and would still carry some weight.

It's noteworthy to mention how my yearning to get married was influenced by my friends who got married before me. Anurita was my best friend in school. She was fair and chubby and had her long hair tied in two thick braids. She could easily speak to boys and often made friends with them. In fact, one of these boys would often follow her back home from school. This boy was quite meritorious and everyone thought that he would make it to an IIT. What a stroke of luck! I envied Anu. When I moved to Pune, she went to Benares for her higher studies and we got busy in our own lives. After one full year of working in Mumbai, I had come home for a break.

One evening, when I reclined on the chair in my garden, I saw a familiar-looking girl cross the road with a group of other girls. It was Anu! I called out to her. She heard me yelling and turned towards me. I called her in for some tea. As she sat, I noticed her forehead. There was a thick line of red vermillion in the parting of her hair.

'Anu, you got married!' I was startled.

She gave me a coy look and said yes. For the remainder of the evening she only spoke about how affectionate her husband and in-laws were and how pampered she was in her new house. She didn't talk about her parents or about our old school days. I soon lost interest in her talks. Partly because I was filled with envy. Everyone was getting married except me. I grew impatient.

Baba, on the other hand, was least concerned. In the following days, I gathered the courage to gently remind him to look for a groom for me. In my desperation, I had registered on a matrimonial website and checked out profiles of men from the same caste. When I shortlisted a few, enough to keep Baba busy for a week, I would hand over the list to him. I would lie to him and say that these men had approached me on the website.

I think Baba was irritated by my constant pleas and he decided to put an end to them, once and for all. An acquaintance had informed Baba of a prospective groom. The man seemed alright to him and he decided to take the alliance forward. That evening when Baba came back from office, I was on the drawing room sofa, flipping channels on the television. We would hardly talk unless either of us wanted something from the other. I think it was a matter of extreme pride for him to be the giver and to have his family ducking in front of him. When I graduated from college and landed my first job, I stopped taking money from him but he would still deposit money in my bank account. Given the equation Baba and I shared, I knew that this was not an act of generosity but a struggling attempt to maintain his power over me. He said to me, 'I got to know that he is from a well-to-do family and works in an MNC in Gurgaon. He has done his MBA from IIFM Bhopal.'

I was very particular about the academic qualifications of the groom. Call it societal conditioning or peer observation, only a man who is from an A-list college would qualify to become my suitor. I would match character with qualification. I thought someone with a degree would automatically be a good person.

IIFM Bhopal was not the best school around. I firmly declined the offer. Baba politely forced me to at least consider meeting the family and the man. 'You won't get a match like this later,' he forewarned me. I was far from being convinced. The next morning Baba asked me to accompany him as he went to get fresh milk from the nearby farm. I knew the purpose but could not refuse him. When we reached the farm, the milkman immediately brought two stools for us to sit on. He then asked his demure, purdah-clad wife to bring us two cups of tea. As he then proceeded to fill the bottles with fresh milk, Baba resumed his attempts at persuasion. This time I could not say no.

Rajan (the man from IIFM) started talking to me as soon as family approval was given. It is strange how in the 21st century romantic liaisons still needed the stamp of the family before the couple could interact. For this particular reason I found arranged marriage nauseating; it seemed all scripted. Man and woman selected by family, marriage date is fixed by the family and the couple is expected to fall in love within the courtship period. What kind of love is predestined and not discovered naturally? But despite the whirlpool of emotions raging inside my enlightened mind, I had to kneel in front of Baba's wishes. With half-hearted attempts, I started reciprocating Rajan's apparently romantic overtures. But as the days unfolded, I realised that it was a terrible match.

I always believed that I was naive and prone to exploitation but meeting Rajan made me realise that I was also a covert schemer. I was not able to develop any interest in his puritanical wooing, where he would indirectly make references to the places he would like to travel with me, after marriage. Come on, I would have fallen head over heels in love with a man who would have directly asked me out on an intimate date. Arranged matches are taxed with moral virtues even when it comes to having sex. His sugar-coated words made me retort by falling back into Vijay's arms. I was secretly hoping that if between these two men, the latter became willing to cement the relationship, I could leave the former without a whimper. The moral baggage was difficult to bear as I saw Rajan off after watching a movie with him and headed straight to meet Vijay at his friend's flat where we passionately made out for hours. I do not consider it selfishness but self-love and think every man or woman deserves their secret world of relationships and sex if they need it and want it.

Rajan's idiocies did not end there. He was curious about my past and indirectly threatened me with serious consequences if I hid any past relationships from him. He tried to cover up his insecurities by telling me a tale of his friend whose wife had lied about her past affairs, and so the friend had abandoned his wife. He said he would have done the same had he been in his friend's place. Hearing him, I shivered with fear. Even though he was an insipid man whom I had no intellectual, sexual interest in, he was still an escape from the domestic upheavals that mired my home. I could not lose him until I found another man. I pacified him and also tried to defend that fictitious friend's wife by saying thing like, 'Past is past.'

I protested but he was adamant. He was of the opinion that all truths belonged to the husband even if they belonged to the wife's past. He would bring this subject up in every fortnightly meeting of ours. Soon enough, I was fed up of lying and hiding and decided to tell the half-naked truth to him. I confessed that I liked a man in the past but nothing happened (no kiss, no French kiss, no intercourse) between us. It was a forgotten affair. Rajan stared at me for some time and then said it was fine. He quipped, 'It's good that you have shared about your past. Let this remain between us and you will never mention this in front of my family.'

I nodded my head wondering if a mere 'liking' could almost wreak havoc in his mind and his family, what would happen if he got to know that I was not a virgin. All hell would break loose. I shirked my thoughts and continued to pretend that I was a virgin. But soon enough, I hit my boiling point when he babbled about an embarrassing condom usage awareness drive in his office where an all-women NGO team demonstrated the usage of a condom to the office workers. He enacted their demonstration by sliding a hypothetical condom rubber up and down on his palm as he explained condom breakage. I was offended!

I dragged the brief relationship with him for a month, interspersing it with brief collisions where I instigated him to break off with me. I started avoiding him, not picking his calls. On one occasion I even told him that I was going to a bar for a fresher's party; it was too much for his frail moralistic heart to handle. I knew that I was deliberately pricking his male ego and moral upbringing by these defiant acts but he kept calm. I think he dreaded the ignominy that would come his way if he spilled the news of our break-up to his family and eventually to the whole community. He kept quiet, I kept testing the limits his patience. His resilience irked me and now I was looking for an opportunity to brutally snap ties with him.

It came and I had to take the recourse of that embarrassing condom incident to prove what kind of an uncouth man he was. I shed tears, hurled accusations against him and blamed him for bringing up the forbidden act in front of a chaste girl. It was an argument that no one could counter. Sex can never have an opposition from those who like it and those who are disgusted by it. Goodbye Rajan.

I tried to fill the emptiness in my life by falling into another man's arms. By this time, I had fallen into three pairs of arms but my life was still empty. I decided an arranged marriage would be the solution. I wanted some kind of guarantee: a guarantee that would prevent the man from running away, leaving me heartbroken. I did not want to be abandoned again. I informed my parents that I was ready to marry whomever they deemed fit. This was when I witnessed in first person the ridiculousness of arranged marriages. But because this memoir is about my vulnerabilities and my sins, I will resist myself from blaming those culturally conditioned families and would rather talk about how I lived my life.

It was February 2009 and I was only 27. I am now 36. Back then, I felt that time was slipping away and I would never find a good groom if I did not get married fast. Because of his dysfunctional marriage with Ma, Baba had stopped taking an interest in our lives.

When I saw Baba not taking any interest in my marriage, I decided to stage a protest. The trigger was an unsuccessful meeting with a potential bridegroom who had to fly out to the States the following day. The man was in India only for a week and had shown an interest in marrying me. Most men had refused to marry me because I was vegetarian and because of my dark skin colour; and here he was, wanting to marry me.

I was very angry when Baba could not meet this man. The man would not be in India for another six months and all marriage discussion had to be stalled. I spent that night and that evening thinking of how I could snap all ties with Baba. I loved Ma and was respectful of her many sacrifices. I decided to take her along with me, back to Pune. My brother already had a job and was sustaining himself. We did not need our Baba any more!

I decided to leave the house but did not have the courage to announce this decision to Baba. I decided to sneak out of house the next day, around 7:00 AM when he would be fast asleep. I told Ma that I'd be waiting for her at the inter-state bus stop and asked her to come meet me at 10:00 AM. I told her, 'We will ride the bus to Jamshedpur at 11:00 AM and in the evening, we will catch the Azad Hind train to Pune.'

At the set time, I left home with a small purse and a handbag. It was the first time I was running away from home and I did not have enough courage to take out my suitcase. It was best to travel light. I left home heavy-hearted and scared of the future that awaited me without the shelter of my Baba. I left nonetheless. Outside, the weather was all foggy. The entire street was desolate except for the turban-wearing milkman with a curly white moustache.

I boarded an autorickshaw. The reality of a harsh life hit me five minutes after leaving home. How would I look after my mother on my meagre salary? Was this the reality that caused millions of women to stay with their husbands? I reached the bus stand and sat on a cement slab under a big banyan tree. In my heart, I was fervently praying for Baba to find me. I started to miss my home. More than an hour had passed. I decided to call Ma.

'Sumi (my nickname)! Where are you? Your phone was not reachable. It's been an hour, your Baba is frantically searching for you along with your uncle. Call him immediately,' she said.

I was deeply happy inside. Baba had noticed my absence and he wanted me back. With trembling fingers, I called him. He had reached the bus stand by then and was searching for me in the tea and snacks shops that lined the bus stop. As our eyes met, I lowered my gaze. The guilt consumed me. Baba was the ultimate power in the house and here, for the first time in my life, I was able to overpower him. I could not look at him. No words were exchanged and I followed him back home.

On returning home, he did not say a word and got ready for office. I went back to my room and snuggled under my warm quilt. I immediately made a decision. It was better to remain a celibate daughter in the comfort of my house than becoming homeless. I was content in my prison.

Luckily a few months later, there was another prospective match. It's difficult to admit this but back then I had become so eager for marriage that I had laid my destiny in the hands of absolute strangers. I was ready to marry any man, provided he met my criteria. I was happy that this time the man did not take a lot of time to take a decision. He decided to marry me in less than half an hour of meeting me. Arranged marriages save time and effort. I was ecstatic! Our families met and the dates and the dowry amount were decided. Seeing Baba's social stature and financial background, my to-be in-laws demanded a dowry of six lakhs. This infuriated Baba since he could not bear to see the colossal gap between their and his social standing. But I was headstrong this time, I was adamant about marrying this man.

I put my foot down and told Baba that the dowry would anyway go to the family I would now be a part of. It will be my new home, so ultimately the money would be spent on my upkeep. Little did I understand then that money is never a precondition for welcoming loved ones into a family. I laugh at my own naivety now and shudder to think how, despite writing countless school essays on the ills of dowry and excelling in academics, I surrendered to this social evil. Not much has changed since then. I think this tradition will continue as long as women continue to take the surname of their husbands. I pity Bollywood actresses who have made it fashionable to take up the surnames of their husbands, all in the name of 'choice'. Little do they know that for millions of other Indian women like me, this ritual only works to diminish our power on our lives.

The talks furthered, our horoscopes were matched; and the date for marriage was fixed for July 2010. A couple of months were left, and I returned to my place of work, Mumbai. For the remaining time, I had to be patient and do my best to keep my fiancé and his family happy. Thus began a series of dates when I cooked for my fiancé and made a series of sugar-coated calls to my to-be mother-in-law.

Though we were getting married, we still did not have a place to satiate our physical urges. My fiancé lived in a shared accommodation and though I had my own rented flat, Ma lived with me. But our repressed sexual urges desperately looked for an outlet to release themselves from our bodies. And we found plenty of opportunities: elevators, seashore, back seats of autorickshaws, corner seats in cinema halls, park swings and even my own apartment, when Ma was away. Sometimes if we became too eager, I would ask Ma to get us glass of water and as she lurched towards the kitchen, I would jump on Prakhar's lap and give him a kiss. Once my mother caught us kissing and I turned pale with embarrassment.

Our sexual sojourns were quick: a quick kiss on lips, a gentle brush of hands on the curve of the waist, through the hair, against the bosom, thighs, knees. Touching each other on parts that are not meant to be touched in public. That was the extent of our sexual exploration. Once, when we were both coming back to Mumbai after our engagement, I slid into his side upper berth. We took the benefit of the golden-brown striped blanket and covered our whole bodies with it. I lay towards the wall and his body covered mine.

As the train whistled forward, with the coach shaking right and left, we made out. We kissed hungrily, insatiably, for minutes. We rubbed each other's necks and sucked each other's lips. My hesitant and obedient fiancé even made an attempt to slide his hand down my salwar. I started getting wet. He used his fingers to touch my vulva. I think, to him, a 30-year-old virgin, it was a big deal to touch a woman's genital. His fingers lay there still, maybe trying to find a way up in silence. Sex in India is always about silence.

In mid-2010, two days before my marriage, Baba had booked a beautician who would come home and give me a haircut and a facial, get the waxing done and do my make-up.

The beautician was a petite lady from the northeast and had amazing white, silky-soft hands. She smiled as she entered my room. 'Let's do the facial first,' she said as she wrapped a peach-coloured cotton towel around my neck. And then poured some herbal powder on a plate and started mixing rose water in it. Her delicate fingers made tiny ripples in the mixture as she smoothened it. She then gently patted the mix on my cheeks, stroking it first upwards towards my forehead and then downwards towards my chin. Saffron nourished my skin pores and my senses were soothed by her nourishing caress. She massaged my face for about 40 minutes. Like a baby, I almost drifted into sleep.

I wore a half-sleeve black t-shirt and a pair of low-rise, flared jeans and folded the hem a foot above my knees as the lady applied hot wax on my legs and pulled the stiff hair with a waxing strip. I nearly shrieked. I had never been fond of waxing and I still don't know why girls get waxed to please their man. After the beautician was done with pulling out the hair on my arms, legs and thighs, she asked me to change into something comfortable like a maxi and remove my underwear.

I then realised that she wanted to wax my pubic area for an unforgettable 'first night'.

'Oh! But I've lived many of those nights before,' I thought with a smug smile.

I was not comfortable baring my private regions to a stranger and hence I declined.

'Are you sure?' the beautician insisted, saying it was included in the bridal package. I was startled! She slyly suggested, 'See, all good girls get it done. It makes their husbands surrender at the altar of sexual bliss.'

She felt that I was making a gross mistake. I could not tell her that I had had sexual relationships before marriage and it no longer interested me. But I was saddened to think about those modest 'homely girls' who had never stepped out of home unassisted, never had any boyfriends and were suddenly expected to bare it all in front of strangers. Back in my maternal village, my cousin got married and gave birth to a child mere nine months after her wedding. While everyone in my family celebrated the arrival of the newborn and congratulated the couple, I was dejected. In villages, the idea of premarital sex even between an engaged couple is frowned upon. Obviously, everyone wants to have sex. Isn't childbirth after just nine months of marriage proof enough that the couple had a sexual urgency to fulfil? I do not know how, after a long, tiring day of wedding rituals and standing for long hours, the couple even had the energy to have sex. Isn't sexual intimacy about the right mood and not urgency? But in this culture of sexual deprivation, especially in villages, can couples afford to wait for the right mood or does sexual intimacy become like an involuntary nightfall?

It certainly happened on my wedding night. I was married into a lower-middle-class family and my husband was the lone earning member. My husband did not know that I was not a virgin, since ours was an arranged marriage. In an arranged marriage, even though the girl and boy meet and talk a lot before marriage, the decision to get married is sealed at the first meeting. In a meeting which is attended by the family members and relatives of either side, how can someone disclose her premarital sex experience? I did not reveal it for the fear of breaking the alliance, and for the months preceding my wedding, I was scared about what my husband would do if he came to know that I wasn't a virgin. On the wedding night, I was prepared to act like a virgin.

The nuptial bed was decorated with bunches of roses. But it did nothing to lift my languished spirits. I was too tired from the ceremonies and from greeting countless relatives. I came back home around midnight and when I finally entered the bedroom, I was ready to fall asleep.

Everything around me was new and alien. I had never sat on the furniture before and their fridge did not have any of the things I liked eating, like jaggery roshogollas from Deshbandhu that Baba always bought for me. I was forlorn with the memory of my Baba's house. I missed the sight of our familiar red carpet and Baba asking me not to watch too much TV. I missed the teakwood sofa on which I sat and lazed around. I even missed the cushions that adorned the sofa, embroidered by Ma with red-blue-green threads. In this new house of mine, I did not know any of the objects. It seemed like a hostel. Even hostels had a mirthful atmosphere as friends giggled, gossiped and cracked jokes. Here I had to be quiet and obedient. The furniture, the windows and the house repulsed me. I longed to sleep in my own home, in the lap of my mother.

Here I did not know anyone. All these people around me: my mother-in-law, who had never cradled me or fed me, was suddenly my second mother. My parents had toiled and spent sleepless nights raising me and caring for me, even before I could pronounce their names. They rightfully deserved to be called my parents, but what had these people done to be called my new set of parents, in a matter of a few months? Had they borne any hardships? Instead, they had taken money to let me into their house. My husband, after consummation, all too happily became the obedient son of his authoritative mother. Keeping up with these dual roles was perhaps back breaking for him.

On the bed in that house, among the hordes of unknown people who were sleeping and snoring in the other room, I had to make love in the first night of my married life. I mentally prepared myself by clenching the muscles of my vulva. My husband did not know about my past sexual affairs and I was too scared to even bring them up. It was better to keep my mouth shut and clench the muscles of my vulva, instead. I also fake groaned to make my husband believe that I was experiencing pain associated with first-time penetration. In reality, I had no pain; I'm a woman who has sat astride her boyfriend several times. A woman on top of a man is a dominant, aggressive position and I loved that.

There was absolutely no reason to feel threatened in a legally sanctioned relationship by a sexually liberated woman but I was playing the moral card to keep up my domestic harmony.

The love I received in marriage was not without abuse. This abuse was not physical but left a deep mark on my self-esteem and self-respect. I had immersed my identity in love, destroying any sense of agency to achieve immortal, eternal, domestic love. And how could I not? I grew up seeing it all around me. My aunts hand-washed the clothes of my uncles, had no social life without them, were practically illiterate and did no jobs. The aunts cooked all day and used to eat leftovers after the men finished eating.

In the mornings, an aunt would get up to prepare breakfast and tiffin for her husband, my uncle, who left for work by 8:00 AM. She packed the tiffin, picked out his clothes from the cupboard and polished his boots. It was that last chore that remained entrenched in my memory. While the uncle also shared some household duties, the polishing of his boot by my aunt seemed way too derogatory to me. Not that I detest the work done by cobblers but in a home, I have never seen a man picking up his wife's shoes and cleaning them.

With these ingrained indoctrinations, I entered marriage. It did not go as well as I had thought. After the initial frenzy of the wedding fanfare and honeymoon, I began to grasp the reality. The real issues had begun before the wedding, had continued through the preparations and had come into their whole being after my marriage. The marriage was emotionally debilitating, morally distressing and financially exhausting. What I missed and desperately sought was my husband's support which would save me from the stinging remarks and irrational demands of my mother-in-law. I suffered through the five years of marriage, only because I was a mother and I feared that quitting this marriage would harm my kid.

I made the choice to become a mother when I was 27. Three days after our wedding, my husband and I spoke about family planning. Both of us had just begun our careers and were struggling to find our footing. A child seemed like a responsibility that neither of us was prepared for. I still wanted to give it a few years and my husband agreed.

When Ma heard about my decision to delay motherhood, she was aghast. I tried to tell her that I had just gott married and that I needed some time for myself before taking on maternal duties. She had her own line of defence: 'Children are the gift of God. They bind the family, make the bond stronger. Further, if you face medical difficulties later, what would you do?'

In her limited world, she had seen married women becoming mothers at the drop of a hat. The ones who couldn't, including herself (I was born after six years of her marriage) had to visit temples, offer prayers, meet gynaecologists secretly. Children complete a family, the more the merrier. I had only one reason in my defence, my freedom. Ma had many to dissuade me. One of my aunts became a mother after two and a half years of her marriage. She also suffered a miscarriage one year into her marriage.

Another aunt, who was a housewife, got married to my uncle who was 12 years older than her. They had a baby a little more than a year after their wedding.

The generation which preceded me comprised of women who stayed at home. Ours was a transitioning generation; we had received education but could not detach ourselves from the roots of patriarchy. I felt Ma was right. I also did not have a precedent in my family to support my logic. So, I gave in to my mother's advice and disclosed to my husband that we needed to shun our previous plan. We started having unprotected sex thereafter and I eagerly waited to hear the little squeaks of a baby.

The arrival of the baby could not mend my marital blues and instead, our fights and disagreements aggravated. We were extremely cash-strapped because of the birth expenses and a huge home loan. The construction of the house that we had purchased was put on halt by the builder. It caused extreme distress to me as all my life savings were put into that house. The financial distress completely took over my life and I could not make myself available for sex. Whenever Prakhar approached me, I made up some excuse to not have sex.

We had been married for four years and Prakhar and my sex life was non-existent. I had been raised to keep my needs and demands passive but I also learnt indirect ways to protest when they were not met. I began to let my baby sleep between Prakhar and me. When I had a caesarian delivery and the doctor asked us not to have sex for three months, I was relieved. I still remember the time when I went to the clinic to get my stitches removed, the gynaecologist asked me to come back after a week to get a copper T installed in my vagina. I wondered, could sex not wait? Did women have to get this installed when they were barely able to move?

I knew at that moment that I was not coming back to get the copper T put in. I remember Prakhar getting eager as the three months were about to get over. I was able to walk and bathe on my own and it appeared to him that I was now fit to have sex. That night I slept facing the wall with our son sleeping between us. Prakhar came to my side and started kissing my neck. The act did not have any impact on me and I pretended to sleep but he was in no mood to give up. He continued.

Reciprocating was unbearable, the best I could do was let him do whatever he wanted to. He continued as I counted the minutes and seconds. I became a corpse for him to devour. The foreplay lasted less than a minute and he now wanted to enter me. I could not take it any more but he was my husband. I cooked up an excuse to avoid sex, 'My abdomen has still not recovered completely from the stitches,' I said.

As a consequence, he insisted on having anal sex from the side. So held me in a spoon and then brought out his penis. He lowered my pajama. I lay there trying not to think what was happening. Thankfully he could not enter me because of the position I was lying in. He tried for a while but had to content himself with rubbing his private part between my buttocks. He then fell asleep.

In the coming three years, refusing Prakhar sex was my only act of agency. Our fights became unbearable. Whenever he tried to come near me, I shirked him off saying I did not want it. Slowly he realised that I was not interested in sex at all. I still desired sex, just not from him. My son protected me from the onslaught of physical assault, ever since the day he was born. I'm grateful to him for that.

While my mind wanted to be celibate, my body had its own desires. My hands automatically went down my pants when I was alone and I started masturbating. It started in the wee hours of a winter morning while I was resting on the bed, my body covered under a striped blanket. The refuge of the blanket helped me unleash my long-suppressed sexual urges. I started slow, real slow with just feeling the skin; a skin that had not been touched for a very long time. It felt good, and then I touched it more. The touching gradually turned into stroking and caressing and then twisting, turning, squeezing, rubbing. It seemed that I had uncorked a soda bottle and now it was becoming difficult to compress the oozing liquid. In my five years of marital togetherness, I had sex only for around six months. First to plan our child, for about five months, and then another one month at the end of the marriage.

I was young, still in my twenties, and considered it immoral to look outside for sexual fulfilment. There was a time when I became friendly with my colleague, a Muslim man. Our work involved talking for long hours and slowly we started talking about our personal lives. I was quite demure but his puckish manners soon made me drop my inhibitions. I would secretly rejoice when he complimented me; unable to reciprocate for I was a married woman. Then once, I was asked to go on a business trip to Bangalore, where he lived. The man sounded ecstatic on the phone as I revealed the news to him. He promised to take me around the city, to his home and make that trip memorable. He was waiting for me with bated breath. I tried remaining calm but my inner peace had been uprooted.

That night, as I slept facing the wall, I started thinking about this man. I started imagining how I would arrive in his city by flight, how he would come and receive me at the airport and then drop me to my hotel. After finishing the day's work, stealing quick glances at each other, and exchanging hushed conversations, I would ride pillion on his Royal Enfield and then he would take me around the city. After our sojourn, he would take me to his house and show me the gilded portrait of Rumi, his spiritual master. And as we stepped into his house, he would hug me and then we would start kissing...

I was jolted out of my imagination. I did not plan to think this way, from where did this thought surface? Though stunned with the idea of enjoying long-forgotten sexual pleasure with a stranger, I liked the tingling feeling in my body that this thought gave birth to. Hesitatingly, I replayed the scene in my head; this time the hug and kiss lingered for a long time. I felt like a ripe mango, my soul filled with sensual love. I longed for the touch of a man, something I had deprived my body of for long. I enacted and re-enacted that imagery till late hours of that night; my body rigid and still but my mind wide awake, active and ebullient. I now realise that most social and moral restrictions can only tame the body, not the mind. That is God's way of reminding us that we still own our minds. Listen to your dreams! Pay attention to them.

The next morning, in the broad daylight, I was filled with remorse. I felt like I had cheated on my husband. It hardly made a difference that the incident was a figment of my imagination and nothing real had taken place. It hardly mattered that I did not share a warm relationship with my husband that made me stumble outside the moral fence. I was deeply shattered and decided to cancel my travel plans. I was sure that if I were to go to Bangalore, I would end up sleeping with that man. My sexuality had awakened but I gagged its feeble voice.

I was not always successful in curbing my infrequent sexual urges. I recall the time when I heavily masturbated. It was uncontrollable and I just did not know how to stop. The more I tried to restrain myself, the more I found myself doing it. My vulva became sore and ached because of excessive rubbing. I applied an antiseptic cream and ice pack to heal the injury and the moment I started feeling better, my hands went down again. The urge to masturbate was so uncontrollable that I couldn't stop masturbating even when I was in office. I would keep my bag on my knees and slide my hands under the table top and then down my pants. During the act, I kept looking over my shoulder to ensure that a CCTV camera was not recording my activity. I was worried and scared then. But now I do not consider masturbation dirty or wrong.

Prakhar and I fought at least once a week. The subject of our fights was the intrusion of his parents. I brought my son into this world to make my marriage work and now I was nurturing him within a dead marriage.

In April 2015, Prakhar was asked to report to an on-site assignment in the US. We decided that he should go; the extra money would be very helpful. This lessened the fights to an extent but the spine of the relationship was broken forever. I wonder if it was ever there to begin with. My husband agreed to go to the US for one and a half years. Ma was against it as she thought I would not be able to manage the household with my son. I also had apprehensions. I wouldn't miss a companion but only a person who would buy groceries, pay bills and help in childcare.

In June 2015, we knew that Prakhar would have to leave in a month. I was anxious. Was it safe there? What about accommodation and people? Was there any racism? I fervently looked up the news on the internet so that I could forewarn him. The next 15 days were spent doing visa formalities, shopping for woollens, essential groceries and plastic containers. Prakhar was going to Missouri for the assignment; a few of his colleagues had already been working there for the past few years and living with their families. Some of his friends' wives had quit their jobs to join their husbands in the US.

I could not quit my job. The visa Prakhar got would not let me work in Missouri. But one and a half years was a long time and his income would surpass our collective incomes. So as a compromise, I decided to join him after a year. I calculated that it would be a good time to take a break. Subconsciously, I was drawing comparisons between the wives of Prakhar's colleagues and me. I could see them happy, settled in marital bliss, raising children, maintaining homes, enjoying the luxury of not chasing deadlines any more. How could I not find fulfilment in doing all those chores? Why was my career more important to me than the companionship of my husband? I did not have any answers.

Only 15 days were left for his departure. It was an early morning flight that departed around 6:00 AM. I was crying like I did every day ever since the news of his departure got confirmed. I was fearful that his absence would heighten the chaos in our lives. What would I do if someone fell ill in the middle of the night? How would I come home alone if there was a long meeting at office? What would I do if some man in the neighbourhood began to stalk me? What if Prakhar got into an accident or fell ill? He saw my welled-up eyes and came close to comfort me. I do not know what happened but all of a sudden, I kissed him. After three long years, I kissed him. Prakhar was not sure if this was an invitation to indulge in an amorous act and he was skeptical that I would turn him down in the middle of us having sex.

I continued the kissing and it took him some time to realise that I was finally in the mood for sex. We had sex that morning. To be honest, I did not relish the lovemaking. It was a need of my mind, not of the heart, not of the body. The heart had dried from the painful atrocities that he had inflicted early on in our marriage. The body had become attuned to the self-imposed shell I had retreated into. The mind was active and required to sustain itself; it needed affirmation that everything was alright. It needed an affirmation from Prakhar and the lovemaking was a medium to seek that.

Soon enough, after the lovemaking was over, I regained my consciousness. The affirmation was accepted but it had ridden me with a deep feeling of guilt. I felt filthy and immediately ran to the bathroom, bolted the door and squatted on the white marble floor. I filled a mug with water and lathered some soap. I then took the lather in both my hands and started rubbing my vagina incessantly with it. I inserted my fingers deep inside the vaginal tunnel where Prakhar's penis had gone in. I wanted to remove all the marks, all the scars, all remnants of his touch from my body. I rubbed and rubbed till the area became sore but I was still unconvinced. How would I erase the humiliation of giving in to this momentary allure? My years of patience and chastity had been beleaguered. I had indulged in casual sex with my own husband.

In July 2015, Prakhar left for the States leaving me and our three-year-old child in Delhi. I mourned his absence for the first week, after which I adapted to his absence. Anyway, there was no love between us but only a checklist of duties that I took over seamlessly.

The love died even before it was born. In arranged marriages, there is hardly any love to begin with, what with your match determined by the elders and your attributes, qualities and pay cheque vetted by the elders. In my marriage, dowry was exchanged. I was initially in favour of acquiescing to all the demands that Prakhar's parents imposed on my father since I wanted to break free of my home at any cost and marriage seemed like a permanent escape. After being married off into another family, I could finally sever my traumatic bond with my father. In my hurry to seek happiness, I forgot about my hapless mother who struggled greatly to educate me amid those dire circumstances. I got married to Prakhar in a jiffy. I was deeply hurt by the series of abandonments, and the permanent legal sanction of marriage proved to be the only recourse. I was confident that if a man remained married to me, I could make him fall in love with me. The problem I identified was that the earlier men did not stay with me.

Yes, my prediction was as bizarre as my relationship education was. My marriage turned into hell with my nagging mother-in-law who kept reminding me of my dysfunctional family, the meagre dowry and my shortcomings. I could not snap at her the way I snapped at my mother. In front of her I was a polite, abiding woman who kept quiet for the welfare of her family. But inside, this disrespect was gnawing at my soul. I turned to Prakhar for support but he dismissed my pain, stating that I should ignore what his mother said to me. I wanted my husband to stand in support and secretly, I also wanted to shame his mother by turning her own son against her. That would be my revenge. I did not want a mere apology but a thumping revenge. It did not happen and I started drifting away from Prakhar, first emotionally and then sexually. Our relationship was relegated to just a mundane exchange of household chores. Who does what? Who gets what? And how do we divide childcare? I compensated for the lack of love in my marriage with overeating and soon from my usual slim self, I became an obese woman weighing 75 kilos. I started destroying myself because maybe I was too ashamed to admit that I was in a disrespectful, loveless marriage. It scavenged on my self-esteem. It is strange that in that model of relationship, Prakhar and I survived five long years and would have probably survived more had it not been for his sudden departure to the US.

I realised that in Prakhar's presence, I had forgotten to operate my internet bank account, pay the house rent and utilities bill and even purchase vegetables. It took me a lot of time to come out of that dependence. For the first time in five years, I was juggling and struggling with home, office and of course a toddler. But something within me was changing. I started feeling blissful! I cut down on eating junk food and started eating a lot of fruits, home-made lunch and drinking plenty of water. Now I ate only when I felt hungry. I became more attuned to my physiology, my body. At the same time, I got in touch with Param. Param was precisely the reason why I quit my marriage. At that time, I still believed that if I got attracted to a man outside my marriage, my marriage was not working.

The Journey of the Acceptance of My Sexuality

The liberating years for my sexuality were 2015–2017. Liberating because I had untied my sexuality from the peg of marriage and had run amok like a wild cow. I locked horns with men and shed the burden of stress. These years marked my long spiral of illicit relationships with married men. Param was a senior at college and later a visiting lecturer. He was different from the rest of our teaching staff. Tall, with light curly hair, feline eyes and puffed cheeks. His voice had a coarse texture probably because of chain smoking. He had an accomplished career that was a precedent among our alumni. He would always assign us tough assignments as homework and ask us questions whose answers nobody knew. We would all be on our computers for hours, fervently searching for the answers to his questions but all our efforts were in vain. It was an amusing sight whenever Param entered the class. He would ask the class how many of them had done the assignment and around five students would raise their hands. Customarily, the rest of the students would walk out of the class. I sometimes tried to trick him by pretending to have done my homework but he would see right through me.

On one of the occasions, I continued to sit in the class without having done my assignment. He walked into the class and asked his usual question. I neither raised my hand nor walked out of the class. I had made up my mind to sit through his class irrespective of his irrational demands. It was not my fault, I thought. The assignments were impractical and I tried my best but could not finish them. Param walked up to my desk and asked me for my assignment. I had nothing to give him. 'Leave!' he demanded. I walked out.

That was how my initial encounters with Param went, best described as walking in followed by walking out of his class. He and I spoke again, after more than a decade. This was a time when he could no longer direct me. What a big leveller time was! Sometimes when you feel that the other person has gained total control of you, you become emotionally dependent on and vulnerable to that person and then a few years down the line, that person ceases to matter. I see our grandparents conveniently forgotten by our parents. I have seen dead spouses being forgotten as their partners move on with their lives.

I was starting a business and happened to talk to him on the phone. The talks were prolonged as he guided me on how to set up a business and advised me on things I should keep in mind. During one of our late-night talks (there was a time zone difference), we started talking about our college life. I fondly remembered the time and managed to tease him on how he would unfailingly evict me from all of his classes. Hearing this, he became remorseful. 'I could not help it. It's a standard I had set for myself. Success is not easy,' he said.

I brushed off his anxieties stating that those things did not affect me any longer. It was after a long time that I was talking to a man at 2:00 AM. Param asked me what happened to my boyfriend from college. I was surprised. How did he know about that? Do teachers know and even bother about their student's private lives?

I told him the age-old story of break-up and moving on. My digging up of personal stories encouraged him to talk about his life. He told me that he found me irresistible in college and often wondered why someone as tall as me did not opt for a modelling career instead. He titillated me by telling me that he used to observe me keenly in the class and that he remembered what my vital statistics were. I did not believe him. '34-24-36,' he said. He was right.

In our later calls, I was completely uninhibited. When he talked, it felt like someone was gently rubbing sand on my whole body. I became so indulgent in our nightly calls that on the day of my wedding anniversary, I forgot to wish Prakhar. It was 12:15 AM and I was on a call with Param. Prakhar called me while I was speaking to him. I dismissed it thinking he was calling to talk about something mundane. But his calls would not stop, there were a total of eight missed calls. I sensed some urgency and answered the call. He said, 'Happy Anniversary!' I was taken by surprise. I had forgotten my own wedding anniversary. Was this the end?

The calls from Param had increased. All my hesitation had crumbled and we would indulge in amorous conversations. Param would tempt me with dreams of a vacation in Mauritius and his fantasies of rubbing honey all over my body and then licking it all with his tongue. He seemed to have a honey fetish. He said he liked the slow motion of honey dripping from a pot. I usually remained quiet through these calls.

Is it a cliché that girls are emotional? Param and I had an age difference of eight years. Between us, he was more experienced: sexually, professionally and financially. He had an influential hold on my past and it was very rare for a person's past to make its way into the present. I was getting romantically involved with someone I knew as my teacher. Add to that my five years of compassionless, sexless marriage. I was desperate. I relied on Param, looking for repose, gratification and emotional attachment. Obviously, these attachments started weighing him down; he was not seeking these things from me. I sought permanence and he could never provide me that. The outcome was disastrous. Param stopped taking my calls and I became a passionate seeker. I believed in perseverance but had conveniently forgotten all pragmatism. You can labour to buy a thing and make it your own, but you can not make a person your own by force.

I persisted for a couple of weeks but soon my patience waned. I got busy with my work and life, forgetting Param. Then one night I got a call from an unknown number. It was him. I was surprised. What made him call me after so many weeks? Param said he would be coming to Delhi in another month for a business meet.

'Is it?' I exclaimed.

In the next 15 days, I stopped eating junk food. In the past and through motherhood, I had gained a lot of weight and I did not want Param to see me like that. That triggered a spontaneous weight loss programme.

I was satiated by dreams of making love to Param. In about three weeks, I lost 11 kilos. Such a miraculous transformation only a fatal attraction was capable of influencing.

The entire world has made the beauty of a woman into such a big business that she thinks if she can get beautiful, then she can get everything she desires. I too thought that if I looked beautiful, any man would bend his penis and then his knees. I was quite open to the idea of sex for I ardently believed that sex beckons love. I mean if you love someone, you want to have sex with them.

On the day we were supposed to meet, I stepped out of the office two hours early. I went to a mall and bought a short dress and a pair of stilettos. Soon the shopping was over and it cost me Rs 6,000, the most I had ever paid for a dress and a pair of shoes. The higher your dreams, larger the price you pay for them. Sometimes in cash, sometimes in kind and sometimes both. I entered the trial room with the purchase bag and changed there. As I came outside in the heels and the short dress, the helpers stared at me. I was conscious of everyone looking at me and would have been disappointed if no one did. Seeing them staring at me was a confirmation that my labour and the preposterous price tag worked. It was all worth it.

My confidence increased and I walked confidently into the dining area of the mall to meet Param and to get laid. It's becoming difficult for me to pen this as it was a terrible experience. For the sake of decency, I am compelled to use refined words to describe my one-night stand but that will amount to faking it. What are one-night stands for? What do you get out of them? Can sex be savoured when it's carried out without any love or respect? Do partners who have sex for a lone night respect each other? The answer for all these questions is a resounding no from my experience. I want to write down this experience, taking the pain of going down that painful memory lane again.

I took the flight of stairs down to meet Param in the central hall. I was quite conscious as I recollected our very sexual conversations. Param looked the same except for some wrinkles on his forehead. He had a small paunch too.

'You have become a little chubbier,' he told me.

Not much of a conversation followed, and he asked me to come to his hotel room almost immediately. I guess we both were clear on the purpose of our meeting but unlike him, I felt a little hesitant to admit it right away. I know I might sound hypocritical but please be considerate; I'm writing from my experience and it's perfectly alright if your experience is different from mine. But there is a deep unrest in my heart and only writing things out will ease it. So please be patient with me. I was conditioned to pretend to be coy; girls like sex but they are taught to never explicitly demand it. They always wait for men to take the lead. That night I went into Param's suite fully knowing that he wanted to have sex with me but I pretended to not know it. And when you pretend to not know something, the results are almost disastrous.

Param was quiet through the entire duration of our commute to the hotel. I tried to make the atmosphere light by smiling purposelessly and giving him loving glances. I was also uncomfortable in that short dress and in sitting so close to practically a stranger. Once we reached his room, I sat on the edge of his bed, knees joined together. I placed my bag on my thighs to keep the bare skin hidden. Param loosened his tie and quipped as he stuffed his large black suitcase with the clothes that lay scattered on the sofa. 'See, the place is quite untidy. I hope you don't mind it,' he said.

I replied to him with a feeble smile. By now, I could no longer pretend. I was anxious to see how Param would start the amorous campaign. As he took off his large indigo coat, he came near me and opened his arms. 'What do I do now?' I thought. I had gone there for a purpose but I was no longer sure. Could decisions be made only to be regretted later? I could not stand up. Pretending to not know what was going on had landed me in discomfort. What do I do now? I was in a conundrum.

Seeing me not standing up, Param sat down beside me. The moment had come and the objective had to be fulfilled at the earliest. Param tried to move my face towards his and then gently touched my lips with his. I think that sealed the bridge of lust between us. Soon, we were fiery and passionate in each other's arms: embracing, kissing, caressing, fondling, feeling, clasping. I run out of verbs to describe our union of lust. He laid me on the bed and undressed me and then he undressed himself. I was too shy to be the dominant one in this erotic pursuit. I liked to be taken. It's weird if you think of it. Our moral upbringing says that women who choose to go for one-night stands are horny, kinky and know no shame. But here I was, I had chosen to go for a lust-laden date and yet I was uncomfortable. Perhaps more than lust it was my sexual starvation that had led me in. It was akin to scouring a garbage bin for leftovers. I was like a person who hadn't eaten in a very long time. Was I wrong?

In between our lovemaking, Param was frantically focused on getting more of my body and I am at a loss for words to describe that feeling. I finally felt that there were sexual feelings in my body. The body is just not there to work, it is also to enjoy sex. But its suddenness made me giddy in that dark room with heavy curtains. It was perplexing. For someone who hadn't had sex in three years, I should have been ravenous but I was icy-cold. As Param continued his conquest, he was eager to enter me. I stopped him and asked if he had a condom. He said no. The lovemaking had made me cheerful and I teased him, 'It's good that you don't have a condom. Now I will get pregnant. And I'll later reveal this truth to your wife and get her to divorce you. And then both of us can get married and stay together.'

I was obviously joking but Param took this very strangely. I tried to persuade him to enter me and come inside me, but he couldn't. He seemed be to be preoccupied and stressed. I now realise how silly I was; I did not fear HIV or sexually transmitted diseases. How could I have trusted him so much to let him enter me without protection? Param asked me to perform oral sex on him and finally the feminist instinct, the lost honour inside me, awakened. I said to him in a clear tone that I would not do that since I barely knew him. Post lovemaking, Param immediately sat on the bed and turned to the other side, near the chair where his trousers were hanging. He picked up his pants and put them on. Soon after, there was the sound of the zipper.

I was still lying on the bed, unable to decide what to do. Could detaching be so easy after intercourse? Maybe because it was just a union of bodies and not hearts. I had thought that the lovemaking would win over his love and now I lay alone on that bed, naked and lonely.

There was no afterplay; there was barely any foreplay except for a quick French kiss to hasten the lovemaking. The main focus was the act of penetration which was prematurely thwarted, thanks to my pregnancy joke. Param was detached and in a whim, he started praising his wife. I was puzzled at this sudden turn of events. What was I doing on his bed if his wife was the queen of his life? Param advised me not to break my marriage with Prakhar because it was very difficult to live alone. 'You need a companion in your old age. Someone who can take care of you; else you will be very lonely,' he said.

He had clearly switched off the intimacy; in fact I doubt there was any intimacy to begin with. I felt filthy and inconsequential as I changed into my clothes. Param had got dressed swiftly. It was weird and awkward. Years later, I did inform his wife of our secret, illicit rendezvous on chat. I think for less courageous people like us, technology serves as a refuge and lets us avoid direct confrontations. I was quite naive to expect that his wife would thank me for my honesty. Instead, she blamed me for seducing her husband. 'What if I said that you offered him a deal. Whether he accepted it or not is secondary. By the way, in 2015, we were trying for a baby, so he was with me throughout. I know you guys met in Delhi once because we spoke at the time,' she told me.

It made me despondent. Yes, I was seeking revenge against a man for ghosting me but I also did not want another woman to be mistreated by the same man. It is ironical that I did not want to accept charges of infidelity because I like to believe that I was not emotionally involved. I think the rules differ! If marriage has outlived its quota of passion, then a person has every right to look out for support and companionship. Such an act I will sanction but a no-strings-attached one-night stand is calamitous for me. I can never condone such an act. But Param's wife's disclosure brought me peace. I know in my heart that his wife knew that I was saying the truth.

Did I mention that on that night, in order to meet Param, I had to cook up a lie? I was a young mother and I did not want to leave my child alone in the house with an ailing, cataract-blind mother. My married brother-in-law lived quite close to the hotel where I was meeting Param. I dropped my kid and my mother at his home and told everyone that I had a late-night party at office. I wore a long shirt and lycra pants so that no one suspected that I had a date. That day I took double revenge. I had been a devout daughter-in-law all those years but my sacrifices had never been respected. My dreams were butchered in the slaughterhouse of my in-laws' home; it was now my turn to teach them a lesson, but discreetly.

Post Param's exit from my life, I started struggling with his absence. There were no more phone calls, no messages, no promises of amorous meetings. I had forgiven him for that miserable date. After all, I still had someone in my life. It is strange that Param had become more bearable to me than my spineless husband. My marriage had turned from being a failure to an abomination. I just did not like my husband, I was repulsed by him. The marriage was on its last legs.

Once I decided to step out of my marriage, there was no looking back. Marriage, as an institution, as a deeply entrenched belief, had no standing in my life any more. My failed marriage and the covert sexual propositions from married men were enough for me to stop believing in its sanctity. I gave so much to marriage and finally it was time to take back all of that with a heavy interest. In the following years, I experimented openly with men, with different kinds of relationships, and I must say on the basis of that: people, not the things you do with them, add colour and vigour to your life. I met a lot of men, dozens and hundreds of them, but I wasn't an irresponsible mother. I had to make sure that whatever I did, it did not have a detrimental impact on my son.

I was a free bird that year, untethered. I got myself enrolled in an entrepreneurship programme to have a social life outside my monotonous day job. This was a one-year program that taught us business skills to launch successful start-ups. On the first day of class, the institute had organised a party in a chic pub. I wore a short dress and was hopeful of catching a fish. I reached the place late as I had to finish work at office. I was given a blue band by the people at the reception and shown the way to the party venue.

Standing at the door, I stretched my skin-tight dress till my knees and sashayed inside. Inside, the party was brimming with fervour, drinks were flowing and young men and women in their early twenties were dancing on the floor. I was disheartened looking at them. Even though I was 32, I felt like an old aunty, the ugly duckling in front of these young crusaders. I could not make a flirtatious pass at a 24-year-old boy. Yeah, they were still boys, not men. In that state of trepidation, I quickly looked across the floor to spot a man who seemed closer to my age. Yeah, 28 or 29 will do, I thought. In a few minutes, I spotted a boy-man who was asking the bartender to make a drink. He seemed like he was 27, ah the perfect match! I quickly tiptoed towards him, running my fingers through my hair. He was undoubtedly the most flamboyant man in that batch. Bypassing my forced effort to smile and chat about uninteresting subjects, we bonded well.

Soon, some other youngsters huddled around me and I left the scene. I scanned the hall and found a 40-something man talking to another 50-something man in a corner. My eyes lit up. I was not alone. In fact, compared to these two gentlemen, I was way younger. My confidence lifted and at the same time I found myself attracted to a lean and tall man standing in the corner. He did not seem to be a student. I asked Abhiroop (the 27-year-old I was speaking to) and I came to know that he was the programme leader of our batch. His name was Vibhaas. I do not remember much of that night. I had a few drinks and left for home. Everyone else stayed. They were all unmarried and I was a mother; I had to get back home in time for my child. I regretted being bound to my motherly duties. Yes, I was the black sheep in that frenzied gathering.

Soon after, our training resumed and I got to know each member of our batch. They were young, lively and spirited. At their age, I recalled, I was busy only spilling tears for men. I was surprised to see that their generation was far more enterprising than I ever was in my youth. I even met Vibhaas in our class. He would arrive at the same time I did but stayed outdoors most of the time, arranging for lunch or other necessities like speaker travel. As the programme leader, he was responsible for the smooth functioning of the class. For his age, he was very fit: tummy tucked inside, chest with defined masculine contour and light black hair. He had a Roman nose, straight and flawless with a slight curvy tip, and hooded eyes. He was no doubt attractive and by the manner he flirted with girls, it did not seem that he was married.

I enquired about him from my other classmates and got to know that he had got married only recently. This was his second marriage after his former spouse passed away due to kidney failure. He had my sympathies and with a heavy heart I bid my romantic dreams goodbye. The next six months, we carried on with our weekly classes. Having shed the layers of inhibition and dropping oodles of weight, I always wore short dresses to the classes. I was so involved in this newfound spirited existence that it never came across my mind that I was the only woman wearing such short dresses. Vibhaas did not pay me any attention until one day, at a party, we got talking.

It so happened that during our lunch break someone suggested having an informal get-together. It had been three months since we had our induction party in a pub. Everyone agreed and orders for beer crates were placed almost instantly. It was nearing dusk and the party was in full vigour in our basement hall. People were chatting and drinking while I refrained from having beer. I was sitting in a corner alone when Vibhaas came and started talking to me. I felt good. Someone whose attention I had been trying to capture all this while had come to me on his own. In that little time, he talked about his wife's demise and also gave an indirect hint that his second marriage was proving to be a bad decision. I was relieved but knew that he would never go for a third marriage.

In about the same time, I was attracted to a married man. My falling for married men was more of chance than choice. I was 33 and at that age, most Indian men are already married. I had to either search for someone younger or go with someone who was married. I had reached the moral low of my life when I fell for Samarth, my married colleague in my new office in Gurgaon. I had joined as a manager, customer support operations, after quitting my previous day job. That was an idyllic phase. For the first time in my life I was drawing a salary that none of my family members would earn. A whopping 14 lakhs per annum in 2015! I had also bought myself the respect of my in-laws because everyone understands the language and power of money. On the night I was informed by the HR manager of my appointment, I jumped in merriment, deliberately making my in-laws jealous with my display of happiness. It worked and they were tongue-tied, unable to react. They understood money and I had it, a lot of it now. I experienced my nirvana-like bliss in that sweet revenge!

Samarth and I bonded over our common love for poetry and literature. He encouraged me to write more and more. It was a time when I was desperate for love and I think I'd have got attracted to anyone who showed me some affection. I did not think much before deciding that I was head over heels in love with him. I had been with many men but none of those relationships lasted long, leaving me drained, dry and thirsty for more. I was too eager to win another man's heart, mind and body to fill up the emptiness in my life. I instantly knew that poetry was my cupid in disguise. I remember once I sent Samarth a poem and he remarked, 'Do me a favour, stand in front of the mirror and admire yourself for as much time as you can'.

I started misreading his friendly gestures. I thought he was hiding his feelings for me and I wanted him to confess them. I would send him romantic text messages but he would not reciprocate. Finally, I was exhausted and felt it was best to distance myself from him. So, I stopped talking to him, texting him and sharing poetry. We sat in different cubicles, so we barely ran into one another.

A week had passed and I was at Karol Bagh market shopping for saris. I was feeling dejected and thought that shopping would help ease my discomfort. I was trying my best to avoid Samarth but, in the process, I was becoming weary and forlorn. I shopped for a few hours and by the time I exited the market, I felt much happier.

I realise that material comforts may reduce our unhappiness but it may not lead to a proportionate increase in happiness. Happiness is not the reverse of unhappiness, happiness is a kind of utopia, that state when we are perfectly fine and are free from all worries. That kind of happiness can be momentary or it can be for a lifetime. Unhappiness, on the other hand, can attain all forms and shapes and faces. It can be displeasure, resentment, deprivation, anger, tears and anything murky that makes you feel your self-worth is less. So, when I stepped out of the store, I was content but not ecstatic. As I exited the store, I received a text from Samarth.

Where are you?

I saw the screen blink with his name and did not lose a second to reply. I forgot that I had pledged to keep myself away from him.

I'm at Karol Bagh. Shopping for saris.

Samarth knew about my love for saris and adored me for it. He always felt bad that his wife did not like wearing saris. Samarth loved my long hair and was sad that his wife had decided to cut her hair. While I loved poetry, his wife did not understand it at all. I felt we were far more compatible than he and his wife. But I forgot one thing: sometimes you need no reasons to love and sometimes you have all the reasons to not love.

I missed you the entire day. He texted again.

It was this text which made me break all the dams I had built to obstruct the flood of attraction from my side. I could not contain it any more and I felt that he was finally confessing his love for me.

You are a stone-hearted guy. You never understand what I feel for you. I texted.

I vomited all my feelings into this one cryptic text. He read it but did not reply. It was obvious that he did not feel for me the way I felt for him. All the pleasure gained so painstakingly after spending almost one-tenth of my salary on saris had waned. I walked with heavy feet towards the metro.

As I walked, I ruminated over the sudden revelation of my feelings. I thought to myself how I could be so wrong in interpreting what he felt about me. I did not care about his wife; for me, it was only Samarth and me in a fictitious world of love that I created so painstakingly. I reached the station, dropped the token at the entry gate and climbed the long flight of stairs to arrive at the platform. Once the train came, I boarded it and found myself a seat in the corner. Once I sat down, I started thinking that Samarth would soon realise his true feelings for me, the way he realised my absence today. I endearingly read his text repeatedly and tried to find a hidden meaning behind the words. I was sure that one could only 'miss' their beloved.

Days passed and Samarth did not text. I was getting weary and impatient. I always made it a point to be the last one to leave a text unattended. This bolstered my faltering ego, indicating that I was the sought after. But this time, the rule fell flat on its face. It was Samarth who did not reply to my text. It might seem like a small thing but for me, it was this idiosyncratic perfection that kept my disarrayed life in harmony. I could only be an object of pursuit and not a pursuer. I decided to text him, in the hope that as soon as he replied, I'd go quiet.

He did reply but this time there was a change in his tone. It was more guarded and restrained, he was not his usual open self where he showered me with praise. I was not sure why I was attaching so much importance to a man who was married to someone else. Days passed and we barely spoke. He started working at a different location and we would only meet once a month during our monthly review.

'Samarth, you don't miss me at all?'

'Pallo, I do miss you. You know there can never be anyone like you. What a command on vocabulary you have! Do you recollect that you promised to send me a new word every day? But you have stopped doing that. I still wait for that word. And I miss your poetry too. You know that I have an artistic heart, a creative heart and I'm not surrounded by anyone like you. All my acquaintances and loved ones are ordinary people. They slog their lives away doing passionless work and then die. You are destined to do something better and valuable. And I know you have the courage to do that. There are only 2% people like you, like us in this world: artistic, tender-hearted, believing in goodness. Don't ever lose yourself Pallo. Be the way you are.'

The surge of his words melted my pain of rejection. I could see myself in a new light in the flame of his words. Where was I all these days? No one had told me this before, ever. That was the decisive moment of my relationship with Samarth. I realised that the truest friends are the ones who know you and don't judge you. They see you as a person, define you by who you are and not by what other people think of you. Samarth made me realise this and saved our relationship. We were destined to be friends, not lovers.

I was still legally married and Prakhar still chipped in towards the house rent and other bills. Though we were not in talking terms, he still bore the majority of the expenses in a feeble hope of keeping the relationship alive. I was in bliss, I was earning a large sum of money, my bills were split between me and my estranged husband and I was young and free to date anyone without fear. In those days, I met Pushkar, my ex-colleague, for a beer date. Not just him, I would meet many men who had good humour, good looks and earned well. I wanted to break past the shell of social aloofness I had created around me for years. Now I was hungry, thirsty to meet people, explore them. I wanted to make up for the lost time. Pushkar and I worked together in a real estate firm and he was one of the few handsome men working there. When we worked together, I was a fat, socially reclusive woman who only wore kurtas (no other outfit fitted me). After I left that office, I had lost oodles of weight. I was more vibrant, joyful, suave and I made sure it all reflected on my social media accounts. Pushkar was attracted to me seeing my remarkable transformation.

I chose a skimpy, blue dotted dress when I went to meet him. He was stunned to see me. 'You have lost a lot of weight,' he said. I blushed. We got into a bar where I asked him to order our drinks. He ordered a round of beer and then shots of tequila, each costing Rs 600. It was then that he opened up about his affairs outside marriage. I was startled! I thought he was happily married. He confessed that he enjoyed a special chemistry with his girlfriend, which was absent with his wife. He met his girlfriend a few times a year and they'd usually go travelling together. They would make wild love for days. 'Our lovemaking goes on for hours,' he told me.

He sighed as he fondly recollected about his girlfriend. The grand moral idea of marriage was crumbling down right in front of my eyes. Marriages are glorified, affairs are vilified, but some people find a way of balancing both. For their partners, ignorance is bliss. Pushkar offered me a drive back home and I was all too happy to take it up. I had expected him to foot the bill but we ended up splitting. As he drove through the wide roads, he gently held my hand. I was thrilled to feel that. More attention from a man: this was the real thrill of my life, who cared about companionship!

I immersed myself in the moment. His car veered through Delhi roads and into a dark alley in central Noida. It was 10:00 PM and the entire lane was deserted. Pushkar took out a cigarette and lit one for himself and me. It was surreal; the smoke rings filled the car and I asked him to slide down the window. He came close to me and started caressing my neck. I did not stop him, I knew the language of one-night stands very well by then. If the man came closer and the woman did not object, she was asking him to continue. But why could she not tell him directly? Soon, he started kissing me on my lips. It was my first lip-lock after kissing Param. I was drenched in the rain of his moist kisses. I felt fulfilled physically but something unexpected happened immediately.

Pushkar slid his hands under my dress and started lowering my underwear. I stopped him but he did not relent. He wanted to have sex and I asked him if he had a condom and he said that he would pull out quickly. I was horrified. How could I make this monster stop? I had to exert a lot of force to stop him. He did eventually and dropped me back home. As I walked back home, I felt liberated. I was independent and had a son and a loving mother waiting for me at home. But the next morning as I woke up, I started feeling empty inside. There was a lull in the atmosphere and the fan was still. The sunlight pierced through my skin. Everything had changed from the night before. I was no longer wearing the same pretty dress, sitting in that chic pub, smoking cigarettes and getting undivided attention from a flamboyant man. I was alone, my son had gone to school and Ma was busy in the kitchen.

In my anxiety, I texted Pushkar. I tried to not show my disappointment but said that I looked forward to meeting him again. Was he missing me, were his days also incomplete, boring and lifeless? I did not want companionship but just wanted to know if there was another person whose life was as sad as mine. Pushkar sounded nonchalant and busy.

In my despair, I called up Rahas, the man I had met just three days ago at a play in which he performed. I was in contact with him over launching my art review website. He was the only man I was talking to in those days other than the other exploitative men in my life. I had to turn my attention away from Pushkar. Rahas agreed to meet but called me to his shoot, which was taking place 15 kilometres away from my office. I agreed. He said he was taking auditions and wouldn't have much time to meet, but I still agreed. I was not sure what was pulling me towards him but I wanted a break from thinking about Pushkar. I did not want to kiss him but just to spend some time talking to him. A piece of my heart had died and needed some comforting. Rahas had asked me to meet him at a temple near the location of his shoot. I went to meet him in a short dress and the passers-by looked at me. He brought this to my notice and I revelled in all that attention.

'They should be focusing on their prayers,' I said.

I got him some canned fruit juice as I was aware of his frugal condition. He was all of 26, trying to make a mark in films, and I was 33 with a decade-long work experience. In him I saw my years-old dead dream of becoming an actor. I could not pursue that because of pressing responsibilities and domestic upheavals. Seeing him struggle at this young age inspired me to help him. I wanted to help him as much as I could. I was delighted to get a break from the chilling abandonment of the prior evening and my ego took over. I bragged to Rahas, 'I kissed someone in a car yesterday. I was all drunk.'

He asked me to keep these secrets to myself. I liked Rahas and I did not want him to think worse of me because I was going around the town kissing men in cars. I promised myself to never tell him these things again. Soon I began a relationship with him. He seemed confident and poised and had a promising career ahead of him. I betted high on him as I squandered my savings and credit cards on his increasing needs. He wanted to buy a MacBook followed by an iPhone. I tried to cajole him into buying a different brand of laptop and phone because it was economical for me but he remained steadfast in his demands. He argued that he needed a high precision and speed that was not possible in other brands of laptop. I did not have that much money to dispense and so he pressurised me into getting a credit card with a higher spending limit. I was aghast! In a matter of few months after meeting him, my healthy financial condition tumbled and I could not do anything. I felt helpless!

I was in a relationship where I was supporting Rahas. We both complemented each other in the sense that I provided him with the resources to practice his art and he helped me meet high-profile artists and filmmakers. I did not mind initially supporting Rahas as he strived to make a mark. It is what Baba did for me and his younger sister.

Rahas had become a partner in the true sense; he would take care of household stuff, be there during my emotional and financial upheavals. Having him around made life a lot easier for me. I have never condemned the loving partnership of two people, what I have a problem with is the compulsory need to socially and legally validate this bond. In my opinion, we make something legal when we want an external intervention to keep it intact.

Whenever I thought of marrying Rahas, I stopped myself. The respect and desire we had for each other did not need legal validation. I was also wary of stepping into a marriage after just having come out of a failed one. I was an independent person and did not want to define myself by the relationship I was in.

There are some conversations which we can only have with ourselves, partly because we fear being judged by others and partly because no one understands ourselves better than us. We are our own best friends. My sexuality is a subject about which I am extremely honest to myself. It used to disturb me in the beginning when I found myself being attracted to different men. I would always get sad over former love affairs but I came clean to myself and discovered that I could not let a man become the centre of my life. The stability of a relationship, the certainty of togetherness, the final acquisition of a person definitely makes life comfortable but I would always miss the thrill of desiring other men and being desired by them.

I have shades of grey in me, and Rahas was a very uptight person. He dreamed of having a family. But I, to date, don't know what a perfect family looks like. I think flaws are inherent in all of us and nothing is perfect in this world. Not even families. The varying emotions and imperfections make our worlds more interesting. If everything was perfect, this world would be sterile.

I have tried to conform, multiple times, to the societal expectations of being committed to one partner. I did it out of the dependency that I had developed on that one partner accompanied by the fear that I would never find someone as good again. I had not and still have not learnt to live on my own. I have always wanted a place called home, with all the people whom I could call my own.

Rahas had been a constant companion, a safety net that held me through all the turmoils of life. But the problem was I could not make him the centre of my life and forget about all other men. From being my strength, he eventually became my weakness.

There were both positives and negatives, but I had to make a decision: either I had to leave Rahas or live with him. Should I seek newer adventures or should I stick to the comfortable, the familiar? Was there a middle path? There was the middle path of polyamory but with Rahas, that was out of the question. The only option left was infidelity, a secret sexual and emotional excursion without Rahas knowing. The question was, was I ready for it?

What happens when you do not want to be with a person you are with? I was facing this question in my life and I was not feeling guilty or ashamed. I think in the world of relationships, we all chase an elusive idea of a 'forever.' Couples who stick together forever are now very rare. I've always been a believer of nature and I believe that all things have a natural way to progress.

All things come to an end: trees shed their leaves in autumn to bear new leaves, a snake sheds its skin. Nothing is permanent: birds fly from twig to twig, one branch to another, day merges into night and everything that is awake goes to sleep.

It is rare but sometimes loneliness feels dear to me. Most of the time, I want to be with someone but sometimes I want to be on my own. I feel that in society, customs takes precedence over an individual. People get to hear the news of someone getting married and they come and congratulate the couple. But what for? People who get married stop having any time for themselves. I might sound selfish, but I have too little time for myself. So how can I start sharing it with dozens of other people that a marriage brings into my life? Secondly, we marry just one person, not the whole extended family. How can anyone start liking multiple groups of strangers in a couple of minutes?

As I noticed Rahas tending to the most insignificant things at home like fixing the broken window pane, the jammed door, the leaking tap, I realised that I had ignored those little things for so long, things which prevented my home from being a perfect one. Maybe more than longing for a man, it was my longing for a sheltered home that made me dependent on Rahas. Our days and nights were coalesced together and he was more than happy to become my unofficial better half. He made me do my morning jog, meditate, drink lukewarm water with lemon and honey and told me not to badmouth my mother. He proved to be that anchor upon which I could found my dreams. I relished our time together, his constant presence. But as they say, there is no perfect world. Rahas remained strangely oblivious to the nature of our relationship. I would often ask him what he thought of me and he would avoid that question. It made me impatient, restless and feel used. I was in a moral panic; I was sleeping with this man for over six months, spending on him, he was also taking extreme care of me but I was still no one in his life. Who was I?

I ran to Samarth for help and for affirming that I was not corrupt, for assuring me that Rahas would commit. I think more than love, it was obstinacy that made it impossible for me to even think of losing Rahas. Samarth assuaged my fears, dismissed my anxiety and repeated this whenever I had a moral attack. I was really fortunate to find a friend in Samarth but this friendship did not come easy to me as I always jumped into falling in love with men, owing to my insecurities and lack of validation. I went to do the same with Samarth when I first met him but he jolted me out of it. At that moment, I realised that in our rush to form intimate relationships, we fall for love and sex ignoring the subtle but more lasting relationships. I was glad to have a friend with whom I had lesser chances of breaking up.

Who decides right and wrong? Who decided it's alright to smile openly but not to cry? The infant cries when it is hungry, it cries openly, oblivious of anyone's presence. But as it grows, it is taught to suppress its natural craving. It is taught to adhere to what is considered right. No one knows who created these rights and wrongs. The child is the closest to the ultimate God. I have a child and I could see the difference between him and me. When he was six months old, all he wanted was to sleep and to get fed. But as he grows, he develops a liking towards toys, processed food, money. The vicious spiral of indoctrination starts debilitating the child's natural behaviour.

The child becomes an adult, conditioned by dogmatic and didactic teachings and preachings of the society, families and surroundings. He becomes guarded with everyone, sometimes retracting so much that he shies away from his own presence, his own desires, his own self. This child lives in each one of us.

Life is hard, difficult and some people around us make it even worse. You cannot alone sustain this life, forget being happy in it. There are financial fracas, pain of migration, pain of growth and you need a shoulder to lean on, to cry on. A relationship is that anchor with which you can sail your wrecked ship in the turbulent sea of life. I look back and look at all my previous relationships. They all started on a high note.

If I'm bothered by something, I don't get respite unless I find a solution. In relationships, if there's something disturbing my peace, I talk it out. Same happened with Samarth when I fell for him sometime back. Samarth refused my indirect proposition because he was steadfastly committed to his wife. That phase when I was turned down by him, I decided to stop talking to him. Sometimes being incommunicado is the only coping mechanism we are left with to deal with rejection and the discomfort caused by it. But even that did not give me peace. With time, I could overcome my ego and also I started missing his friendship. I could finally see that he was quite upright when he stood firm on his stance of not looking outside marriage. At least he was way better than the rest of the wayward men like Param who lied to their spouses and objectified other women.

As soon as I realised this, I became restless to sort it out with him at the earliest. One Sunday, when I was in office and there was minimal staff, I couldn't contain myself and dialled his number. He picked up the phone and greeted me in his usual tone. I was quite irked hearing his cheerful voice. Was he so unaffected by my misery? All men are like this: insensitive, heartless. I blurted out a flurry of abuses to calm myself. It still did not help and I decided to lay down my guard and ask him openly.

Sometimes life surprises us. I was in a committed relationship with Rahas when I met Sulabh. Strangely enough it was Rahas who introduced us. Sulabh was quite an influential man from a bureaucrat family and had a big 4-BHK flat in Mumbai. Rahas would often stay with him when he visited Mumbai. Once when I was in Mumbai, Rahas took me to Sulabh's flat for having a creative discussion with the budding filmmaker. He was heaping praises on Sulabh. I was enamoured by the description of his work, his choice of making hard-hitting films and of course his affluence. When I walked inside his home, I found two other men sitting beside him. They were all wearing casual t-shirt and jeans and here I was, looking like an old woman in a sari. I was disappointed at what I was wearing. In a haste, I tried to redo whatever little I could to make myself look more chic in the old-fashioned sari. I completely forgot that I always chose to wear saris for their sensuality. I flipped my hair on one side of my neck so that my shoulder would be exposed and also tossed my *pallu* so that it exposed my bare arms. It did not matter if I won him over but at least I wanted to leave a mark in Sulabh's mind and body when I left that place. He should know whom he had met.

Sulabh was a young filmmaker and had one film to his credit. I saw his short film *Kitab Wallah* and was impressed by his subject, his thought process, his approach and his ability to weave emotions into his narrative. He had earned my respect, something most guys I met failed to achieve. I wanted to review his film on my blog. I could clearly see that he was among those rare filmmakers who attempted to make hard-hitting films. Enthused, I mailed him some samples of my poetry on Facebook. Yes, Facebook is a cupid that can seal lust in one tap of a finger. I was over the moon when he called me up the next day to tell me that he liked them. This is what he said then, 'I didn't sleep the entire night, I kept reading your poems.'

I never could have imagined what was about to happen next. In a twist of fate, he was visiting Delhi for some personal work. We met to discuss his work and ended up discussing everything other than work. It was winter and the afternoon sun shined warmly.

We decided to meet at Karol Bagh. I was excited about meeting him. I wore a maroon knee-length dress and kept my hair loose. I reached the market and saw it was crowded. In that melee, I stood waiting impatiently for Sulabh's arrival. He was late!

Fifteen minutes had passed by when Sulabh called to say that his car was stuck in a traffic jam. He called up again and asked me to cross the road. I walked up and found my heart beating fast as I was about to face him. I was amused by this feeling since I had never met him like this before. Where was this strange mix of anxiety and happiness coming from?

I walked a few steps and found his car. It was a silver Toyota and he was in the driver's seat. Our eyes met and we smiled. I opened the door of the car and sat inside. He was indeed good-looking, I thought. Sulabh was wearing a pair of blue jeans and a white t-shirt, paired with a dark blue jacket. His hair was slightly curly and he had a fair complexion and light stubble on his cheeks. We started talking about grooming and fashion.

As I sat, Sulabh drove. He asked me if I had a lunch place in mind. It was 2:30 PM and there were butterflies in my stomach. I said no but mentioned that I was a vegetarian. He suggested we go to a street-side dhaba near Mandi House. We reached that place, he parked his car at a distance and we walked over. It was a wide, clean road flanked by big white houses.

Sulabh said that despite being affluent, he had a deep love for street food. When we reached the dhaba, he pulled out a chair for me to sit on. Even though I knew that was a fairly common gesture, not too many men

I dated followed that etiquette. Here was a handsome, chivalrous man who loved my poems. Life could not get any better than this. For me, life was all about these thrills. Could you get that thrill living with the same person throughout your life? I was in a continuous pursuit of new companionship, an unfamiliar face, an unfelt body: a new emotional landscape to explore, a new life to dive into. Sulabh and I shared similar tastes and that point of time, I wanted to stay a little longer in that dhaba than him. It's strange how intimacy can develop between two strangers in a span of few hours. I think this intimacy has more to do with us shedding our layers that protect our vulnerability from judgement. Sulabh had no expectations from me that I had to fulfil, neither did I. Also, the charm of meeting a new person that you also find attractive adds spark to that intimacy. He sipped my being with his eyes and my heart swelled with pleasure!

After having our lunch of roti and paneer butter masala, we left the dhaba for a stroll. While I walked with him, I did not pay attention to the direction we were moving in. My thoughts were immersed in our conversation and I felt intoxicated. After 10 minutes of walking and talking, we reached a tea stall adjoining Mandi House. The place was full of drama school students and other pedestrians. The tea vendor had a busy time stirring the boiling tea in the saucepan. He had a helper who grinded the ginger and then ferried little plastic teacups to the customers. Sulabh was right, the ease and openness of that tea stall mimicked what I wanted from life. I wanted my life to be open and warm like the tea in those little teacups.

He then drove me back to my office. I loved the ease with which he talked on our way. He told me stories of his youth as we drove through.

'Bangla Sahib Marg, I stayed on the street that overlooked it when I came to Delhi in 2009.'

'This road, Kasturba Gandhi Marg, this is where I directed my first play in The British Council in 2012.'

On our way, finding an empty corner, he parked his car and took out his mobile phone. It was then that he revealed that he was in a five-year-old relationship with a theatre actress who loved him insanely. He also confessed that sometimes he felt that they were not meant to be together and feared that they would break up. But her limitless love and service made him go back to her every time. He said no one could ever love him and be with him despite all his flaws other than this girlfriend. I was envious. He made a video call to his girlfriend and made us chat for a while. That two-minute-long chat was exhausting for me as I tried my best to force a smile on my face.

Sulabh was five years younger than me and as he reminisced about his youth, I stealthily matched my own life to his. Where was I when he was doing all this? A woman's brain is intricately built like a complicated maze of thoughts and feelings. In 2009, I was anxious to get married at the age of 26. In 2012, I became a mother. The roads unfolded the age chasm between him and me. I felt unsure and undeserving of his affections. How could I, a mother in her early thirties, desire a bachelor in his late twenties. I was so disturbed that I decided to uplift my cowering self-esteem by prodding him about my age. I knew that I looked much younger than I really was.

Sulabh, like any other man, was clueless about the enigmatic feminine charm. Women always outdo men in arousing their curiosity by playfully devised coquetry and a magical spell of innocence and confident charm. My spirit was now adamant about crushing the age gap between us. My body was a lush landscape the gates to which had been closed for him. I asked him one seemingly innocent question to bring his carnal feelings to boil. I read his countenance.

'Guess my age, Sulabh?'

Sulabh looked confused. '28?' he asked.

Ah! The contentment I reaped from this answer was indescribable. As if someone had showered my aching body with petals of tuberose and jasmine. I had become indefatigable, I was invincible. Age had finally taken a bow in front of my mettle and zest for life. I thanked the treadmill and the free fruits in the office that helped me retain my looks. Money could buy you youth, I thought. I flashed a smile and said that I was 32. I was actually 33.

With the age saga over, I was nearing my destination as he drove. We both could sense a rising attraction. Our eyes met for a moment and then stayed there for two more seconds. No words were spoken because words were not required. The most intense relationships are those where words become unnecessary. The initial phases of all intimate relationships are such. In this phase, body becomes the language. The eyes, the hands, the lips. A kiss can reveal so much more than words can. Kiss a man and you don't need to tell him that you love him.

The courtship went one step at a time, starting from the sizzling gaze. Sulabh gently clutched my hands. He changed gears holding my hands in his. I did not say a word. At that time, a tornado of emotions twirled around my mushy heart. I wanted to move forward and kiss him. But the moment slipped.

'Come home for a drink? I have a nice home in Khidki,' he said.

I think it's an innate talent that women use to sense if a male suitor is taking things too fast. My past relationships had taught me to take things slow. I would inevitably end up having sex if I went to his house but we had just met.

'Some other day, maybe?' I said.

He was disappointed. He continued, 'Come on, it's not far and my sister is also not here. She is coming back after two days and it will be difficult after that.'

'Listen! I think it's too early. Plus I have to get back to work. I just came for a quick meet-up during my office lunch. I do not have so much liberty at office,' I sighed.

'Why are you fearful? It's all mutual right! I'm a decent man and I'm not going to touch you if you don't want it. All I thought was that maybe we could have a few drinks in my house and enjoy some cosy time.'

I still did not yield. I had been in this situation with Param before. Lots of questions crowded my mind. Why was he insisting so hard? I knew that he wanted physical intimacy and going to his flat was just a pretext. I declined.

The next morning, as I woke up, my mind was fresh and pulsating from the moments of togetherness spent with Sulabh the previous day. He was all over my mind and I found it difficult to accept his absence in my day. I was sad that I was not going to meet him that day. Expectations can build up in a jiffy and can become monumental in no time. I was at the mercy of those expectations. My mind was acting like a morphine addict and Sulabh was the drug I was addicted to. Thankfully it was a weekend so I was saved from the double whammy of a burning heart and office toil.

I started thinking about all the reasons I could invent to call him, to get in touch with him. And then I remembered that he had discussed some script ideas for his next film and wanted my help with them. Exuberant, I called him up to inform that I had a basic idea for the script. I was dejected when I sensed his drowsy voice. He was a late riser and was in deep slumber when I called. I had woken him up from his sleep and he told me that he would call me back after sometime. The first reality check!

Sulabh called me after three hours, his voice still drowsy. On learning that I made the first draft of the script, he complimented me but did not profess his desire for me. Did I leave no impact on him? I still did not give up and decided to ask him to meet. On hearing this, he sounded excited, 'Yeah, why not! Let's meet at my home.'

I was in a quandary. Just the day before, I had decided to not go to his house. And today I was going to do the same thing.

I had reached the landmark he had told me about. It was a cold winter night and the wind howled around the trees. I was shivering in a turquoise green sari.

I had not worn any sweater as I had none that matched the sari. I could feel my frosting body that ached under the merciless chill. I was in distress; the cold frost was eating me up and the man hadn't turned up to provide me with the warmth of his hug. I waited for 15 minutes and then called him. But he did not answer the phone; exasperated I called him again and again but it went unanswered each time. The frigid cold burned me and I felt my body tearing, falling apart, fainting, crumbling into shards of snowflakes.

I made up my mind to leave the place. There was no one in the streets, not even a dog. I stood there for a while, feeling abandoned. It was time for me to go back home and pretend that nothing had happened. I turned back and lumbered towards the metro station when my phone rang. It was him. My happiness knew no bounds. He was feeling sorry and explained his situation; a crucial staff of his family-owned restaurant had absconded and they were not being able to fulfil all the orders. I could not understand much of it but I was happy that I did not have to go back home without kissing him, hugging him, making some kind of love to him. Yes! The wait had now made me impatient. I felt like a hungry lioness who wanted to devour her prey. I was ready to make love. It was strange! The prospect of rejection had transformed me from an unwilling woman to a woman who was impatiently yearning to be loved. One cannot make sense of an erotic force; it is the most uncertain, illogical, irrational emotion. Eroticism doesn't obey rules and morals. It is its own rule.

Sulabh stood near the metro station and smiled at me from a distance. He had a radiant smile. He came in and hugged me with his left arm. I felt good on being rescued. I wanted to be held and snuggled, I wanted to surrender. He saw me shivering and asked me to wear his black overcoat that was lying on the rear seat of his car. I grabbed it and wore it. As I sat in the car, he gazed at me and said I looked beautiful in his coat. I blushed.

Inside the car, the temperature soared as our warm bodies reluctantly sat at a distance. Sulabh took me to a small Chinese outlet and ordered two small bowls of vegetable soup with herb-buttered croutons. As I savoured the soup, I could not decide which one tasted yummier, the soup or the touch of the fingers that served me the soup. We had our soup but he was not finished with his dining excursion.

'Let's eat some more,' he said.

For me it was a sheer relief to be treated like this. For the last one year, I had only been paying for all of Rahas' expenses. It felt good that I didn't have to worry about the bill and that someone else was there to take care of it. I must confess that a rich man (notwithstanding his creative abilities) does spark a deep interest in me. It has more to do with being tended for, being looked after.

In fact, this reminds me of an Indian soap opera from the mid-90s, *Swabhimaan*, that was the story of a rich industrialist who passed away leaving behind a son and a mistress. The serial was about the power struggle between the son and the mistress, both of whom got an equal share of his property and assets. As a young child, I was fascinated by that serial. The mistress was young and hardly a few years older than the son. It seemed to me that if a woman is much younger than her beloved, she is pampered and cared for.

I felt treasured that day and Sulabh seemed like an eager suitor.

After we finished our dinner, Sulabh murmured that he had a bottle of Old Monk in his house and that we could drink that and listen to Urdu poetry. He said that he had a nice collection of vintage records and it would be good to hear them on a record player. I agreed. To be honest, I would have agreed even if there were no records or any rum. The lure of intimacy was like a drug. For Sulabh as well, it was a pretext to placate our rising sexual urges held captive in his car. At that moment, our sexual energies were at a terrifically high level and it was only the fear of social judgement that kept us from ripping off each other's clothes.

Together we went to his flat. It was located in a dingy neighbourhood and had a swirling staircase. I cautiously climbed the stairs holding his hand. Though I was adept at walking around in a sari and could have climbed those stairs without any help, holding his hand was a way of feeling intimacy. What I did not know then was that in less than an hour, I would be forced into having sex with him.

Inside his house, it was all warm. He lit a cigarette and picked up an old ashtray from the top of his refrigerator. He did not light two cigarettes but just one. His idea was to share the cigarette while we hummed along with the couplets and sipped rum in steel glasses. It was a sight to behold. We both sat on the sofa; the record player was placed on the glass table in front of us, near the ashtray. He took a puff and passed the cigarette to me and we smoked it till there was nothing left to smoke.

'I want more,' I said.

He took out another cigarette from the packet and lit it for us. A mild unrest was slowly building up and it was only a matter of time before we touched each other. I was ready to take the carnal plunge but waited to be led. Girls and women are taught that to be pursued is special. Sulabh eventually took the lead in wooing, seducing and finally forcing me to have sex.

Why do we numb our genuineness in the name of love? Romantic love has been aggrandised to the extent that we surrender our self-esteem, our dissenting desires, our conflicting dreams in the name of love. It is assumed that love needs cohesion, that two people need to have similar attitudes to sustain that love. I have rarely ever heard of couples having an open and transparent discourse on how they are different as individuals. At that moment, I had a different perspective towards intimacy with Sulabh. Yes, I did want to experience intimacy but through a completely different process. In the name of attraction and love which has always been thought of as unifying, I failed to articulate my different physical need to him.

Sulabh started fiddling with my fingers and I let him do that. He leaned forth and we had the most explosive, magical, sticky kiss. I wonder, how a new touch could make the same old ritual feel new. I had been kissed many times before but this kiss was different; a never before experienced treasure. Why was Rahas unable to arouse me in the way Sulabh did?

Getting attracted to someone doesn't mean that there is an inherent flaw in our partner. I think it is the essential moral conflict that makes us stick to one partner for life and stops us from looking elsewhere.

Human beings have two innate life needs, need for stability and need for adventure. We make things certain to make them stable: our jobs, our house, our partner. But we also need adventure, real thrill and risk to make life tempting. We want novelty, unpredictability in our otherwise regular and bored lives. A person with whom we have an amorous relationship is like a new life. The thrill and ecstasy of being with someone you don't know completely and don't own at all is insurmountable.

It's unfortunate that the natural human instinct of needing diversity in love and sex is termed as immoral. I know, there have been millions of people advocating marriage, living by the dream of eternal, everlasting love and perpetual attraction for each other; to even think of someone outside marriage is prohibited let alone desiring someone and ultimately having physical intimacy with that person outside your regular relationship. This is branded as infidelity, as immorality and as per the social norms the straying (are we dogs?) person is punished severely, granted a divorce or a break-up and subjected to mental anguish. Why are our rules so rigid for love? Why is tolerance for other people not practised in our sexual relationships? I see that in every other part of life, we have similar relationships with more than one person. We have two parents, two or more siblings, two or more friends, countless relatives, two or more children. Why then is our lover supposed to be only one person throughout our life? I feel it has more to do with social balance and our own mental balance. Yes, love is vulnerable. You get exposed and dependent on a person on whom you have very less control. It is a threatening situation and thus you set off to increase control on that vulnerable situation to safeguard not the relationship but your being.

The dopamine levels in my body surged as Sulabh continued kissing me. All I could feel were his hands clutching my back and a mouth that was melting into mine vigorously. Sulabh then made me lie on the couch. Though I had considerable sexual experience, I still preferred being guided in the lovemaking ritual. I was kissed, I was made to lie down, I was being loved. I liked to surrender completely to my lover. I felt tender and supple like a ripened mango. Sulabh was baring its skin, the rigid layers of boredom and unsheathing the erotic energy inside. I was rejuvenated under the shower of his wet, cigarette-flavoured kisses. It was a breathtaking experience.

I lay on the couch with my eyes closed.

In that passionate, intense lovemaking, my long lustrous hair got entangled across my face and it became ticklish for him to kiss my face. He lifted his right hand and with his small, hard fingers cleared my face. Like a dexterous lover, he picked each thick black strand of hair and moved it away. His fingers felt like brush strokes that were painting me in a rainbow of ecstasy. Sulabh was gazing at my face as I murmured little sighs.

'This face, these gazelle-like eyes, this long lustrous hair. I cannot believe that I have you,' he said.

Sulabh held my hand and led me to his bedroom. As I lay down on his bed, he switched off all the lights.

He started undressing me. He tried to unhook my blouse but was stuck. I had gained weight since I got that blouse stitched and it had gotten tighter, making it difficult for him to undo the hooks. These days women rarely wear saris and Sulabh definitely seemed to lack the experience of unhooking blouses. My breasts had become heavier and plumper. It seemed that the arousal had increased the blood flow inside and my nipples became erect and the area around the nipples distended.

Sulabh made multiple attempts to unhook the blouse and finally succeeded in unhooking three out of the six hooks. It was a moment of awkwardness for me. Here I was on a bed with a total stranger and he was finding it hard to undress me. Our eyes met and he faintly smiled out of impatience.

Seeing Sulabh unable to unfasten the last hook and becoming restless in that still awkwardness, I helped him undo it. The room was dark and both of us sat up to undo that one annoying hook that was holding things up. To be frank, I was frightened as he undid the hook. I was in a quandary: do I want it or not? I liked kissing him undoubtedly and I liked lying with him, feeling his touch, his entire body but I was uncomfortable with this undressing. Is this what they call the grey area of consent?

I couldn't say no to him as I thought I would not have intercourse. Having a man already in my life, I was bound by unassailable chains of monogamy, of loyalty. I felt kissing was still less intimate and more forgivable than sex. Having intercourse was like leaving signs of his penis inside my vagina or the testament of our sex. I was still in a relationship with Rahas and was scared of infidelity. I was still able to condone the foreplay but not the physical penetration. It was weird that at the time of the lovemaking with Sulabh, all this was flashing inside my mind. I was scared! I wanted to relish the moment, immerse in his embrace and the shelter of his body but I was afraid of the world that awaited me the moment I exited his door.

Sulabh opened my blouse and flung my bra in the air. The blouse lay in a corner of the bed while the bra dropped on the floor. I could see from the corner of my eye that it was on the floor and was getting dirty. But I ignored it. I wish we had a careless way of lovemaking. Straddling, waddling and rolling in a thick puddle of mud. Ripping each other's waterlogged clothes, throwing handfuls of mud at each other. Smearing each other's cheeks and forehead lovingly with the muck and then wiping it off gently. This kind of lovemaking had to wait till an eternity, so I had to be content with the hushed, quiet lovemaking inside the confines of that bedroom.

I was naked and so was he. I could not bear to see his naked body. It was still too early for me to allow a man access to my body and to see his. I could correlate this feeling to peeling an unripe mango simply because we cannot resist its flavour. Our lust was flavourful but the trust had not yet ripened. With closed eyes, I could feel his skin on mine. I felt little stars of electric charge pulsating and bursting into fireworks. In my mind, my body had lifted up from that bed and was levitating. Sulabh was holding my spirit and my body. Two bare, cold bodies were soaking in the warmth of each other. His warm embrace made me feel how much detached I had been from my femininity before. He helped me discover the pent-up love inside me, which had screeched before but was gagged by the cultural threats of monogamy. 'I'm not a monogamous person,' my soul screamed out.

He gently nibbled my nipples with his small but sharp teeth, I groaned out of pleasure and pain. Then he squeezed my breasts and sucked them. He was besotted by my ripe mango-like breasts. These breasts had been touched and fondled by many men before with their rugged, coarse hands but nothing had felt this good before.

I could feel the fragrance of his perfume filling me. Sulabh was a well-bred man from a well-to-do family. His upbringing could be made out from the choice of his perfume. I remembered having sex with Rahas and his perfume. Also the times when he did not use any. The thought of his body odour repulsed me now. Comparisons are not always bad if done in a vulnerable moment of lovemaking.

Sulabh undid the string of my petticoat and I responded to it with a deep sigh! Now, I was becoming fearful. How do I eviscerate this morality that had been injected deep in my blood? Even though no one was witness to our voracious lovemaking. He was hard to stop and he wanted it all. He was slowly and gently inching up to my vagina. I confess again, intercourse is my way of surrendering to my man, my emotions, my wretchedness, my being. A man will become my master if he manages to have sex with me. I'm a slave to sexual love; I'm also a slave to my secrets and no secret can be more profound and insidious than an illicit sexual affair with a man outside one's supposed monogamous relationship. I resisted feebly. Sulabh persisted.

'Let me enter once. Only once. I won't ejaculate,' he said.

He felt that I was fearful of getting pregnant. What neither of us feared was getting afflicted with an STD or an STI. But what about my secrets, threats to my existing relationship? Who would bear the burden of my monotonous life, who would invigorate my dull moments with his constant presence and laughter, who would make my loneliness less unbearable? Rahas was the answer to all these questions. What I feel now is that when you make a person fill in an empty space of 'who' in your life, he becomes a role. A role with all its responsibilities and obligations; yes with responsibilities come obligations. What if he is not a who, he is just he. When someone asks me, who is he, rather than replying he is my husband, I should say, he is he. I detest roles. I feel someone is strangulating me, my independence, with the noose of roles. In this life you are bound to become a slave, either you become a slave of your role or of your independence.

Sulabh was insisting, as if sex was the final destination without which all our lovemaking would be meaningless. I could not muster the courage to say no to him, so I had to cook up an excuse to avoid sex. I told him that I was not ready to have unprotected sex despite all his assurances. It was strange that my refusal did not seem enough for him to stop. Why did I need to find excuses? That night, in that bedroom, my inability to say no to him was an outcome of decades of submissiveness and reticence. He replied, 'Just wait for two minutes. I'm going downstairs to buy condoms.'

He immediately hopped off the bed and slid into his jeans, wore his shirt and ran towards the door. I was in a perplexed state, lying spread-eagled on his king-sized bed alone. I half-draped my naked body with a blanket. It felt odd to be naked in a stranger's house. What if his servants or his sister knocked on the door? I was deeply immersed in these thoughts when Sulabh came back with a pack of condoms in his hand. His face gleamed as he saw me and he flashed the pink packet to announce his triumph. I felt numb. It was apparent that I did not want to have sex with him.

Sulabh hurriedly lifted my petticoat, slipped on the condom and entered me. I was numb; there was no pleasure felt and no moans. I surrendered and let him do whatever he wanted to do. I faintly remember that after I surrendered, a contentment glimmered in my heart. I was his. He had taken me. What would I tell myself? That I have been raped? That I was violated without my consent? It was too hard for me to face these questions my innocent soul was trying to ask.

In the coming week, I met Sulabh thrice, on alternate days. Each time we met at his home and each time we had sex. My friend Dr Gaurav Deka later gave me the reasoning behind such self-destructive behaviour of falling for emotionally unavailable, bad men. He said that as grown-ups, we mimic the relationship modelled by our parents. Because it feels comfortable and familiar even if it is an abusive relationship. And that is why, coming from a dysfunctional home, I fell for those disparaging relationships.

In our subsequent jaunts, I started enjoying sex with Sulabh. As we got closer, he confided that doggy style was his favourite position. I was initially uncomfortable to get into that position because of my heavy buttocks and because the position required me to take onus. I was perturbed about my body image. My buttocks were dark, riddled with freckles and blackish bumps and were massive like big watermelons. Sulabh had a small buttock.

What will he think of my buttocks?

In my discomfort, I asked him to switch off the light in his drawing room, but keep the one in his bedroom on. That served the dual purpose of hiding my body as well as letting some light on for us to sensually feel and see each other. Throughout his thrusts I was conscious of my buttocks. I felt I had lost my right on him just because of my disformed buttocks. But this unusual position had its upside too. I had never tried it before. Sex is as much about owning pleasure as it is about giving pleasure. With this new position, I felt something ecstatic. I moaned loudly as I said, 'Sulabh, it feels amazing. I have never had such an experience before. What a skilled lover you are. You know how to make a woman reach her heaven.' Sulabh was bemused. He did not believe he had done something exceptional. Little did I know that, that day during intercourse, he had hit my G-spot.

Sulabh had given me a spare key to his flat so I could come in even when he was away on vendor meetings. I would wait in that spare time and scribble poems to recite along with him while lying down on the couch and resting my head on his lap once he came back. That period of wait was redolent with thoughts of sex.

I feel now that no matter how much we talk about equality in a relationship, a relationship is and has always been about changing poles of power. Equality could mean partners alternating in wielding power at different times. Because a relationship is about surrender, you cannot receive unless you stretch your hands out. Yes, sometimes you receive and sometimes you offer. Even during sex, one partner receives and the other provides, in different moments of lovemaking. If we talk about equality, can we use a measurement scale to check if both partners derive equal amounts of pleasure or does it vary in intensities?

I relished that lone time in Sulabh's house, pining for him and scribbling poems in his small notepad. Sulabh would always take an hour to reach home and the wait would make me want to devour him at once, the moment he rang the bell. But my feminine coyness made me resist my desperation and wait for him to make the first move. I remember once I was in his house and I wore a tight-fitting shirt. He took longer to arrive and I started feeling uneasy in that shirt.

I stood up and opened his cupboard and brought out some shirts to try out. There was a hooded shirt with red and black stripes which I liked. I smelled its underarm and it smelled of his sweat. I sniffed the smell of his shirt and it reminded me of him. Contented, I happily changed into his shirt and waited on the couch to surprise him when he got back.

But what is commitment? Is it about being there for each other, in the ups and downs of life, in health, in sickness, in richness and penury as the priest sermons in marriage rituals? Is it about not leaving and staying with each other despite disagreements, fights, arguments? Is it about not straying outside and breaking the monogamous contract? What if I decide to create a new kind of commitment? I choose to support my beloved but I also claim the freedom to drift. Relationships become stagnant if there are no ripples. Sulabh was the ripple in my relationship with Rahas. I was clear on what I was getting from both these men. Rahas provided me security, stability, constancy, belonging and emotional support. Sulabh ushered in poetry and enlightenment. I look at it from a vantage point and see that the thirst for enlightenment had outdone the other elements of a relationship and pushed me to move out of my secure zone to tread into a highly uncertain, riskier and insecure terrain. Am I to be blamed or was this the course of nature?

On our last day of school, 18 years back, students were busy getting their slam books filled by their classmates. I also had bought a red slam book and for the first time in my entire school life, I talked to almost everyone in my class. Maybe because the purpose was very clear. The purpose was to get my slam book filled by my classmates, with their writings, their likings. In effect, because I would no longer meet them in person, I wanted to get their beings inscribed on these pages. One of my classmates, Ritika, wrote about her inability to say no.

I was the same way. I had grown up in an abusive home where I was always instructed, suppressed and humiliated by Baba, who himself was battling a failing, adulterous marriage. When he was home on Sundays, the rest of us would speak in hushed undertones and when he was out, we would all be loud and happy. I had learnt to suppress myself, told myself that I could never say no. It was my inability to say no that was playing havoc in the love triangle between Rahas, Sulabh and me. My uprightness, to not tell a complete lie, also worsened this situation. My attraction for Sulabh had markedly increased after Rahas left for a theatre tour in Hyderabad. In that week, I met Sulabh almost every day, had sex with him on all those days, all behind Rahas' back. I tasted unrestrained freedom; there was no one to question me, no one to monitor and follow my moves. I owned my life. Yes, in that one week I owned my life.

When Rahas came back to the city and met me, I was a changed girl; a girl who was no more in love with him. He took me to the basement of a suburban metro station. Since we were lovers with no place to stay at night, that was our go-to place, far from the melee and its clamour. I was unusually quiet as I stood there; my head was lowered and a deep anxiety embittered my heart. Rahas had grown up in a patriarchal family and often fondly recollected how his mother shivered in front of his father. I could see the flashes of that patriarchal blood surging in the veins of his clenched face. I was frightened! On that night Rahas stood in front of me and looked at me with suspicion. The basement was deserted and I was frightened to the core. I trembled more. The fear of getting caught was all over my face. I felt like a thief standing in the witness box and Rahas was the judge who was about to announce my sentence.

Rahas questioned me, 'Are you OK?'

I looked up at him meekly and murmured that I wanted to share something with him. Looking at my dreariness, Rahas could make out that I was hiding something from him. I turned morose and told him a partial lie, 'I am attracted to Sulabh. I met him while you were away.' I withheld from him that we also had sex.

Rahas stared at me for a long time while I cowered in a corner and trembled in the aftermath of my confession. After a minute of stillness, he came near me, bent to look me in the eye and questioned me again, 'I know that you met him. Did he touch you, kiss you? Did you sleep with him? Swear on your son.'

I had no courage to tell him the truth. What would he do if I told him? Kill me, beat me, desert me? I do not know the accurate answer. In one second, I was demoted from my independent identity to become someone who was at the mercy of social norms. I meekly said no, putting all his fears to rest. Rahas was relieved to know that my body was still his property. He came closer to me and embraced me in a tight hug.

'Don't panic. It's alright. But now don't talk to him any more,' he said.

I nodded to appease him. I would have done anything to not let Rahas abandon me. He had been my constant companion; he never said no when I wanted to meet him. I feared loneliness; I had grown addicted to and dependent on Rahas' presence. My identity, my need for self-dependence, something that I had painstakingly built after Prakhar left, was in threat with this growing addiction and dependence. And in that moment, I saw myself standing at a crossroads with two divergent paths leading to different directions. The path of self-dependence and the path of companionship locked horns with each other. I made the pragmatic, conscious choice of companionship. Survival was more important than pleasure.

I went back home content over my defeat. I did not gain anything in this settlement but I had lost my independence and my agency. I had also lost the threat of loneliness. That night I slept with the fond memories of lovemaking with Sulabh. The next morning, as I woke up with a fresh mind, I rethought my decision to cut off all ties with Sulabh. The thought created a monstrous angst in me.

'Can I make my identity kneel to fulfil the command of a man? Don't I have the agency to decide for things that I like? Can I not get stability and independence at the same time?'

My mind revolted. It finally sunk in that I had made an adjustment to survive. I immediately decided to make amends and reclaim my own voice. I decided to not cut off connections with someone just because Rahas had asked me to. Where was my own judgement and free will? Exasperated at how I was reduced to being a minion the previous night, I called up Rahas to announce my decision. He picked up the phone and spoke to me softly. Upon hearing my decision of continuing to talk to Sulabh, he asked me, 'You are OK with me leaving you but you cannot leave him?'

I talked to Rahas from a firm ground of logic and rationale. It became hard for me to understand why I could not make a choice. What was the worst that could happen? I might make a wrong choice and end up getting hurt emotionally or physically but I would live and learn. I remembered the books I read in my childhood where the female protagonists made daring choices; they were never supported by the society and ended up getting hurt and abused. But they never regretted it because it was they who made their choices instead of their pall-bearers.

I was in a limbo; the attraction to Sulabh was part out of interest and part out of stubbornness. Rahas was clearly not comfortable with me being sexual with Sulabh. I had to devise a lie. I hated telling lies but this time I had to lie to protect both my relationships. The stakes were high and someone's trust was at stake. Throughout my life, I had lived according to other people's whims and fancies. I started spinning a cobweb of lies and realised that I was a dexterous spinner. Though I was nervous when I lied to Rahas whenever I went to meet with Sulabh, I eventually escaped undetected.

But I could not escape the ringing bell on my mobile. Rahas used to call me intermittently during the day and it was difficult to not answer his calls. Even if I avoided picking up his call, I had to call him back in an hour or he would call me back.

One day after work, Sulabh came to the metro station to pick me up. My whole body brimmed with joy as I saw him.

He walked up to me and escorted me to his car. His Toyota, worth 18 lakhs, had caught my fancy. As a child, I was always fascinated by the cars wheeling on our streets; I would go near those cars and make signs and marks with my fingers on the dust-tinted windows. That child inside me never died and I still carried that awe for cars. When Sulabh drove me around in his car, I felt like a princess from *Ramayana* riding her *pushpak viman*. As he turned his head over his shoulder and looked at me, I was under his spell. Rahas had cautioned me earlier about Sulabh, about his dark side, but I didn't care. For me it was the dark side that attracted me towards him and other men in my life.

My phone rang. It was Rahas. I was stunned at his interference. Nervous, I explained to Sulabh what had happened before we met. I mumbled that Rahas did not want me to see him. It was a huge disclosure and I should not have done that. Sulabh calmed me down and said he would handle it. Rahas had called Sulabh to invite him for a get-together with the promise of ample booze and roasted chicken. Rahas was a teetotaller so I knew that all this was just a masquerade. Rahas knew that I had left home to meet Sulabh and he was making all attempts to keep Sulabh away from me. Sulabh sensed the seriousness of the situation and accepted the invite, as I looked at him helplessly. I told him, 'I'm not going to go back.'

In essence, I meant that I was not going to go back without having sex with Sulabh. Even for Sulabh it was a terrible proposition to leave without fucking and sucking me. Both of us wanted to experience the powerful climax of lust.

Sulabh handed me the keys to his flat and left to meet Rahas. I waited alone in his flat, afraid of someone stomping in. I had cheated on my saviour and my lover and could not call him to rescue me. I barely knew Sulabh beyond his body. Could he help me survive the hurricanes of life? Reality was sinking in too fast in that solitude! I calmed myself with the thoughts of Sulabh and making love with a frantic, insatiable urgency. After an hour, Rahas called to check on me. I picked the phone and lied to him, 'I'm at home.'

This tempestuous, hide-and-seek affair continued with Sulabh amidst ever-increasing lies. One evening I sat with Rahas and sobbed over our impending separation; he had to go home to his family for a month. But immediately after he left, I wiped my tears and called Sulabh to inform him that I was coming to see him. I had a natural inclination and passion for Sulabh and it converted me into a liar.

The only constant is change, and thus it becomes incredibly debilitating to deal with uncertainties in love. So, we set out to fix love and fix all insecurities that arise from it. It's a dangerous contradiction because thrill and joy reside in insecurity, risk and uncertainty and once you fix those, you bring in predictability and permanence. I was facing a similar fate. My relationship with Sulabh was sensational because of its impropriety and now the same impropriety was making me dependent on an emotionally unavailable man. It was terrible!

In that forbidden relationship too, I demanded loyalty. How absurd was this? I had always taken pride in saying that I give my man ample space and that included ample sexual space. The problem of jealousy should not have arisen in me but it did. It did on the day I lay on Sulabh's couch while he was in the kitchen of his home-delivery service. He asked me to wait. That day he forgot his phone on the table and I found it. Inquisitively I picked it up and unlocked the phone. I knew his password. He did not say it to me on his own but shared it when I asked him in a moment of rising intimacy. I wanted to see if with increasing sexual encounters, I was also coming closer to reigning over his heart.

Passwords are an important metric to judge the success of a relationship. The more intimate a relationship becomes, the more passwords are exchanged. The sharing leads to the deleting of a lot of records. Sulabh always deleted his chats with me because his long-distance partner Sahira would keep an eye on him. And I was OK with that. I never wanted to confine or own a man, I found it too naive a way to prove my worthiness. Also, any man, if he wants to stay with me, should do this out of his free choice and not any compulsion.

I wanted to dethrone his partner and become Sulabh's only object of desire. So, when he shared his phone password with me, I experienced a small triumph. That day, when his phone was lying unattended on the table, I unlocked it and started reading through his chats with his partner, Sahira. A new world unveiled in front of me where I witnessed his insanely passionate love for her. I was in a delirium. All this time, I thought that this man was carrying the weight of this relationship because he could not bear to hurt her. But I was wrong. Sulabh lied to a liar. Our passionate love affair was no longer exclusive, it was shared among two women and a man. He always lamented his loss of freedom and his never-ending string of lies after getting in a relationship with Sahira. This made me believe that perhaps he was not happy with her and was dragging the relationship for the lack of an escape. But the intensely intimate chats where he showered emojis of kisses on Sahira turned my beliefs upside down. The man seemed privileged, and women were at the mercy of his attention and his willingness. The thought repulsed me.

When Sulabh came back from work, he noticed my glum countenance. He leaned in closer for a kiss but I retracted; the mixed feelings of jealousy and unease kept stirring in my heart. I showed him the message in his mobile phone where he had showered emojis of kisses on his steady partner. I thought Sulabh would be embarrassed on being caught but his reaction was different, 'You also have a partner. You want to keep that relationship intact with him but want me to leave her. Don't you think that is unfair?'

His words stung me. It was a false accusation. By meeting Sulabh, I was risking my relationship with Rahas. I had asked Sulabh many times if he really wanted to be with me but he declined each time. Sometimes by saying that his family would not approve of the relationship and sometimes by saying that our attraction had lasted only because our relationship was forbidden. He told me once, 'You are only after me for the pursuit. The moment you own me in a relationship, you will lose interest in me and will leave me.'

He was right. He was the only man who had seen my dark side. I wanted to own Sulabh irrespective of what he said. Was that my obstinacy or was it a natural drive for humans to want to own someone they loved?

The jealousy was coming in the way of that conquest. I wanted to distance myself from him. I wanted to hurt him back for the hurt he caused me. I wanted to take revenge. Sulabh could not make sense of my sudden changed behaviour. 'You knew it all the time. Didn't you?' he asked.

So what? I had not signed up to be logically correct all the time? I was hurt and that was it! I could be insane,

I could go back on my words. I was genuinely hurt and it did not matter what I had promised in the past. Things change, people change! Now Sulabh had to tide through this jagged turf and cajole me. He had to say that his messages were just a compromise to keep the relationship alive. He had to persuade me that what I saw was indeed a lie and that our forbidden relationship was the truth. I think when we see a blatant truth and we cannot come to terms with it, we run towards someone who can lie to us and make us believe it. We gag our own instinct and pass on the baton to a different person. Our fears defy our individuality.

But Sulabh did nothing of that sort. That hurt me more. Soon it was time for us to part as I had to go back. I sat with him in the car but remained quiet as he drove. Sulabh could make out that I was terribly unhappy with the sudden revelation of the chemistry between him and Sahira. The emojis flooded my mind and distanced me from him. Unlike other days, when we shared a smoke on our way back and I kissed him on his neck and held his hand, I remained quiet. Such was the hurry to get away from him that I left my book and train tickets in his car. As I reached home, I was in tears; my castle of passion had collapsed into rubble in a moment. I could feel the pain of betrayal but surprisingly I did not feel any remorse for the lies I told Rahas.

There is a thin line between being sexually liberal and sexually used. In my zest to experience unrestrained sexuality, I overlooked other key elements of a relationship. Of course, I never endorse one-night stands with strangers, but I also like the idea of having simultaneous intimate relationships with multiple men.

Though I decided to have an intimate relationship with Sulabh, I failed to check if he was the right person. I wanted closeness from him but he always remained elusive. In those moments, I clung to Rahas for the feeling of security. And when I recouped, I went back to Sulabh in secrecy. I was having the best of both worlds but I had to trade this double happiness for a web of lies.

I realised I was depressed. Depression is different from sadness; it is much more severe. It is malignant in the way it spreads through our body and soul like cancer, steadily and stealthily. Indeed, it is cancer of the soul and mind. Of course, there are initial signs or behavioural lumps which look innocuous in appearance and hence we do not pay attention to them. Emotional outbursts, mood swings, sadness, pessimism, self-doubt, anger, all of these come across as part of the normal human behavioural spectrum. But there is a difference between emotional behaviour and depression; the former is an experience, the latter is a disease. The experiences change, they come and go like day and night, but a disease festers on unless treated.

Sadness is evident, depression is not. I can say this as I have experienced both. It's easy to break away from sadness but depression eats up your soul and it is hard to escape it. Strangely, in my case, extreme happiness preceded depression. I was in a state of eternal bliss when I was seeing Sulabh. Our chemistry was explosive as was the emotional connect, the physical attraction, the lovemaking, the conversations; all of it was matchless. With him, I experienced the highest physical compatibility I ever had with a partner.

But there was a catch. This bliss was only a result of the coming together of two people and was dependent on the emotional contract between these two people. So, when one of them changed the terms of their emotional contract, the bliss ended. I started getting cues prior to the grand arrival of depression. The relationship with Sulabh was in a turbulent phase. His availability, emotional and physical, was sporadic. We would only meet once a week or once in two weeks. My emotional state was determined by his presence in my life. I was happy when he was with me and dejected when he was not.

I could not gauge what this dependency on him was doing to me. I had given someone else the keys to the vehicle of my happiness. That meant I had to depend on that person to drive me to and from happiness. I should not have done that. I should have kept the keys with me. I was so intoxicated with his love that I chose to remain oblivious to the fact that a day would come when Sulabh would leave. He was not from Delhi. I was so happy that I chose to turn a blind eye to the future, though the future kept knocking at my door. That day had to come when we would separate, and it did.

It was a nice windy evening, around 7:30 PM. I packed up and left from office. I had texted Sulabh in the morning, expressing my desire to meet him. He had not replied. I rarely called him but that day, I just could not restrain myself and called him up. He picked up the call. I started off by chastising him.

'You are ignoring me, Sulabh.'

'No! I am not. I am leaving for Mumbai today.'

His words wreaked havoc inside me. I was taken aback.

'It was sudden!' he assured me, 'I'll come back in five days. Some urgent work has come up.'

The news transformed me from a strong woman to an anxious lover.

'You are leaving and you did not even bother to inform me.'

'It happened all of a sudden. I decided to go just half an hour back.'

He had only given me access to his body, not his life and decisions. I disconnected the call. In a flash of a second, this revelation changed something in me. I continued to walk but felt as though someone had tied weights to my feet. I crossed the road and reached the mall which was on my way to the metro station. I saw a sweet corn stall and felt the urge to eat. I needed a break to reinstate my normalcy. I felt eating would help me ward off the despondent feeling. I ordered a small portion and ate perfunctorily. After I finished, I took the metro. Through the entire journey of one and a half hours, I was numb. I never anticipated that Sulabh's departure would create such a huge dent in my life.

There were initial symptoms of depression. From a happy-go-lucky, confident, ambitious woman, I had transformed into a despondent, miserable person who had little faith in life and her abilities. My smile had vanished and was replaced by a blank expression. I stopped reacting and became completely passive. I did not cry as I did not feel the urge to cry, instead I brooded. At that time Rahas was in Mumbai and I felt worse. There was no shoulder to lean on and cry. How important this support was in my life!

I felt like time had frozen and that I was stuck in it forever. I felt like something was eating my soul and my identity. I became disinterested in work and glanced at the screen of my laptop for hours without doing anything. My energy was drained, my arms and legs hurt. I tried to distract myself by eating and reading, but it was all in vain.

I felt at ease only in darkness; with my ever-nagging mother and three-year-old mischievous child sleeping, I enjoyed my solitude and prayed for the night to never end. Subconsciously, with each passing day, I was growing accustomed to depression and felt comfort in its presence. The more I tried to break through it, the more I panicked. The more I surrendered myself to its fate, the more still I became. Stillness was better than panic as it kept me transfixed in a state where my senses ceased to work, akin to a lifeless stone.

A lot of who I was was determined by my relationships. I have always had an apathy towards anything that can control me. I always got attracted to people who exert no control on my life. People related by blood often get hurt or offended by my actions but they do not threaten to leave me. Samarth was a well-wisher in whom I confided my deepest feelings, but to him it did not matter what I did or what I did not. The trickiest relationship I have is with him. It threatens my sanity.

Expectations can build or break bonds. Love is not a territory which can be conquered by someone. It is a feeling and feelings are independent. I cannot see or touch my feelings and that is why I find it difficult to control them. You can merely experience feelings, enjoy them, but cannot own them. You can breathe air but cannot own it, because it transcends physical form, it cannot be captured or controlled. Water, unlike air, has a clear physical form and so human beings conspire and aspire to control it, to own it. History boasts of countless wars that were fought between states, between empires to claim rivers. Unlike air, water can be confined. I think it's a human tendency to try and own things it can confine. Love cannot be confined. I can love someone and as long as it stays in my heart as a feeling, no one can detect it. I have continued to desire Sulabh for about a year and never encountered a problem because I have done nothing to express those feelings. People who become a part of your life vie for these expressions of love and sooner and later, you become a creature who is constantly expressing feelings that you wanted to keep to yourself.

I have somehow fallen in this trap, although I have always tried to keep my feelings private. It is not by virtue of force but comfort. Comfort is a devious creature. Feelings of love are spiritual, manifestations of those feelings are not. Manifestations can be enhanced or condensed. By virtue of this spiritual love, I tend to feel for every child on this planet. But when I choose to manifest, to give a better life, better means, better comforts, I choose only my son. There is a man-made competition on this planet, to claim, to win, to own. There cannot be many winners but there can be many losers because the competition is to eliminate. I wonder, how and when did this competition arise and who created it?

I think there are enough resources, space and people on this planet for everyone. There is no need for competition. Still we clamour because we see everyone else doing it. Because what we see as prominent, we believe in it. Rahas and many of us are a victim of this conditioning. Sex is a manifestation, an action and thus it seeks to be controlled. If I have platonic feelings for tens of men in this world, deep in my heart forever, it hardly matters to anyone, the court, the priest or the legal spouse. But if I seek to manifest this feeling in the physical form of a conjugal union that can be photographed, that can be recorded, I'm digging a grave for myself. In essence, my body becomes a property to be owned; monogamy precisely means that.

But there is a difference between being sexually liberated and sexually exploited, though apparently, they seem to be the same. I think I began my sexual rebirth as a sexually liberated person but somewhere down the way I got sexually exploited. It was hard and traumatic and the pain has not eroded even after two years. On that fateful day, I gave Rahas a good excuse for me to meet Sulabh. I had left my books and train tickets in Sulabh's car and had to get them back. In my heart, I was excited at the prospect of meeting Sulabh with all social sanctions. Rahas could not disagree as the reason was strong but he asked me to leave for his place early and asked me to keep calling him in between. I'm having a hearty laugh right now as I'm writing this. Sometimes, in our pursuit of dedication to a relationship, we don't realise that we become a donkey laden with the burden of responsibilities.

I reached Sulabh's home before him, it was 7:40 PM. Sulabh had changed homes and had asked his servant to accompany me to the new place. I felt short of breath as I reached the doorstep. This new home had no associated memories for me. It was strange! Along with Sulabh, I had also fallen in love with his tiny house. His new home was larger, with large windows, bigger rooms, high ceilings. I felt threatened by its expanse; my secrets could not be contained here. The openness of that house was smothering my little dark secret. I waited for about an hour, taking calls from both Sulabh and Rahas. Sulabh was running late and Rahas was getting impatient about my extended stay in his house. I pacified him, 'I'm not alone, his mother and aunt are here in this house.'

But Rahas was far from convinced. I asked him to wait until 9:00 PM. If Sulabh was not back by then, I would leave. This calmed Rahas and I heaved a sigh of relief. In just about five minutes, my wait came to an end. Sulabh called me to say that he was downstairs. Ebullient, I paced upstairs and looked down from the terrace to see him. It had been 15 days since we last met and the wait was unbearable. I felt like a parched land bereft of rains. The time had come to soak myself in the spring showers of his love. These were the ephemeral spring showers that would not last forever but who could decline a temporal happiness? The joy of this long wait tasted sweeter.

I rushed back downstairs to meet him as he took the small lift inside the house. Our eyes met and all the pain inside me was gone. I was love-blind and I relished the thrill of meandering on the unfamiliar terrain of love;

except I did not know that I could fall and hurt myself, like I did. Sulabh took me inside from the drawing room to survey the spacious, lighted rooms of his new home and introduced me to the women in his family. There were three of them, his aunt, sister and cousin.

Their presence was one of the factors which would enable me to prolong my stay at his house. I stealthily clicked their pictures and sent them to Rahas just to make him feel at ease. But in my mind, I was looking for a remote corner where I could devour this fair-skinned man with jet black curls. The same fire was burning in Sulabh's heart as he took me to the terrace. A cool breeze was blowing from all directions and I could hear the cacophony of the children who were playing on the adjacent terraces. There was no one on the terrace but Sulabh was acutely cautious of any passer-by who could discover us sitting alone on the terrace edge. He looked right and left but was unable to stop himself from exploring my body; addiction befalls all.

I too was addicted to his kiss; the whole purpose of coming to his home was to savour the taste of his lips. Our lips rubbed against one another's; he touched the insides of my mouth with his tongue and I was lost in the moment. He dabbed an exotic perfume on his hairy chest and whenever I leaned in to kiss him, the scent would fill up my lungs. I loved twisting and rolling his chest hair as I kissed him. The passion was unsurmountable when our lips came together for the last time; we kissed for an eternity, detaching only in the intervals when it was absolutely necessary to take a quick gasp of air. I wanted to keep kissing him but

Sulabh declined. He was wary of getting caught in the act by the neighbours.

It was strange! He had been having more sex with me than with his partner and yet he was trying to project that he was celibate. Why do we pretend that sex is not happening around us? I think it is because it will be intensely difficult for us to live in a house where we consciously know that our parents have sex and a lot of sex. Can we deal with the fact that our mother wakes up the next day and limps around with a burning sensation at the meeting of her thighs and when asked the reason, she murmurs that she had rough sex with our father last night? Isn't this a hypocrisy? And that hypocrisy zapped my dream of a firewhisky kiss with Sulabh that evening.

But the same hypocrisy leads to repression and that is far more insidious. You become a slave to your carnal desires because you are asked not to have sex; you become obsessed with sex. Because of Sulabh's steadfast denial of an urge, of the emotion to connect with another human being, and his refusal to acknowledge this as sacred, he fell prey to it and he made it a disease. He was sick! And I bore the brunt of that appalling mental repression. He sexually abused me and dishonoured my body. It began with a wordless exchange. He gestured me to come under the derelict roof of the terrace and held me from behind. I was wearing a short pinstriped dress. He then lifted the dress from behind and lowered my underwear. At that time, I was a thirsty soul stranded in the Sahara desert. Any touch of his was a balm to my sexually yearning body.

I didn't know what he was going to do next, how he would love my body. I surrendered in lovemaking; I always liked being passive and dominated. Sulabh took out his shaft and almost drilled it into my anus. I tried to scream with pain but I couldn't. The fear of being caught made me numb my cries as my body writhed and wringed in pain. He continued his thrusts and I squealed softly in pain. It made no difference to Sulabh. He was continually thrusting, harder and harder each time. Those 10 seconds, I felt like I was in a public slaughterhouse and that my end was near. I almost lost consciousness and I was in tears. He came out and then zipped his pants. He asked me to adjust my clothes. It is a travesty that on the one hand he refused to kiss me because our faces were visible in the moonlight but on the other had anal sex with me as our bottoms were inconspicuous in the dark terrace.

I asked him the way to the washroom as I wanted to check on my aching buttocks. I lowered my underwear and gently brushed my palm around the parting of the buttocks. I did this for a while and felt better. I then pulled out my hand to wash his spattered semen. When I brought my hands near the flowing tap water, I was mortified! My entire hand was smeared with blood. It was my own blood. I bled during the forceful intercourse. I was in acute pain when he was thrusting into me and I did convey it to him through my feeble cries but he was too self-centred to pay any heed to my cries. My servility had brought me an unimaginable misery. I was sexually assaulted!

I don't know why I can never have resentment for someone; someone who had even abused me. I did not resent Prakhar and had empathised with him because I was immensely guilty about leaving him. It was I who wanted a divorce. The greatest relationship is with the self not just in a spiritual way but also in a pleasurable way. I keep my pleasure ahead of everyone and that is why I have to make compromises; I know I was making them. The lust I had for Sulabh and the compromise I had with Rahas to make this life bearable; I know the exact reasons why I chose to be with the two men. I cannot lust while in love. Predictability bores me to death. I want newness in relationships but I also want my home that brims with compassion and comfort.

I remember just a week back I went to my neighbour's home for a religious ceremony that was to mark the auspicious date of birth of their son. The entire family was decked up in vibrant clothes and there were a lot of sweets and delicious dishes being cooked in the kitchen. I felt jealous. As a single mother, I did not get to have these festivities in my house because there was hardly anyone to invite.

Nonetheless in this conflict of social and personal you tend to lose hold of discernment and thus I got abused by Sulabh. The presence of a family is a grounding factor in an individual's life and here I was a free bird, answerable to no one. I was responsible for my happiness as well as my hurt. But my feelings didn't wither away immediately. It was 10:00 PM and there were a lot of unanswered calls from Rahas.

I was scared! I had had sex with another man and I was worried whether Sulabh had recorded the act with a hidden camera. I called Rahas.

'Why are you still there?' he asked.

OK, I had to go back to being a good girl from a bad girl. I asked Sulabh to drop me home and he became furious and screamed at me.

'Will you stop prodding me? You are not his slave that he is commanding you to leave anytime he wants you to. You are earning much more than him and yet he is controlling you?'

His words were right but not his intent. He was not there to sermonise on feminism. It was for his own convenience that he tried to trick me into believing that Rahas was abusing me. After forcing himself on me! I dropped into a deafening silence. I lost my voice. Maybe the physical trauma that I had experienced moments ago had shut me down. That day as I reached home and gained consciousness of what had just happened with me, I snapped all ties with Sulabh.

I was overcome with the guilt of lying and the pain of being abused. I could not bear the weight of this heavy heart at home and ran to the park for succour. It was a summer afternoon and leaves bloomed on trees and the wind was mellower. I sat on the ground and called up Rahas. He picked up the phone in 10 seconds and as soon as I heard a 'Hello', I began to wail. My heart was profusely bleeding and I helplessly looked up to him to salvage me from this ignominy. Rahas was unaware of what had happened to me and tried his best to offer healing words. I was brutally hurt and I kept asking him if he was in my life, like a maniac.

'Yes, I am there with you.'

With Rahas, I had developed an attachment more than love, over time. I was scared of being alone as a single mother in this merciless world. With time, I started to believe that I could not do without him, that his presence was crucial for my survival. Specially with the sexual awareness work I had embarked on, I felt I could be preyed on anytime by lusty men, who had already started to stalk me online. Sometimes, I also feared what if I died before time, who would take care of my kid. It was a vicious grip of fear that became more powerful than love that once existed. It did not happen on its own. Rahas had slowly and consistently injected fears of abandonment and abuse in my heart, my mind. I began to believe the day he would leave me, us, we would have no chance of survival. The men will hunt and nab me down and there would be no one to look after me, us.

With time, things began to deteriorate. I stuck to his presence because of 'needs' and not desires. Our fights began to escalate over trivial issues. Sometimes we would quarrel so much that three days later I would not even remember what was it that we fought about. Rahas looked down upon me and my work with contempt but at the same time forced me to shell out money. In the house, he would pick up spare change lying around or devise tricks to take money from me. I slowly lost all respect for him, it was just the fear of unknown abuse from the outside world that was making me stick to him.

I was lying on the floor of our storeroom. The mosquitoes and the fear of crawling insects were not letting me sleep. I did not fear mosquitoes as much as I feared dengue. I did not have enough money to pay for my medical expenses. Thinking of money made me cry. It made me realise that my young child who had started understanding and yearning for material pleasures, which he rightfully deserved, had to be content with his mediocre toys. He told me of his friend's car and the tablet his father owned and expressed the desire to have them. My passion of pursuing sexual expression had landed me in a financial soup. I was living off my savings and was in no position to splurge.

It was painful! There I was alone on the storeroom floor while Rahas, the man I had chosen to share my life with, was sleeping peacefully in our master bedroom. Was this what they call love? I will be honest here and will share what had landed me on the storeroom floor. Since my childhood, I had always pleased others; that was my fate as a woman. I was scared of Baba and because I was deprived of his love from an early age, I tried to compensate for it by falling frequently and repeatedly in love with emotionally unavailable men, searching for that security, love, attachment which I was denied in my childhood. The time had come for me to stop doing that and I was inspired from within to stop pleasing people when they were wrong.

That day, my young son was killing mosquitoes with an electric racket in our bathroom. When the mosquitoes hit the racket, they got trapped in the wire mesh and made a popping sound because of the battery-operated electric current. My child jumped in joy on hearing those popping sounds and the victory of eliminating mosquitoes made him frequent our bathroom. Killing mosquitoes had become both his and my pastime in those days of penury. That day as my son swiped the racket on the wall on which a mosquito clung, there was a knock at the door. It was Rahas. My arthritis-afflicted mother commanded my kid to open the door and, in a jiffy, he ran out. I was in the other room working on my laptop. Rahas came and went to bathroom to change his clothes. And then I heard him roar, 'Can you come here immediately?'

I was startled! I was in the middle of some work and couldn't understand why he was shouting at me. I told him to soften his voice. I believed that I deserved respect and that no person should talk to me in a demeaning tone. Rahas was unruffled; he again called out to me. I forcibly got up and paced to bathroom.

In the bathroom, the sight was gory. There was an electric immersion rod plugged in and the switch was turned on. The immersion rod had become red-hot, ember-like and it seemed that it had remained switched on for a long time. Rahas then started shouting at me. I couldn't understand how it was my fault. It was an accident and he too was responsible. Because of his frenzied banging on the door, my son might have switched the rod on. This was a conjecture but surely, I did not deserve such a treatment. Just that morning, I had told him that every man on this earth is subconsciously intimidated by women because she is the creator, she is the expression of nature. That is why men feel the need to confine women to the household. Here I was, surprised at how true the axiom had turned out to be. He was internally threatened by my refusal to bend.

The mosquitoes were biting me on every bare place they could find on my fully covered body. On the waist as the shirt slid up, on my foot, on my elbows resting on the floor, on the neck and the neckline. Plenty of bare spots.

Writing this I feel why do we look for genital stimulation in the act of penetration to derive sensual joy? As I could see, there were plenty of bare spots on my body that had never been explored. These form a part of my body and are meant to be touched and enjoyed but no man had ever thought of touching and caressing my elbows, foot, waist, neck. The focus had always been on the hidden parts of the body. I won't say that I do something exceptional when it comes to lovemaking, I too yearn for penetration. I think it has to do with our conditioning of sexual shaming and the influence of uncreditable alternatives like media and porn; how we think love should be rather than how it should be. Growing up, I watched images of lovemaking in porn and I too began to believe in quick gratification.

I felt dejected looking at the closed door; was there a shadow approaching from behind the door? I had faint hopes that Rahas would come and apologise for hurting me. At that moment, my reality was that I was sitting alone in that room and yet I dreamed of things getting better, of him initiating truce. But I was clear about one thing, that I would not change my stance, come what may. It was not about being obstinate, I could still fall at the feet of Rahas and surrender to him but it was to enlighten him with the light of understanding and compassion. Being a man raised in a patriarchal household in UP, he had not seen women arguing with men or standing equal to men. It would take a lot of time for him to mould from his stiff bearings.

I remembered, a few months back Rahas had left a plugged-in iron on the bed after he got a phone call to report to the studio half an hour before the appointed time. He was ironing his shirt and hurriedly left to the other room to change. Rahas left for work and the iron remained plugged in; gradually the bedsheet burnt in a streak of chocolate brown colour. I was engrossed in my writing work and couldn't see that streak enlarging. It was my idle, semi-literate Ma who kept a tab on every little movement, spoken word and rotten vegetable in the house, who noticed the pungent smell coming from the bed. She screamed!

I took off the iron and mumbled that he might have left in a rush. That night as I lay on the floor, the old thoughts came to my mind. How sometimes I could be rational and forgive the other person. I think between a couple, it is a constant war of words. Who wins what and who loses what? The medallion is bestowed to the man or the woman? The other day, I did not choose to trigger a war but buried the matter peacefully but I must confess, not all days were like that. There were some days when I lashed out at him because something else was disturbing me from within.

It was 1:00 AM and I had lost all hopes of his return. It was a great dishonour for me; no one was paying me any attention as I lay unattended. And thus, thoughts of vengeance began to spurt in my mind. If he did not come to seek forgiveness before morning, I was going to break up with him. I was determined! I prided myself on the fact that even though I was sleeping on the floor in the storeroom, despite owning this house, I was allowing him to sleep in the air-conditioned bedroom. In India we treat our guests with utmost respect. He was not a family member but only an outsider, a guest. How much anger I felt! I had to contain it and allow him to sleep. I couldn't be inhumane. But my hurt ego was bull-headed and wanted me to redress the damage by seeking revenge.

But I was stuck in this relationship with Rahas for the long haul. Sometimes I did take a fight as an opportunity to quit the relationship. I'm being completely honest here; I did not like the restrictions posed by him in my life. I liked to be wild, to be unchained from any responsibilities. Responsibilities had overwhelmed me and I now wanted to live on my own for some time. As tempting as this freedom sounded, I was also afraid of hardships that this real world offered and this fear made me recoil into my suffocating shell. True! Freedom requires a lot of courage and ammunition. I sometimes wondered what if I had loving parents, a brother who would not break ties with me even if I were an infidel? What if I had a lot of money? I would have got love and protection. Yes, I felt I didn't need a husband; I needed loving and supportive parents, a brother and a monogamous lover who would be content with the non-monogamous me. Was it too much to ask for?

It was not until I exercised my sexual freedom that I believed I was indeed free. There were a string of short intense affairs riding high on physical want and emotional highs. I would call them random as none of them lasted more than three weeks. I think most of these relationships were unique in the way they made me discover a side of myself. Most of them continued in succession, with one spillover leading to the other. It was my way of coping with the aftermath of my divorce. To forget one, I moved to another and to forget another, I moved to the other.

Vibhaas and I had been friends for three years; we did not meet frequently but were in touch. I liked that he never made a pass at me and always kept a respectable distance from me. We did talk about intimate subjects: my looks, his fondness for me, but he ensured not to go overboard. It was obvious that he was enamoured by me but I never brought it up since I was already reeling under the headache of another affair and could not afford to manage a new obsession.

I remember once I went with him to watch a film. That day, I wore a clay-coloured short dress which made the contours of my body visible. The dress ended a little above my knees and made visible my plump, round, waxed thighs and legs. As I entered his car and sat beside him, he complimented me on my looks. The film raised the sexual tension further. In one of the lovemaking scenes, the hero thrusted into the heroine's vagina, with their naked thighs in sight on screen. I felt terrible discomfort watching the scene with Vibhaas. There was a set pattern in our meetings: we met in the evenings at Connaught Place, went for long strolls, shared a cigarette, ate *paan*, sipped coffee and talked intensely. It was a ritual for him to click a picture of me just before we parted. Our relationship was equal in every sense; there was a silent meeting of our eyes, pulsing sexual tension, civil platonic communion and sharing of bills.

He was a man who was not eager to claim my body though his desire was apparent. But both of us were satisfied with the current situation. Both of us, for different reasons, were in no hurry to get physical. In a span of two years, our lips finally met. In a way, I also had silently harboured a desire for him that went back to the days when he managed our entrepreneurship class. There were beer get-togethers where I kept a distance from the core group, instead loitering around the snacks table. Vibhaas would never notice my presence though he and I belonged to similar backgrounds: we were of nearly the same age, while the rest were youngsters in their early twenties and talking to them sent a grim reminder of my diminishing youth. I secretly yearned for Vibhaas' admiration but never got it in the one year of our entrepreneurship class.

Thus, this secret wish to be desired by him lay buried in my heart but very much alive. It finally came to fruition. I was reeling under the rejection from a man, whose name I no longer recall, and called Vibhaas to meet me at a quick notice. My affable friend came and the drinks and talks helped me alleviate the stress. On an impulse, out of gratitude, I leaned in and we kissed. It was mutual then. This is where I went wrong; if something happens between two people, it does not mean that there is blanket consent for all successive intimate encounters between the same two people. A moment of shared intimacy is when two people actually get involved and consent to a certain act. In our next meeting, I overlooked the signals of his refusal. I assumed his consent to be implicit. Consent always has to be explicit. I flirted with him, kissed him but failed to notice that he was not reciprocating. I failed to see that because I believed that men were all sexual beasts.

It was Monday. I had a sudden urge to meet him.

I was in his car in a parking lot in the morning. Since it was a weekday morning, the parking lot was deserted. I looked at him coyly and signalled him to touch me. He did hold my arm but I was not content. I was in haste that day, eager to do something, to feel something, and I was clueless about the fact that he was not eager at all. I could still not underpin the exact feeling that made me move forward and kiss him. He was clearly uncomfortable and I sensed this immediately after our quick kiss. I was guilt-ridden. I said to him that I should not have kissed him and he was very courteous. He asked me to stop thinking about it but it got on my nerves. The whole day I could not focus on my work, cursing myself for this kiss. The saving grace was that he did desire me physically; he even fantasised about me once, but consent is important in every relationship. What about a partner who is not in the mood? These were my parting words to him.

'No, it is not your mistake. I was too much in my zone to even think that I'm causing any unease. All my life, I have played the victim card. It was difficult for me to even think for a moment that a man can be sensitive.'

I Want You on My Bed Right Now

I was anxiously expending my orgasmic energy on the keyboard of my laptop. Half an hour back, I was taking anxious turns on my bed in the memory of a man I had met just yesterday and now the thoughts of our passionate lovemaking were making me restless. The man is a public figure and a star. We connected over our mutual thoughts on the obsoleteness of marriage: how marriage eventually becomes an airtight container and how people choose childless marriages. He invited me to a luxe 5-star hotel for lunch, an invitation that elevated my status from a middle-class woman to someone who hobnobbed with the rich and famous. I opened my cupboard and looked for the best-looking sari to wear on that afternoon. I picked up a black-and-red-striped Sambalpuri sari. That was the costliest and prettiest sari I had. I paired it with a deep-neck sleeveless black blouse. The fabric was soft as a pillow and I felt as if I was in the arms of a lover. Saris were an unbeatable weapon of seduction I used on men I desired. They upped my oomph, my confidence as a seductress without risking my reputation. With growing age and self-awareness, I realised that it's far easier to look and feel sensual in a sari than exposing your body in short skirts and feeling uncomfortable in the exposed skin as men leer at you. I liked to be covered outside and naked inside the house of my lover.

I draped the sari and checked myself out in a mirror. I, by no angle, looked like a diva. How would I seduce him? Determined, I began to disrobe and searched for another sari. I finally settled on my most recent acquisition: a rainbow-coloured cotton handloom sari. I looked much better. Time was running out so I applied some light make-up and sauntered out.

In our discussions in the lunch area of the hotel he was staying in, he mentioned how he got married at the age of 31 when he was still a virgin but over time, his thoughts matured and he had a better sense of relationships, lust and desire. His living of those experiences shaped his thoughts about the institution of marriage and the emotion of love and sex. It pacified me. The profound, deep-rooted connection I felt with the man sitting across an elaborately laden table was not baseless. This emotion might defy the traditional definition of love and monogamy but this emotion was coming from the deep recesses of my heart. I was in a trance! Here was a superstar sitting in front of me and I had to talk to him. How would I? His fame had uplifted him from the ranks of us mere mortals and on top of that, I wanted him to surrender to my charms.

'Marriage is unnatural, Pallavi. It's a social institution made to determine lineage, property, paternity and to control women. It is impossible to stay sexually and emotionally exclusive to only one person throughout your life. Then in India, marriage is not just of two persons, it is a mesh of families, extended families, responsibilities, bonds, properties, children and so on.

Today I can divorce my wife and live an independent life. But today my mother talks to me for five minutes and to my wife for half an hour. Then we co-own our NGO. It becomes very difficult to break up and for what? Is it worth it? So, I asked myself what can I do? I live my life the way I want. At several occasions, I have also spoken about non-monogamy. I think monogamy is unnatural. I would have loved to live a life like you, on a public level, but it will hurt my family, my wife. The day I realised that my thoughts have changed, I made my family and wife sit together and told them. My wife has reached a stage where she understands it but she is still uncomfortable with a public acceptance of non-monogamy.'

He had to take an early leave and he dropped me at the station. As we departed, he took my hands and gave them a gentle squeeze. Ah! That first touch! how desperately I wanted it to prolong. Sometimes playing a decorous woman had its own pitfalls. It was unbearable! I came back home with his presence all over me. I went to meet him alone and I came back with his memory. It was distressing! I had always been calm with men but today, I was agitated. I wanted to cuddle him, kiss him, lie with him on my side on the giant double bed of his hotel suite. I tried to shirk off the feeling and focus on my work; but the very nature of lust is it is overpowering. Being a conscious person, I decided to come clean to him, hoping it'd give me some relief. Also, I wanted to see his reaction. I wrote back to him on chat on Facebook. It was where we first met and interacted and I wanted to keep myself in those limits only. Never asking more or expecting more. It saved me from any hurt and damage to my self-esteem.

'I felt liberated and orgasmic to meet you. Yeah initially it was difficult as I was struck by your larger-than-life on-screen persona but then I reminded myself that you are a person first. It became easier to interact then. I hope to grow more and meet you more often. I'm smitten!'

Pat came his reply.

'Just read your message. Let me confess, I felt equally orgasmic. It's very hard to find such sorted people. Especially women (because they are traditionally suppressed more). I'm so sorry that I had to leave abruptly. But I honestly meant it when I said let's meet again. I'm glad you too feel the same way. Let the journey begin.'

A glimmer of hope? He seemed optimistic. Our heart becomes irrational in love; as they say, love is blind. We distort the reality, magnify the strengths and slash the differences. I tried to decode his message, reading each and every word, trying to segregate the words and assemble them in such a fashion that it became an answer to my unasked question. I know its futility, its hopelessness but I was driven by desires. In one day, from being desirable I shrunk to being desiring and I was happy. Sometimes, losing your status brings you happiness. Such a parody of life!

The desperation increased the following day. I tried to work the entire day, reading and writing, but my self-awareness had taught me that the more you suppress your emotions, the more severe their impact becomes. Our emotions want to flow and we should not clench them. Thinking this I again wrote to him, 'I have to purge this feeling. Deeply attracted to you since yesterday. The polarity of a man and a woman is so amazing. There can be nothing more beautiful than this experience. That first touch and the spark when two minds meet. The eroticism is... I don't have words. Though I know that your stature plays a role in this dire attraction and I'm not happy about it. But let it be.'

Pat came his reply, this time shorter but it echoed whatever was brewing in my heart.

'Well, I must confess it's mutual then. Very much.'

Oh! again. I felt on the top of this world. His reply filled my heart with ecstasy. I felt orgasmic! Yeah that was my state of being. Orgasm is an all-embracing emotion; to me it means being connected to the essence of life, not negating it, not disowning it, not suppressing it. I felt orgasmic in this moment because my heart knew love, it was open to love, and this heart was unbound by social norms. There was a deeply internal process of the creation of thoughts and emotions that happened inside me and I did not let it get adulterated by social conditioning. My emotions were mine, my happiness was mine, I had stopped staking my happiness at the altar of social acceptance. I now practised self-love. I was still in pain because I could not hug him and kiss him. But this desire to do so was orgasmic. I was stirred by those emotions and sent a voice note to that man.

'Please ignore the snoring sound of my son. I feel that orgasm is in every moment. It is not about genital stimulation. Right now! I feel orgasm with you because I was talking to someone on the phone and he was telling me a story. I was not interested in the story. I wanted him to wrap up the call as quickly as possible and his words were unintelligible for me because I wanted to send you my thoughts. I was very much impatient to talk to you; that I wanted to talk to you was orgasm for me. In that state of anticipation, I was biting my nails. I have never bitten my nails, so that is orgasm for me. When I saw your message, my heart fluttered. I felt like a teenage girl with butterflies in my stomach. That is orgasm for me.'

My voice letters to him continued; I wanted him to notice my carnal suffering, my emotional strife to embark on a passionate journey with him. Once, I was so let down by my own booming desires that I broke down. I wanted to cry in the bathroom. The silence and succour it offers is perfect for us to free ourselves of our tears. But I soon figured out that crying in the bathroom is also a luxury. As I paced up to open the bathroom door, I discovered that Ma was washing herself, so I had to go back to my room. I waited for her to come out and she came out after 15 minutes. My tears had dried up by then.

The man did invite me over a mere three days after our first meeting. But something had changed in between. I was in an internal turmoil, drawn at the two opposite ends of duty and desire. The doctrine of monogamy, loyalty on one end and wild, untamed desires on the other. I was oscillating between the two ends, but was more inclined to go with the latter. Adherence to monogamy was more out of fear. I was not rich and I had dependents.

Distraught! I chose an indirect route to make Rahas comfortable with the idea of extra-relational emotional and physical intimacy. I talked to him about psychological, scientific theories that substantiate attraction and refute monogamy as a universal choice. I shared anecdotal evidence of popular people staying in partnerships and having publicly admitted affairs. Rahas was a smart chap and he could make out that, behind all this pep talk, I wanted to say that I wanted to have sex with other men. Yes, I did not have the courage to hurt him and neither did I want to lie to him. I was messed up! But he eventually became comfortable with me meeting other men and was not spying all the time.

I was ecstatic as the star called me and asked me to meet him at his hotel. He was a big star and so a nobody like me had to go all the way to his hotel, travelling an hour and a half by train in the heat. That's the one thing I learnt that day; power differences do come into play in a relationship. I was smitten by his aura, his stature, and thus made all the effort for him. Our conditioning has fed us that a beautiful woman needs to be wooed. To be honest, I felt a bitter pang in my heart that I was going all the way to his hotel to meet this man, not once but twice. But I turned a deaf ear to the social conditioning brewing in my mind. I took a long shower, shampooed my hair and picked up the best clothes in my cupboard and showed them to Ma for her opinion. I applied some *kajal*, a little fairness cream and some compact powder. In my hurry, I forgot to dab the pheromone perfume my friend Raj had gifted me.

I reached his hotel. He too was keen on meeting me, perceptible from his frequent messages during my one-and-a-half-hour commute.

'Come to the restaurant S3, where we had our lunch last time. There is a metal tree in the right corner. Come further and you will find an elevator. Stay near the elevator. I will be there.'

Do I have to go to his room? I thought but then dismissed my consternation by reminding myself that I was too desperate to make love to him, to taste his body, his lips and to have his hands wrapped around my back. I remembered poignantly how the previous night, as I slept with Rahas, I yearned for his touch. As Rahas kissed me, I imagined that man's face. I wanted to stage a pretext for the physical act by having a coffee together and then maybe he would invite me to his room. I pacified my bursting thoughts and waited near the elevator. As I walked, I saw him standing at a distance. He was looking at me and I felt hesitant. I was in awe of his stature and it was difficult for me to look at him. I looked sideways most of the time as I inched closer to him, occasionally giving him a swift glance but pulling back soon after. He was more at ease looking at me; his eyes were fixated on me, and that made me more uncomfortable. I increased my pace and heaved an inner sigh of relief once I stood right next to him. We exchanged customary hellos and then he took me to his large suite.

The entire passage was desolate. It made me a little uneasy. I started missing the warmth of my home and its hustle bustle. The silence was discomforting. The actor led me to his room. It was a super-luxurious suite with a king-sized double bed, upholstered armchair, kitchenette and a work area. The large windows offered a panoramic view of the skyscrapers of Gurgaon. The room was filled with silence. I slumped on the sofa facing him as he sat on the chair near his work table. And we started talking. In fact, it was not me talking but him elaborating the dos and don'ts of a casual sex encounter with a famed actor.

'Pallavi I am a public figure and unlike the other men in your life, people know me. If there's some kind of sexual rumour linked to me, it will tarnish my reputation as well as bring pain to my family. So, I want you to keep this discreet. While I would have loved to live the life of a hunter-gatherer, having sex for no reasons other than having sex, the society I'm a part of is not like that. So, what can I do? I can best do what I like and it is no one else's business to know what I do in my life. I also do not believe in expectations though I feel responsible for the women I'm intimate with. Like me, they too have their families, marriages and children and we respect each other's privacy and space.'

I was bewildered as he spoke; why is it that people have to form so many layers around them to enjoy a natural erotic desire. I told him that I agreed with him on the part that sexuality need not be traded for comfort, resources and finances. But I understood his compulsions and agreed not to divulge our sexual encounter to anyone. We spoke on sexuality, cultural restrictions on sex, judgements on sex and half-truths. He asked me how Rahas dealt with my open sexuality because his wife was still in ignorance about most affairs of his life. I admitted that it was tough to mould the rigidity of a staunch monogamous person like Rahas but I keep enlightening him with theories around non-monogamy. It had started to make an impact where at least he was comfortable with me experiencing gentle physical intimacy with other men. Secondly, I wanted to change the mindset of the people of my family around sex and monogamy. I also relied on half-truths: so if I kissed a man, I would tell my partner that I was attracted to that man; if I made out with a man, I would tell him that I kissed that man. It helped me soothe my conscience. The actor laughed as he heard me say this.

'I don't believe in a conscience,' he said.

I was not sure what to say to him at that time. Did I know what a conscience meant? Is conscience just morality or does it depend on the individual? I quipped that I had a conscience but I did not know what it meant to have one exactly. In that flustered state of mind, our talks went on but no one took a lead to start the lovemaking. I was silently counting minutes to our kiss but it remained elusive. He took the lead by asking, 'Can I sit near you on this sofa, if you don't mind?'

His words seemed like incantation breaking the sexual unease and the atypical quiet of that room. I reflexively muttered yes. He stood up from his chair and sat near me, our bodies close to each other for the first time. He took my hands in his and started caressing each of my fingers with his finger. His fingers were slender and had a light wrinkled texture and a genteel quiver. He was about 15 years older than me. His touch made me quiver with excitement and spawned a torrent of sexual energy throughout my body. I could not wait for more and asked him to kiss me.

His lips! How do I describe them? I can only go back and feel the soft rub of his lips on mine. The gentle nibbling and sucking of my lips by his. Can there be something more beautiful than this? I doubt! His lips fed my lips the orgasmic juice bursting like little stars from the edges of his lips. I was lost in the moment, lost in him. His touch made me realise that my lips were thirsty and this thirst could only be satiated by his lips. I had been kissed a hundred times before but it all seemed redundant; the lure of the forbidden, the unknown was magical. I want to be kissed by him and only him for a hundred nights more. The diffidence had broken and greediness had increased. I wanted more of him, more of his body. Thus, I murmured, 'Can we go to the bed?'

I stood up first and holding his hands, trod to the bed. I lay on the bed and he climbed on top of me, his legs stretched out of the bed horizontally in the air. And we began kissing again. It was now more passionate, with all barriers of reticence being broken, and we both hungrily devoured the other person through our lips. Time came to a standstill; the room ceased to exist and so did all fears of being caught. In that moment, I did not even care if Rahas came to know about this illicit liaison. It was not just my lips but my entire being that was being soaked in his saliva. Our hands reached out to undress each other. He went first. He removed my kurta and unhooked my bra as I looked down on the mattress. I was shy! At that moment, I cautioned him, 'Look! We cannot have sex because I'm menstruating.'

I felt good when he didn't insist on sex after knowing that. He was a decent man. There was a fear in my heart; what if the man overpowered me and forcefully got me to do things I don't like. He left it to my convenience and that made me desperate to love him more, for hours. I immersed myself in his spell, his aura.

Take me in! My heart fluttered, inaudible to him. He made the lovemaking more passionate by his gentle groans and moans. For the first time in my life I saw a man moaning and it thrilled me. He gently pecked on both my eyes, making me swim in the stream of ecstasy! Our fingers were tightly intertwined and our legs remained clasped to each other as we made love. I stroked and lightly scratched the back of his leg with my toes.

I thought I would win him over by applying all the skills of seduction I had learnt so far. I had read about the specific spots in a male body and the method of arousal. I gave him gentle love bites around his neck; circled his nipples with my fingertips and gently sucked them. I had read that some men can have nipple orgasms. Thinking that my sexual prowess would make him dependent on me for sexual excitement, I went on and on. But I was wrong! He didn't like to be bitten as he had a very low threshold of pain. He was quite orthodox when it came to lovemaking, preferring only the missionary position. It was awkward. My confidence level was at an all-time low.

It turned worse after he ejaculated. I had already told him that I could not have sex because I was menstruating. Well that was a half-truth! It was my third day and so I was not bleeding profusely. I wanted him to enter me but was unsure. Of late, I did not allow men I did not trust to enter me. He had knocked on my heart but he had not opened its doors. Knowing that he could not enter me, he spread a white towel on the bed and started vigorously stroking his penis up and down, moaning as he did it. I was stiff and stared at him blankly as a pale stream of semen emitted from the tip of his penis. One loud moan and he was done. It felt weird when a man had to come on his own in the presence of a woman.

He might have felt weird too. He quickly went to the bathroom to dispose of the wet towel while I quickly wore my bra and kurta in that moment. To be honest, I felt hesitant in changing clothes in front of him.

'I hope you are not getting late,' he said as he wore his jeans.

His words left me in a state of shock and disbelief. How humiliating it was for me! In that moment, his detached words made me feel like a sex worker. I was in love with this man and I had decided to share my body with him. I could not leave yet, I decided. So I stayed over for half an hour. We didn't speak much. He slumped into his cushioned aristocratic chair and took to reading something on his iPad. I stared at him, hoping he would begin a nice intellectual conversation and exchange ideas on cultural restrictions around sex and love.

I took a pillow and rested my elbows on it. The room had started to haunt me; this person who was sitting across from me seemed to be someone who was not interested in me any more. I looked like an accessory that he didn't need any more. I was heartbroken. I did not want to be with him forever but one also longs for shared moments of intimacy. That is a nourishment for the aching soul and the body. I felt like a doormat.

Half an hour had passed and I could not take it any more. I told him that I would be leaving and he came along to see me off, his face hidden under a cap. I was amused. Thankfully, there was something hilarious in this macabre ending of our illicit love tale.

It was a day of disillusionment. A self-sworn romantic, I did not have a single man in my life whom I could feel love for. Men would just enter and exit my life as per their choice. I opened the door of my heart to anyone who came knocking, hoping that the person would stay and fill my heart with mirth. The person brought gifts of mirth but these were the gifts which got over soon and all I was left with was the wrapper of memories. I was in a pitch-dark place, fearful and desperate to lend entry to a visitor who might stay, this time for long.

I had met Arun, a month back, in a poets' get-together at his house. It was an invite from an acquaintance since a legendary poet was coming. I did not want to miss this chance to meet him. I was skeptical initially as it was a men-only meet with alcohol and I barely knew any of them. I kept wondering if I should go before finally relenting to my heart's desire. I went to Arun's place.

The place was far away and was not as near my house as I had assumed it to be. We first waited at a metro station where the gentleman's friend was to arrive. But then he gave us a call and instructed us to reach a shopping complex where he would meet us. As we tried to cross the road to reach the opposite side, the traffic signal turned green and a string of vehicles passed by. It was getting difficult to cross the road and we stood there waiting. There were a couple of rickshaw pullers standing at the side of the road, waiting for commuters. Among them was a drunkard who, seeing us struggling, came near us. And what he did then was unexpected. He went right in the middle of the road and started shooing and yelling at vehicle riders to halt so that we could cross. He became a live speed breaker on the road. It was dangerous as a few vehicles were at a high speed and the drunkard could get hit. I tried stopping him, but he turned a deaf ear. Finally, he succeeded in stopping the vehicles as all the riders got scared by his daredevilry. Courage is a virtue few possess and those who possess it do not fear. The riders were fearful that if the drunkard got hit by their vehicle, they might get embroiled in a police case. The drunkard on the other hand had dissolved his fears of death, of accident, in the pint of alcohol he had swallowed.

I was dazed by his antics to help us and his courage, which was not his own but an aftereffect of liquor that he had drunk. It is known that people lose their consciousness, their ability to decide, after a spell of alcohol. The drunkard lurched on the road, yelled, and his head spun. But he did something unique, which all aware people did not. He tried to help us, risking his own life in the bargain. Would someone do that for a stranger? Since the drunkard was not in his senses, he helped us—did it mean that it is our senses that restrain us from showing unprofitable attention to someone with whom we have no business, someone we do not know, someone who can dent our comfort if we decide to help him or her? How have we acquired such senses? A newborn does not distinguish between his or her own and the other. With time we learn to strongly distinguish, strongly prioritise tribes of people, in makeshift tents of affection from which some people exit and into which some enter. I wish we could unlearn these barriers which make us differentiate between people, who are all humans, who all have the same number of limbs, same lifespan, same struggles and same sorrows. Who are more alike than unlike. Not just this, there was a deeply personal reason I liked his eccentric behaviour. I was so used to lack of attention from men that, that day the drunkard made me feel worthy of care.

When I met my acquaintance and his friend, they wanted to find a wine shop to buy ice and beer bottles. At that time, I felt out of place, an unworthy addition to a group of men who seemed to have no interest in gazing at a beautiful woman like me. I was suspicious, fearful, doubtful. I almost imagined a scene of rape and even a murder. Who would take care of my child if I died? My imagination ran wild until we arrived at Arun's place. His home was on the first floor and on the ground floor, was a dimly lit grocery shop where a few men stood. Those men stared at me as I walked into the house. Did they think I was a prostitute? My imagination hollered again. My fears were laid to rest as I entered the house.

The house was modest and was littered with books, newspapers, emptied bottles and plastic cups. Two men sat on a rug on the floor and Farhat Saheb, the evening's guest of honour, was seated on a sofa-chair. The men cheered enthusiastically as Farhat Saheb hummed some couplets from his prized oeuvre. I sat beside Farhat Saheb, away from the group of men, who huddled together in a corner. Between us was a spread of vodka and whisky and a big packet of potato chips. Arun offered me a drink which I politely declined. I was never a liquor addict.

The *mehfil* peaked and the recitation of couplets paced. The men too started reciting their own couplets decorated with praises and applauses. I was a loner there with no voice. No one looked at me. Instead of taking note of the sole woman present in the room, the men turned their affections to a 60-year-old poet. Suddenly,

Farhat Sahab asked me to share some of my writings. I recited a poem that I had written.

After my recital, I noticed that the men were warming up to my presence. People started talking about subjects like love and marriage. I asked Farhat Sahab why marriage was given such a sanctimonious status in the society and why love had to be exclusive and monogamous? Amit, a 40-something man attending the *mehfil*, had a pragmatic answer to that: marriage is good for children, and society thrives and grows on life's succession.

In between, I made furtive glances at Arun who looked like the youngest of them all. Just as I got ready to leave, he insisted that I have dinner. I could not agree to his request as I was getting late, but he did not give in. Finally, he let me go. The next day, he invited me to a poetry slam where he was performing. In the days that followed, Arun and I made plans to meet but somehow the plans kept getting cancelled. I kept postponing and revising the meeting date, but he didn't seem to mind, a gesture which brought him closer to my heart. One night, I was writing when he called up. We talked for three hours that night, which made me amazed. With Rahas, I felt it difficult to keep a conversation alive for even three minutes.

After we spoke for three hours, we both felt our sexual energies flowing through the receiver of the phone and we were gasping and yearning to receive love. Arun suddenly wanted to meet me the next day, a proposal I was secretly waiting for. He asked me to come to his house, but I wanted to meet him outside. I had the fear that if I met him in his house, we would not be able to resist making out. I shared this fear and he assured me. He said that he would keep a safe distance and would make me sit on the sofa while he would sit on a mat. I then told him that I did not fear him but I feared myself. Just the utterance of the word 'home' had stoked in me amorous emotions and I imagined him cuddling and kissing me. Arun and I had an age difference of 11 years but being a poet and performer, he was way mature than his age and we bonded over our ideas, desires and the subtle prospect of love. As he hung up that night, a new person emerged from me. A person who was head over heels in carnal love with Arun. I now wonder that my emotions were so tender and vulnerable that a three-hour-long phone call could make me go weak in my knees.

The next day, Arun called me up early morning to check if I was coming. Yes, I replied. I then embarked on an elaborate beauty ritual to look my best. I oiled my hair with olive oil and applied a mud pack on my face followed by a sprinkle of rose water. Then I picked up a black sari and ironed it to remove all creases. A gentle puff of powder, a light touch of lipstick and a line of *kajal*. I looked at myself in the mirror and my face was radiating. I was pleased with the result. I then took a taxi and left for the metro station where Arun promised to meet me. Through the short trip, my mind was preoccupied with thoughts of Arun. We would first shake hands and then sit in a dimly lit room. He would recite poetry from one of his books as I'd lie on the floor listening to him. In between we would have intense eye contact. Then he would kiss me, hug me, our bodies would get entangled like a wild creeper. Soon enough, he would undress me and our naked bodies would dissipate in the darkness of his room.

The imagination was sensuous but somehow, I was not convinced with the cliffhanger. I felt it was imposed and was not coming naturally to me. Usually I'm quite numb to what I feel but this time my doubts rang loud in my head. I decided to not pretend any more. The intensity of that feeling snowballed in the next couple of minutes; I anxiously checked my watch. It was almost five and I had to take a decision: to go or not to go. I think I was already moving towards a no but I was taking time to admit it to myself. By the time it was five, I was ready with a firm answer. I did not have the courage to call and inform him so I surreptitiously took out my phone and messaged him.

'You should have told me in the beginning. I was awake the entire night waiting for you,' he texted.

I was relieved to get a narrow escape. It was clear that I needed time to boil up my erotic desires. I was content that I did not have to pursue the erotic trajectory of another person who had a much smaller appetite for erotic excitement. I detest hook-ups for this very reason: sexual intimacy that is devoid of emotional intimacy is akin to dehumanising a person. I am glad that that night, my instincts saved me from the ignominy I would have faced if I had been enslaved to my carnal desires.

Fears of a Single Mother

Love is not one's sole companion. The hard truths of life impact its well-being and transform it from one phase, one form to another, often distinct. Two people can remain bonded because of their needs and can become enemies as one of them ceases to fulfil the other or the other person gets an escape route. All kinds of love can change its course, take different forms, and a mother's love is no exception. Yes! The holiest, the most selfless, everlasting love of a mother can change too. It did for me. For me, being a mother made me responsible when it came to expressing my sexuality. Ever since I rediscovered myself, came out of my marriage, I cherished the feeling of being free. I'm not sure if I ever wanted to be caught up in bonds again. What do bonds do? They root us and limit us. How would we achieve transcendence if we are tethered and tied down?

Our kids are lovely parasites. Sorry to use that word, but this is what I feel. I gave birth to a cuddly being that feeds on me and my miniscule finances that were barely enough to support me through my life. Is bringing a child into this world a big enough happiness to suffer this loss? I dare think not.

It was all well up to six months back, when I was still working and earning, when I withstood the abuse of countless managers who would gossip behind my back. But I would tolerate all that because of the promise of a pay cheque. I was now an unemployed single mother, by choice. My exit from the company I worked in was sudden. I was unprepared for the sudden notice, financially and emotionally. But I knew that it was coming. I had stopped focusing on my work and instead started preparing for my entrepreneurial venture. I had thought that a day would come when backed by ample savings and a set-up business, I would make the big leap towards entrepreneurship smoothly. I had hoped for a smooth transition but your fate is not always in your control.

I could not meet my KRAs and received a three-month warning email in my inbox. A mail that was lost in the volume of emails I received every day at work. I was unaware that I had come under the spotlight and thus I carried on with my indifferent attitude at work. My days at the company did not last long and one fine day I was asked to give in an involuntary resignation. Not just that, I was asked to leave the office the same day. I was filled with humiliation and stealthily packed my bag and took the lift. I was red-faced with shame. As I reached downstairs, I ran up to the main gate until I was short of breath. As I exited the main gate of the building where my office was, I looked back with pain and forlornness. Life had moved on for me. I was on my own, without a husband, without a job.

In the next six months, I saw my son grow up, unaware of the depleting finances in my bank. He demanded small luxuries which would, over time, increase with his age. Back in my youth, when I heard hapless parents singing paeans to their own sacrifices to bring up their children, I dismissed that as something middle-aged people say.

I was quite harsh to those parents. Now, I felt the heat. My child demanded toy cars and chocolates that were cheap but his demands were growing. It takes a lot of effort to bring up a child.

The other day he saw an expensive car on the road and exclaimed, 'Look Mama, Papa has this car. Buy it for me also.'

In that moment I turned cold as I realised that his demands were growing. I could see the future. At 34, I had finally learnt to see the future. I calmed myself as I held on to the little one's hand and kept reminding myself that I had bought a house for us and it was something my parents had never done for me! After all, my son would not ever have to worry about not having a roof over his head. I didn't expect him to be grateful but I wished he would stop fussing over things.

Can a woman's individual self survive within the identity of a mother? I think people are right when they say that a woman becomes a mother; it's one or the other, never mother-woman or a woman-mother. One identity is subsumed by the other. Motherhood is lauded, honoured and prized. One becomes a mother and, in the process, renounces her unbridled sexuality. I became desexualised after my son's birth.

My son slept peacefully on the upholstered bed. When Rahas was in the house, he was made to sleep facing the wall so he didn't witness the amorous lovemaking between two adults. On other days when Rahas was not home, we snuggled and cuddled. He slept before me and every night, I spent a lot of time staring at his moon-like face.

Life seemed pretty long. In all my 35 years I had noticed that when you were happy, when everything went well, time flew. I saw my son, who had seen the separation of his parents, see his mother struggling to do part-time jobs and dealing with an obstinate and chauvinistic stepdad (he thought of Rahas as his dad), and yet being happy and content with his games and toy cars. Sometimes I wished to be like him and unlearn all the pain of rejection and unmet expectations which my adulthood had taught me. Sometimes I wished to be a child again.

There were days when I seethed in pain, when my pain got the better of me, when I thought that I could no longer put up a fight against my painful life. The more I tried to cope with pain, the more it increased. My pains started with my desire to assert my identity and it had cost me all I had. Specially because I had an innate interest in meeting new people and particularly men. Not that I was looking for sexual liaisons but I always developed a certain chemistry with intellectual men. I did have great women friends but they all got left behind in the journey of life. Some time back, I met an erudite, divorced Bengali man named Rishabh on a Durga Pujo walk. He had quit his job and had been organising cultural walks in different locations. His walks served as a great excuse to meet new people with similar interests in culture, food and history. I was enthralled by the experience.

I wanted to meet Rishabh again. The week we decided to meet, I had a terrible viral infection and had to cancel on him. Then I was travelling and the meet was postponed for another two weeks. When I came back, I called him to ask if he would be free for breakfast soon. I fancied the idea of sipping warm tea and eating lettuce and tomato sandwiches under a buttery golden sun, breathing the tranquil morning air. Rishabh was a historian and a master of storytelling, especially when it came to our golden past, stories of kings and queens, stories of wars and dynasties, stories of monuments. I wanted to hear those stories at peace. I think Rishabh too wanted to meet me, so he instantly agreed. The only impediment was that Rahas was home and he did not like me meeting other men. I decided to disclose my plans of meeting Rishabh to him, right before we were going to sleep the previous night.

Things happened as I had predicted, Rahas fumed and started abusing me. I, on the other hand, did not lose my cool but was heartbroken from those snide remarks. He tried to pull my mother on his team to prove he was right, a feat that was not hard to accomplish. Ma always sided with men when it came to tough decisions; although she believed that women should educate themselves and work, she also believed that all education and work should be used to improve one's domestic life. Ma fumed when she saw me going out on weekends to meet people, attend workshops; she expected me to devote all my spare time to my son.

The fight took an ugly turn when I roared at Rahas and asked him to leave the room. The air became heavier and venomous and I had difficulty breathing. I wanted some peace and silence, away from people who failed to understand me, who failed to read my soul. Rahas left the room in disgust. He came from a household where women observed purdah and were dependent on the male householder. His upbringing of decades could not be overturned in some years. I debated with him whenever he showered praise on the women of his family on how they kept the whole house soaked in love. I argued that there was no conflict when one partner was financially dependent on the other. I have seen from my experience, that an imperishable friction exists between two poles of power in the household when the woman is educated and does not count on her husband for the final decision.

Rahas complained about me to Ma, seeking validation on his objection to me meeting another man. He had her unanimous support. She pitied her own state of being, relegated to a nanny for her grandson.

My child Chiku's innocence sometimes sent shivers down my spine. He was growing up and was trying to make sense of why his parents didn't stay together. Sometimes he told me things like, 'Papa must have gotten a new job and that's why he has moved to a place near his office.' It pained me more because my son had ceased to be a priority for Prakhar, who was anyway an apathetic person. He had only stuck to the legal responsibilities of sharing half of our son's educational and medical expenses, nothing more or nothing less. Once I sent him the bill for a bicycle that I bought for our son. To my disgust, he answered back saying that as per the legal agreement, he was only supposed to contribute towards our son's school fees. It had been a year since he had bought any clothes or toys for his son despite earning well, while I kept struggling to make sure my kid did not have to compromise on his little desires. On some days, I got exasperated by Prakhar's ruthlessness and in one heated moment I texted him that I did right by divorcing him. Later I deleted that chat out of fear.

I shed tears of shock and tried my best to compensate for the absence of a father figure for my son but I was not always successful because I ran short of money. Prakhar's absence in my son's life was never a problem when I was earning well; I could afford frequent flights and travelled with my son to different parts of the world. I knew, as a single parent, I was capable of keeping my son happy if I had money. But thanks to my new entrepreneurial stint of sexuality education, I didn't have much money left.

Every Saturday, my son went to meet Prakhar. Since I didn't own a car, the biggest attraction for my son was Prakhar's car. Usually when he came back from his father, he looked sad and dejected. When I asked him what had happened, he just remained silent and lay down on the bed. He was learning a new way of protesting in silence. I felt a deep pain in my heart. On repeated probing, he finally said that he had asked Prakhar to buy him something, perhaps a remote-controlled toy car, but he had refused. How could I tell my child that his father was cold-hearted? Especially when I saw him write letters to his father every night. He sketched and coloured pictures on his school drawing book and mailed them to Prakhar but never got a reply. The child didn't mind. I think when the heart is pure, it offers love unconditionally.

The weekends were a pain in my heart. On weekdays, my son went to the school and thus half the day was spent there, followed by his tuition and then a trip to the playground. But on weekends, kids from other families went for vacations or leisure trips to restaurants or relatives' places. My child fondly remembered his paternal uncles but everyone had forgotten him. I wanted to fill all the gaps in his innocent life before he came to realise that no one in Prakhar's family liked him. The child was so mirthful, he never complained to his father, never asked him to take him along to his uncle's place. I tried everything in my limited means to give him everything he desired. On Sundays, I took him to a nearby market and bought him things that he needed. Sometimes we ate out and gorged on *dosas* and ice-creams. On one such Sunday, he spotted a big toy store and insisted on going in. I definitely could not afford to buy anything from the shop. He played with every available toy in that shop: from a giant football to a remote-controlled aeroplane, from a toy guitar to a Lego set. Seeing him play with these expensive toys, I stood in a corner and cried.

Every day, I went for an evening stroll. Ever since I had quit working in an office, my life had become sedentary. So, I decided to take small breaks to kill the boredom of being home all day. As I reached the park on weekends, I was filled with a heaviness. The park was mostly empty since all the people were home, spending time with their families.

Was it just about those happy-go-lucky, chirpy women or was there more to the heaviness forming inside my heart? I wondered. Was it a subconscious feeling of loss at not having a perfect home? Not having a husband who stayed with me? Was the husband so important? A Saturday evening made me ponder on this again. I realised that at times, it becomes important to open the stopgaps imposed on our hearts and rant freely.

I had an inherent dislike towards these homemaker women simply because their life was easy because of their ignorance. They did not have to compete or prove to be equal to their husbands. They were happy playing the second fiddle and the home was at peace and harmony. I couldn't do this. My parents had me educated and now I demanded equality at home. This was making my life difficult as expectations had increased. I took out my anger on those hapless, dependent women.

Sometimes I saw Ma sitting on a park bench. When she had no one her age to talk to, she would sit and watch the kids play. One of them was my son but the others? Weren't they all mine? Could kids be disowned by someone? I love all kids like they're mine and I wondered if other women love my kid in the same way.

I sometimes looked up and saw the trees that flanked the gravel path on which I walked. To me, those branches appeared like hands that held on to each other. When I saw a neem tree with yellow and green leaves, I remembered my childhood. When we lived in small quarters, there would always be neem trees growing in the vicinity. As kids, my friends and I would jump all around them. Some women would sit and chat under their shade and sometimes there would be a mynah perched on a tree and I would mimic its chirp. Evenings were when many people came together in harmony. I snapped out of my train of nostalgia. This neem tree had no children playing around it, no women sitting in its shade and no mynah.

There was an eerie stillness in the park. Leaves on trees were left covered with soot from cars. Unfamiliar people crossed me as they jogged; one of them was an old lady in a green cotton sari. She looks frail like my grandmother. I was filled with longing as she came closer to me. How beautiful it would be if I could sink my face into her lap and sob my heart out. I wish I was closer to her. She had judged me so much that it had splintered my heart into burning embers. I yearned to be a child again.

Becoming a mother had unleashed memories of my own childhood. I could see my child growing up and being socially conditioned. When he was born—this little bundle of soft cotton with pink cheeks and twinkling black eyes—I had held him in my arms and felt that all my pains had washed away. Then he started growing, inch by inch, his mind started absorbing situations, conversations and emotions from the world around him. I remember once I slapped him out of anger because of some mischief and later I slapped myself out of guilt. Then one day he had broken a teacup and I was livid. I scolded him and he threatened me saying that he would slap himself. I was taken aback, how quickly he had learnt the tricks of the trade!

That outburst is completely unrelated to the situation and the doer, the receiver and the observer are all clueless. I call it karma, no one can escape from that. For this reason, I like the existence of death, the ultimate leveller and emancipator from all suffering, all sins, all guilt and all regret. I love life as much as I love death. I do not fear it. Let it come when it will, I will welcome it with open arms. But wait death, till my son grows up. I desire for him a life of bliss, till now it has been possible barring some uncommon scolding. But he has not realised that the world is evil. I want to be his shelter, his umbrella. I dream this because I have suffered. I have chosen a profession that makes people drop their jaws.

You Are Getting Exploited

I remember being slapped by Baba once, when I was in the second standard. I kept making mistakes while memorising multiplication tables and he lost his temper. He had never raised his hand on me before. Ma, on the other hand, used to beat me with anything she could get her hands on—mops, pencil boxes, rolling pins. But with time, I got accustomed to her anger and learnt how to avoid her beatings. Often, I would run away to our neighbour's house. With time, I began to resist her and asked her to stop hitting me. The last she hit me was when I was in the eighth standard.

In a nutshell, it had never been physical abuse that was directed to annihilate my self-worth. They were all innocuous childhood beatings that do not quite qualify to be physical abuse in my books. But when it comes to financial and emotional abuse, I have experienced that plenty!

I did experience financial abuse in my first year of college at Pune from Viplav, my then-boyfriend who would be completely dependent on my money to support his lifestyle—dining, shopping, travelling. But soon enough we broke up and the subsequent men I had relationships with were all self-dependent, including my former husband, Prakhar. But the relationship with Rahas changed all that. He came into my life when he had high hopes of fame, money and security. He promised me commitment and love and said he wanted nothing in return. Money was never discussed but I always ended up giving him more and more of it. I always believed that one could detect abuse when one faced it but I now believe that one only knows abuse in retrospect.

In the beginning, I offered him financial help because I wanted to give him wings to fly. I bought him a MacBook, an iPhone, shared his rent, paid his bills and bought flight tickets. I also ordered his groceries. In those days, he told me that he often had to skip meals or go to a *langar* as he did not have money to buy food. In the last three years we had been together, he did not have to skip a single meal. I was determined to improve his life: from the kind of clothes he wore to the meals he ate, I changed everything. I once accompanied him to a flea market where he bought a shirt for Rs 200: it was wrinkled and faded. I could not bear the thought of my beloved wearing a cheap shirt when I was wearing Tommy Hilfiger and other expensive brands.

Immediately afterwards, I asked him his shirt size and bought an expensive Lee shirt and shipped it to Mumbai, where he had moved to look for opportunities in films. His days of penury were over and I willingly took him under my wings. Soon enough, his demands increased, and he asked for an iPad. I was debt-ridden by then because I had separated from Prakhar and he had stopped paying home expenses.

Rahas had become an ungrateful, obstinate sucker. The incessant extravagant spending came to a standstill when I lost my job. He supported me emotionally for those two months and I soon got back on my feet as a self-employed professional. But this time my income had shrunk considerably. I borrowed money, did part-time jobs and barely earned enough to survive. I still ended up spending around Rs 5,000 on him every month. I did not mind him asking for more but somewhere this had caused an inferiority complex in him and he had begun to pinpoint my flaws and say rude things about my age, past relationships and my broken family. He also said terrible things about my looks.

I was a fool to believe all that he said and it added to my woes. In essence, I had grown addicted to his company and it was causing great harm to my happiness and confidence. I felt I that I could go nowhere without his support. He had created a great fear inside me and I believed that I was unsafe without him. Like I said, the abuse was always indirect. I started fearing for my life. Rahas took more money from me and said he would return it later. That never happened. I had grown tired of being a provider. I wanted to be pampered by a man; someone who would take me out to shop and I wouldn't have to worry about the bills. It had been three years since Prakhar had left us and I had forgotten how it was to be with a man who spent on me.

To add to that, Rahas and I had huge fights and most often, the subject was his family. He barely talked about his family and when he did, he said only good things about them. I highly doubted that because every family has its own issues. I said to him, 'I find it hard to believe that in the 22-member joint family of yours, there has not been a single fight in the last 28 years.'

He continued to insist that his was a family from heaven and I continued to believe him. On the professional front I was able to keep afloat and he was a failure. So I could barely relate to him though I still supported him financially. Two people are brought closer when they share their wounds. I did see some rifts in Rahas' family: his father was the lowest-earning member in the whole family. His cousins were all engineers but Rahas and his siblings barely had enough money to finish their undergraduate studies. His family was clearly poor. I had managed his bank account and not a single penny was ever given to him by his family. Whenever he used to go to his home in a small town in UP, he asked me for money. That money was his way of trying to fix a broken home. Sometimes I would walk in on his calls with people back home and I would overhear him talking about some dispute in the family. When I probed him, he got abusive and his face turned red with anger. It is a strange coincidence that all the men I have been in relationships with, have guarded the matters of their home from me, making me feel like an outsider. How can love develop in such a situation?

Things came to a pause when Baba arrived at our home. He asked me if I was saving enough being a single mother and I disclosed that I was supporting Rahas financially for years. In return, I was getting abused and looked down upon. Baba was startled; he asked me to stop giving Rahas money immediately and to distance myself from him. I tried to do it but then Rahas came home and I could not resist him. I did not speak to him for an entire day and fought with him. I had grown sick and tired of Rahas and his dependence on me but it withered in front of my dependence on him. I secretly wished that someday a man would come and rescue me from the clutches of that self-imposed addiction. A worthy man who was intelligent, successful and rich! Was that too much to ask for?

Meaning of Life

Oh sure. Let's have a chat. Always great to have an informal discussion as two friends discussing RedWomb's potential without any baggage. Looking forward to this. Does late in the night, after completing the daily drudgery, suit you?

I was talking to Bhibhu who showed an interest to join me in my sex-positive start-up RedWomb. I told Bhibhu that I was a pleasure specialist, so drudgery was hard to come by for me. What better work than something that revolves around the purest of our carnal desires? For the uninitiated, I never chose this profession but the profession chose me. I was bored but content and coward enough to not leave my regular day job. But life happened, I ended up spending five long years in a sexless marriage and diverting all my energies into work. I felt old at 30, I was obese and had no social life. I was a mess inside while living up to social expectations on the outside. It took me five years and some luck to come out of this trap. Once I was out of my marriage, I discovered that I was attracting the attention of a lot of married men.

Initially, I was happy to receive this attention after a long period of sexual drought but later, with much disgust and disappointment, I found that all that these men were looking for were flings. It made me wonder why marriages don't work and how they continue to thrive even when there is so much unhappiness on the inside? I wondered why people were so obsessed with sex and how they had managed to dehumanise it to a point where emotions and mutual respect had ceased to matter. The questions started giving me sleepless nights and I was befuddled for a long time until I discovered that the shame, taboo and repression attached to sex had turned it into an obsession for people.

I was aghast! It felt bitter when, in my desperate hope to find suitors, every man I met would proposition me for sex. As a result of that, I chose to become a sex educator, to eradicate the social ill of sexual taboos. I was mistaken to be a sex-hungry woman who openly invited sexual proposals, and I wanted to change that negative perception. My thoughtful social media posts on sexual pleasure, yearnings and desires were conveniently misinterpreted by a large section of men and women. Men stealthily flooded my inbox with sexual requests and women from my social circle pretended to not know me. But I was determined! Every incident of sexual objectification and public hesitation about my work made me more resolute. My mentor Gautam says, 'Pallavi, I will distribute chocolates for free if there comes a day when you don't write a controversial post.' He is right! But I did not set out to mock social customs, I was only being true to myself and my inner feelings. I pay the heavy price for the truth every day but I love the relief it brings me.

My unemployed partner, who depended on me for money, had created deep fears in me out of his sense of insecurity. He made me feel that I was being watched and was under continuous surveillance. Even when I went to this friend's house to make out with him, my feet froze with fear. What if he found out? The fear of mental and emotional abuse was imminent. However, I went to his apartment because I did not want to lose the potential of sexual proximity with a man. It had been three years since I had had sex with anyone other than Rahas, my ex-partner, and the boredom was killing me. I felt as if my body was stamped to be accessed only by Rahas and I was desperate to break free of the shackles imposed upon my sexual liberty. I found it difficult to understand how one can commit monogamously. How can love for one man close the doors for all the other people in this world? Love is like light; can you curtail the flow of light? In my soul, I was clear that I was not doing any wrong but the fear of getting caught always lingered at the back of my mind. Social customs decided that I was wrong in pursuing my spontaneous desires. After a day of indecision and shivering, I decided to tell Rahas that I been sexually intimate with another man and sure enough, all hell broke loose after that. It resulted in a violent fight, with him nearly attacking me but then he restrained himself and inflicted harm on himself. I was numb for a while but later, as I regained my awareness, I wanted to let the world know of the pain that a woman is made to feel if she pursues her desires. I was not wrong! Here is an old post of mine that I wrote after that incident.

Hmm...sex, I underestimated your power. You caused a BIG fight between me and my partner yesterday. I was called a whore, a prostitute because I mouth kissed someone. And I don't blame my partner. The social conditioning runs high in everyone's blood. Even lame authors, poets, sex educators, priests. And will I be forgiven if I dare challenge sex? No way. I went to bed without having my dinner yesterday. Contemplating on what I have done. A kiss? A kiss is enough to make my partner leave me. And he loves me a lot. Unflinching, immeasurable love. He cares for me in every way possible, but always on one condition. My body is a temple he worships. And a temple does not allow unauthorised access.

I was under a lot of emotional turmoil yesterday. My partner slapped himself on his face so many times because he could not deal with my transgression. He shook me violently and cried umpteen tears. Yes, you SEX, you made me bend on my knees and agree with him and say, 'Yes, what I did was wrong.' Because I cannot afford to lose him. In a world of vicious tyrants, I cannot lose him, my true partner. So, I said to him what I did was wrong. Sometimes you have to concede to save the relationship.

But I'm having a hearty laugh now to see the mighty status sex is awarded in our lives. How we cringe at the thought of our beloved kissing, making love to someone else. Well, it's just a series of vaccinations before my spirit, my body and my heart are ready to take a head-on challenge with the disease that we have turned sex into. I'm going back to my lab to dissect every thread of this cobweb to decode sex. And in the end, sex will be reincarnated into a lovely, holy, beautiful, intimate thing, which it always was before we made it into a dirty thing. I believe a day will come when every husband will ask his wife to kiss another man, anyone she likes being intimate with and loved by. The body no longer remains a temple, the body finally belongs to the woman herself.

I eventually left Rahas; it all happened at its destined karmic time. I met Anish around the same time as I was moving out of this abusive relationship. Ironically, I got in touch with him a year back for an interview on his marriage as I was bewitched by his understanding of the dynamics of heterosexual relationships. I thought of posting this wise exchange with him on my platform RedWomb where we talk about the real side of a man–woman relationship. We exchanged long intimate emails on sex, love, relationships and monogamy.

Dear Pallavi,

My apologies for taking so long to get back to you.

It so happened that Denise left for Italy in April and since then we have been in an open relationship. Not really 'married'. She was going through a difficult and confusing time and wished to spend time in Italy to clear things and to 'find herself'. She believes that once she finds herself she will know what her 'self' wants. Till then, I feel it is my responsibility to support her on this journey, even though remotely. We are in regular touch but we do not stay together. At the moment we cannot say when we will meet again, and in what form. I can not answer your questions about our non-existent sexual relationship at the moment. All of this happened after your email and I was waiting to reply to you once I had greater clarity on Denise's programme. For now, she stays in Italy.

But regarding sexuality, I believe that sexual monogamy is a personal choice, but the way things are in society, it has been made into a man-made law, a social obligation...It is not a natural law for homo sapiens...lifelong monogamy is a natural law for a very small minority of animals. For most of the others, polygamy works. But man has a more evolved mind and hence makes more evolved and complex choices regarding sexuality, food and other preferences. While the behaviour of animals is determined by their breed, humans' behaviour is dependent on the individual's 'samskaras' (habit patterns, conditioning).

Denise and I both feel that the very concept of 'marriage' (the way it is understood socially) is man-made and not natural. A natural choice is that which comes from within and is not enforced by society. I really believe that our society will one day evolve to accept and embrace sexuality as it is, among other things. That it will no more be a taboo and that couples will not feel let down when one partner has the urge to be with someone else. That one day we will live in a more open, spontaneous, liberal world. At the same time, let me also caution that sex can overpower a person's mind, like any other drug. No matter how much you take it, you are never satisfied. Like everything in life, sex is best with balance. If the balance tilts either way, there is trouble. In India, sex is a taboo. No one talks about it. No couple holds hands in public (never saw my parents do that). The children are not taught about sex either. Nudity is a no-no even in the peak of summer. Women wear ghungat to hide their faces and men keep wondering what treasures lie behind the ghungat and that choli. The suppressed urge becomes a big monster within our repressed mentality. Thus, rapes happen. While in the West, sexual liberty has emancipated the minds of people and have stopped them from obsessing about sex, but they have not been able to strike the right balance. Many couples continue to have secret affairs. Also, many people spend lifetimes participating in orgies. People there often indulge in excessive sex and are never satisfied. So, neither excess nor scarcity. We need balance.

I wrote back to him.

Hi Anish,

Thank you for this honest sharing. I agree with nearly all of what you have said. The suppression becomes a mental sickness and monogamy, even though it can be a personal choice, ends up being a rule most people are forced to follow.

I understand that you are on your journeys to seek meaning in your lives. I am happy that you could take that route as conventional marriage rules dictate that two people remain with each other until they die. We need space and acceptance to follow our heart's callings. Are rules always needed for this?

I know a man who is really attracted to me. He is sixty years old and has led all his life without any attachments. He now has a 'want' to be possessed and to possess. I completely understand him, having had this 'urge' myself recently. He wants to pursue a relationship with me but if his soulmate disagrees, he has said that he will stop talking to me.

This befuddles me. I am also very possessive and jealous of the man I love. Maybe rules are required for a balance.

What kind of rules?

Anish wrote back.

Dear Pallavi,

Denise and I really appreciate this intimate and meaningful conversation with you. Thank you for asking such pertinent questions and sharing your intimate story. I welcome any question or critique to my answer; in every question and discussion, at least one or both of us stand to learn something or understand something better.

In my little experience, the only rules that apply, and will always apply, are that of Existence... the coexistence of Nature and Space, fused together, like the Divine Yoni and Lingam. Nothing, no God or Godlike being, escapes the rules of Existence for Existence is absolute. Within the union of Yin and Yang, infinite seeds of possibilities from the Masculine realm (Space, Shoonya, Omnipotent, Shiva, Man, Yin) are constantly being turned into reality by the Feminine realm in its womb (Nature, Samsara, Omni-facilitator, Shakti, Yang).

Beyond and outside the rules of existence, there are no rules. Man-made rules are self-inflicted and self-accepted imprisonment in an otherwise free coexistence. And with every rule arises a stronger attachment or attraction to what is not allowed by it. In denial lies an attraction. In suppression lies a rebound. In closing a door lies a curiosity to check what's on the other side of it.

So by putting rules, we may, if luck is on our side, forcefully tame our beloved to behave as we want, but their mind will go exactly to the places where they are not allowed to go. In their minds, they are already breaking the rules, so what if they can't do that physically? Does it make a difference in the mental plane? If a body is with us, but the mind is not, is that soul really with us?

Any rules in a relationship are mere expectations of at least one dissatisfied mind, turning a natural and free relationship into ugly bondage. Expectations are mere conjectures of a mind functioning with assumptions stemming from inexperience, underdeveloped intelligence and incomplete knowledge of Existence.

Such artificially forced, mutually 'negotiated' expectations and rules are like a business deal, that is, 'you have to give me this or I am going to fall "out" of love with you. I will get mad at you. I will leave you. I will not even say hello to you if I cross paths with you.' What suffering we give to ourselves! Then to the world... Only because we are ignorant.

A beloved is not a possession. Any rules aimed at possession and exclusive access are like chains of bondage tied with mutual acceptance. They murder love. Any man-made 'law' carries the seed of 'injustice'. Justice means mutual 'need' fulfilment. Not expectation fulfilment.

A mind trying to impose self-made rules, or expectations upon another is not flowing with Love. It results in degeneration and torture in relationships.

Such rules stem from expectations which in turn stem from unverified assumptions about reality. These, in turn, stem from naturally allowed freedom of thought and imagination. Living with such rules is like living in self-imposed imprisonment, often dragging the beloved along to living hell. Or often, people split up and the relationship is done for good!

Everyone wants the right feelings within relationships. Everyone wants freedom, love, trust-based care, harmony, collaboration. Not rule-based bonded labour to please the other partner who is dissatisfied, incomplete, fragile and needs you to behave in a certain way as per their imagination, to make them feel temporarily happy, complete and satisfied. Rules of nature have allowed full freedom to the human mind in its thinking, imagination and activity. The human mind is very powerful but an underdeveloped mind is a power in the hands of madness. It expresses itself as fear, control, oppression-based chemistry in relationships.

Love, when it happens, gives and begets feelings of unconditional acceptance, trust, nurture, respect, appreciation and devotion in relationships. Affection is reserved for someone special. For love, everyone and everything is special or no one is. In love, harmony, justice, freedom come together in one package. They are a state of being, not doing. Caring is an expression of the Being in affection or love. But with rules, these feelings disappear when the rules are broken or forcefully imposed. Living becomes mechanical instead of transcendental and fluid.

When two people are in love, they don't need any self-imposed rules to ensure justice.

Empathy, mutual care, need fulfilment and growth cannot be set forth as rules. They just happen as an expression of love, a free-flowing harmony.

There is no competition over who wins, who rules, who is right, who is better. There is just oneness.

In the feeling of Oneness, there is no need to impose rules. There is consciousness of the collective and coexistence. There is Sam-Bhoga and Sam-Yoga. There is consciousness and bliss. In my opinion, love and understanding are more valuable to a human relationship than a physical orgasm, though the latter is a very powerful and a pleasurable experience too! :)

What is your understanding on this?

I never replied to this email as it lay buried under a mountain of work but as fate would have it, we met after three months. Anish was in town for some work and he reached out to me complimenting me as a fellow warrior.

He felt that if we met, we could have an enlightening discussion on life, ways of living and people. The idea stoked my desire to meet this person whose thoughtful and incisive email had already left an impact on me. I agreed and we met after a week. In between, we spoke a few times and I personally was dumbfounded to find my curiosity rising about this man. He seemed different from everyone I had met so far, whether a yogi, thinker, social worker, entrepreneur, employed professionals. This man was on to something unique which was aboriginal and yet enriching. It added icing to the cake that he was an excellent poet too.

The day we met, it was raining. We did not speak as much as I expected but whatever little I spoke, my desire to stay close to this man and understand life from its basic precincts increased phenomenally. Anish had passed out from IIT Kanpur and landed a plum job in a big MNC but left it all 10 years back to go back to his roots, in fact, all the roots—the village, forests and nature. I came to know this after I started reading about him, gathering tits and bits from whatever source I had. I was stunned. I had seen people preaching the path of self-discovery and here was this bespectacled man, living the path of self-discovery. What difference did it make? Well, as Anish's mother put it, as I saw her stacking and ironing Anish's clothes, 'He does not iron his clothes.' Anish says that clothes are only to stay protected and not to look glamorous. Isn't this a deep wisdom that most of us have forgotten? I remember buying clothes on a credit card that only added to my monthly loan for each of my public appearances. At one time in my life, I found myself getting addicted to shopping simply because it gave me a temporary high and excitement, or was, as Anish puts it aptly, a 'painkiller'.

But the two days we met were not enough as I had to get back to my house by late evening. I decided, or rather I would say, his naturalness induced me to follow him all the way to the village of Saalig, where he currently lives. As a single mother, solo trips are a luxury for me. So it took me some time to figure out where to keep my family since I wanted this to be a solo journey and wanted to keep aside all the attachments and relationships for a while. The decision came with tremendous guilt since I would be staying away from my eight-year-old son for a long time. His father had already forgotten him and it caused me heartache to leave him with my parents. At least one of the parents should stay with him—which was my rationale—but the growing desire to enter this tunnel of light shown by Anish where I would discover my innate being in the lap of nature amidst the people of the hinterland superseded every guilt I had. In the end, I tried to sabotage my guilt by taking permission from my child about this trip. I nudged him one morning at five as he was in a deep slumber. I asked him, 'Can I go for this trip Chiku? It is really important for me, for this life.' and he replied, half-awake, 'Mama, you go. It's important. You finish your work and come back.' His consent alleviated a lot of guilt and I packed my bags and left for Saalig.

Well, the guilt was not alleviated completely but came back in spurts. As I boarded the bus to Dharamshala, the nearest town to Saalig, I found myself whimpering, longing for my child. But then I managed to control myself and started living the dream and hopes that took me this far. Upon arrival, I felt slightly edgy as Anish was late by almost 45 minutes. The village is a 45-minute drive from the main city of Dharamshala. I was filled with apprehension—how would I live in this village that you cannot even reach through public transport? But even that 45-minute wait in that snowy winter was full of life learnings. I took shelter near the gate of a suburban mall. The guard did not allow me to enter the building since it was not yet the opening time of the mall. 'They will capture everything in the CCTV.' I wondered if there was any rule that could supersede human life. I would surely fall sick if I stood there for a few more minutes. Eventually, my shivering found some empathy in the guard and he let me in.

Finally, Anish came and I merrily dumped my bags in the trunk of the car. We embraced. I felt shy in front of the guards. But the hug washed away all the discomfort I had from the time I left my son until the time I waited in that morning rush of howling winds and raging snowflakes. I reached his house. It was situated at the corner of a road and had a wide verandah and two dogs. I had been terrified of dogs all my life but the Anish said, 'You should not live in assumptions. Look at them. Do you really find them to be your foes, wanting to harm you?' I looked at the dogs and found them to be flawless beings. They would bark at strangers but swerve their tails around the people they know. I learnt a lot from those dogs—Snehi and Kaali. How they waited patiently for their food even if it was mid-noon and never complained. Sometimes, they squinted in a sign of reciprocation if I tried to talk to them.

Those dogs have become an integral part of my life, accompanying me on my walks, guiding me on roads where I lost my way. In a surprise turn of events, I even fed them biscuits from my palm. Anish was right! We tend to live in unverified assumptions. Let assumptions be based on reality as it is. Should I refrain from saying that he is an incredibly charming young man with a sweet effin beard? I smugly confess, initially it was the lure of this man that made me dive deep into the realities of life, social upliftment, the cause of undivided human society that he is living, feeling, seeing and making. Yes, in my quest to accompany this man, all of this attraction sprung from his cause, I readily agreed to offer myself as a volunteer. But as I started living in this village, I started doing sundry household chores such as handwashing clothes, cooking, sweeping, brooming, washing utensils and at the end of the day drew deep fulfilment and contentment. I realised something has changed inside me as I have started to live more naturally. In the evenings, Anish goes to teach children for free in a mud house he has named Gurukul. True to its tradition and founding ethos, Anish inculcates value education and life education in those kids.

Every evening, Anish and I used to teach children for free in a mud house that he had named Gurukul. Upon going to the village, the silence of the mountains and the warmth of the villagers touched my soul. I fell in the love with the simplicity of village life, the spiritual journey of this man, and our intellectual and sexual chemistry as a couple living in the same house. With Anish, I realised the depth of sexual intimacy one can get in a steady relationship. I loved pleasuring him—on every inch of his skin—from head to toe.

Sometimes, during our lovemaking, we used to crack jokes, as I would ask him to seduce me in Punjabi—his native language. Sometimes, I would scream and groan at the top of my voice with pleasure. Sex with him was an unparalleled experience. We would turn off the lights while a giant window would face us with moonlight beaming on the windowpanes.

I had every possible sexual experimentation with Anish. Once, he had recorded our lovemaking while nibbling the side of my neck with his teeth. After that, we watched the film together. He looked like an incarnation of a Greek god and had every possible lovemaking trick in his armour to make me reach zenith of orgasms.

For the first time, I realised that reckless flings with random men stand nowhere in comparison to regular, steady sex with a partner who is full of love, emotion, respect, knowing and getting comfortable with each other's bodies, and talking about the lovemaking and plans to make it richer, better and different. From a reckless pursuit of relationships and trying to get out of the abusive relationship with Rahas, here I was—locked down in the pandemic with Anish for three months. In this forced exile, I discovered new relationships—with self, with children, with nature and with a man. I had been running amok, writing non-stop about sexuality that included vivid details of lovemaking, and I encouraged people to do the same non-anonymously. I felt it was necessary because I was tired of people putting masks and suffering or lusting within because of their sexual fantasies as they could not get social approval.

But this time, I was in a village with a yogi who had forsaken materialistic life and settled for altruism. He was my 'monk who sold his Ferrari' and I fell deeply, madly and crazily in love with him. From being an entrepreneur who was dreaming of raising million-dollar funding for her sextech start-up, getting featured in the most popular publication and working extensively on increasing her PR footprint, I became, in a span of a month, a demure woman who harboured dreams of a home with this yogi—the dream of her own nest. I became so content in doing household work that I lagged in my work, or rather I chose to lag in my work. But Anish was not a typical man; he was usually by himself and it took me a lot of time to give him the space he cherished for himself and thus I found myself all alone. How was I supposed to deal with this solitude? Something in me made me stick to my own space in order to let him enjoy his. It was difficult on the first day. Anish was reading something at his desk and I took a book of poetry and went to the other room.

Inside the room, I sat on an armchair. I opened the book and started reading the lines loudly. It seemed amusing to me as I had never done that before. But I continued reciting it until I started emoting the feelings behind the lines—the pain, the angst, the frustration and the hope. It was a poetry collection by Dushyant Kumar. I spent an hour reciting almost 10 poems in varied emotions. It was my first time by myself in many years not doing work but something else. I was partly successful.

Over time, I morphed my lifestyle around Anish. I would wake up in the morning, do the dishes, clean the house, feed the dogs and then go out for a walk. I was happy seeing this new avatar of mine as throughout my city-bred years, I was an aggressive, workaholic woman. This time, the only work was housework and I started enjoying this domestic life more. I would wipe the kitchen platform thrice a day, stretch the cramped folds on the bedsheet if someone sat on it and even a pint of dust would not escape my eyes. Some days, I would be exhausted after relentlessly doing household chores and would plead with Anish for help. He had become nonchalant after I took up duties, and would often keep his leftover plate on the platform instead in the sink. I took it all on myself, becoming his mother and lover. It was taxing!

Some days, I used to sit and ponder about loss of work, about how I am struggling at work. I would draw satisfaction from teaching the village kids. But it would not compensate for my intellectual pursuits. Anish's love and the mind-boggling sexual chemistry kept these thoughts at bay. Our days were also ridden with conflicts; Anish was fixated on a certain style of thinking, a certain philosophy of life, and was closed to others. He was mostly closed to feedback, even from a well-wisher like me. Anish, because of the influence of his spiritual teachers who considered sex as an obstacle to reach higher dimensions of life, would time and again withdraw sex from me. He decision of becoming a celibate left me puzzled, heartbroken and angry over this sudden change. It also made me sick to find that he equated our sexual intimacy as a mere carnal desire, and I found extremely insulting and juvenile.

I could not adjust to his smoking and drinking pursuits. I had never been with anyone who was a regular smoker or drinker and I found it difficult when a group of men strode inside our house and sat for hours, filling the room with bluish, nicotine-laden exhales. A young man in his twenties once, unable to maintain his state after drinking a full bottle, lurched and yelled in the veranda causing public embarrassment. I was furious and stomped in the room and banged the door with a thud. Anish, in his defensiveness, did not find anything wrong even when I pointed how my eight-year-old child can live in this environment? To my utter dismay, he said it is good for a child to be exposed to all kinds of people (couth and uncouth) so that the child can learn what to emulate and what not to. At that time, I only had sympathy for Anish that he lacked rationale to see through this simple incident.

Anish was going through his own internal struggles. On the outside, his life philosophy dictated that one should be happy in all circumstances. I found it difficult. For me and for all conscious life on this earth, pain and other feelings are equally valid emotions. I could see Anish carrying the mammoth weight of this expectation imposed on his self—to be happy under all circumstances. It made him addicted to smoking and drinking. It made him distant from his life dreams. I wanted to help him by being the symbol of selfless love. I had forgotten myself in the process of loving him. My day would start with him and end with him. It was him and just him. I sometimes feel that this love obsession gives oneself an excuse to distract from other difficulties of life—financial, aspirational, spiritual and otherwise. I lost out on contracts and investments, and kept a part-time job to pay my bills. But I was happy since I was wholeheartedly consumed in the process of loving him. Yes, I loved him 'too much'.

Each time we had a fight, he would withdraw himself sexually from me, which was immensely pain. After we used to make up and reach an agreement (where almost every time, I had to acquiesce), he would again have sex with me. The relationship was completely one-sided. It was all about his philosophy, his choices and his decisions. For me, the sole consolation was that he was there with me. On the upside, I liked his altruism where he did not believe in hoarding money for his self-interest. He was, and still is, a big-hearted man and would help needy villagers in the times of their dire financial needs. If any child who would come home to study forget their lunch, he would eagerly share food with them. Sometimes, I would get irked because other villagers never invited us for meals, and it was us who would treat all our guests with meals upon his insistence. I wanted to ask him why they never invited us in return but did not have the courage to ask that as he would feel bad.

Yes, a relationship is a mirror, and he provided me a mirror to deal with my shortcomings too. I never knew that I have latent anger inside me as the men I dated or was with in all my previous relationships were far more masculine and hot-tempered. I consider it a matter of pride that I still have managed to retain my femininity in a world where women compete with

men by being like them. But Anish was relatively soft-spoken barring episodic outbursts of anger. I remember once I was taking an online session and he was cooking in the kitchen. The clink and clutter of utensils were creating disturbance in proceeding with my client session, and I was fuming with rage. I was angrier as he could not understand this on his own. I lashed out at him by spewing harsh words. I could not comprehend the source of this unjustified anger that originated inside me. It was something more than what had happened that day in the kitchen.

I later realised with the help of my friend Joyee that I was trying too hard to be a good, pristine woman—one who endures everything in her relationship, one who forsakes her personal interests, her rights and her desires to adapt to a man who is less willing to change. A relationship is never a one-sided street; it needs joint effort of two people willing to change, accommodate and bear. Anish could never do that, be it reducing his nicotine or alcohol consumption or focusing more on work and less on inessential village chatter. He just could not change his life for good: I would, on the other hand, try to mend my mistakes whenever he highlighted them. So I always lived on the edge and hence, sometimes, on the most naïve of the occasions, I lost my cool simply because my long-suppressed inner voice emerged. Then, it would not be a reaction but an explosion!

One such explosion became the reason of my untimely exit from his house and probably the dream I had built around him. It was a Sunday and we decided to take assessments of children home-schooling with us. Anish called the children in batches at different slots along with their parents. We had decided that we would wake up early and complete all the housework by 10 am so that we get free for taking tests when the children would arrive. I woke up at 6 am and saw Anish sleeping peacefully, cosily in his blanket. I couldn't bring myself to wake that soul submerged in sleep and decided to do all the housework alone. By 7:30 am, I finished doing the dishes, cleaning and bathing, and I gently prodded him.

'Hey! it's quarter to ten.'

Anish woke up in a jiffy upon hearing this. He then realised that it was a light banter and there was still time aplenty. He then had a glass of warm water and went to the nearby ration shop to buy some groceries. One of the parents were our close family friends and we had invited them for a South Indian lunch of idlis. I then busied myself in the kitchen preparing for the lunch.

At 10 am, his first student Akhil arrived with his father. I did not like that student much since I found him competing for Anish's attention. Once he had suggested Anish for an all-men bath in a far-flung lake. The other kids were smaller and were busy playing among themselves while Akhil sat with Anish mostly. Another reason for not liking him was because of his father who was a compulsive smoker. On earlier occasions too, whenever his father visited our home, he would develop the urge to smoke as soon as he stepped inside the home. I loathed him. But Anish disliked my segregating behaviour with these men and asked me to maintain politeness with them. That day, I tried to do that even when Akhil came inside and asked for a matchbox.

It was for his father who wanted to smoke. I detested his father's impulse for nicotine on the day of his son's test but, nonetheless, I stuck to Anish's philosophy of giving all humans equal respect irrespective of their habits and addictions. I politely refused Akhil and then went to meet his father to greet him and asked him tea to which he declined. In about ten minutes, Anish came out of the bathroom and after dressing up, he sat near Akhil's father. To my utter surprise and anguish, Anish took out a cigarette and offered one to Akhil's father. They both smoked in front of the minor as he took the test. I was crestfallen and seething with rage.

Since morning, I had been running from pillar to post to make all the preparations alone, from cleaning and tidying the house to cooking, and this is the end result of it. I was flabbergasted! To make the matters worse, Akhil was having some difficulty in answering some questions to which I hinted Anish not to smoke in front of the teenager. Anish hit back at me. 'It is because of your interference that he is not able to focus.'

It was enough for me. I went to the kitchen and was determined not to support Anish in the rest of the examination. Soon other parents started arriving and Anish came inside to check on me. I blasted in rage. 'What did you do just now? You smoked on the day of the examination in front of a child?' Anish realised his mistake and said sorry but it was too small a word to cope for my disappointment with him and his love for the company of those compulsive smokers. Instead of helping them transform, he was promoting smoking. I felt it is again a cosmetic sorry and he would soon get back to his old ways of smoking at get-togethers. I don't know why I overreacted this much, perhaps because of months of bottled up pain and anger found an outlet and it exploded. I walked out of the house and went to the house of our neighbour, an 80-year-old widow, and sobbed uncontrollably in front of her. Amma, as we used to fondly call her, was childless and stayed alone. She was curious to know the reason behind my desolate wails and I kept on dismissing it stating that I am missing my son (whom I had left at my parent's home). But she would not believe it. 'You are hiding something,' she claimed rightly.

I stayed at her home for the next three hours talking about her life, her loneliness, as she wept narrating how she had taken to tobacco after her husband's death as it gets her sleep. I helped her apply cement on the floor and then I lied on her warm, rugged cot chatting with her. After some time, I felt relieved and by that time the examination was getting over too. I stood up and left for home. There, parents were going away with their kids and some women asked me where I had been all this while. At that moment, I felt it was a hasty decision for me to walk out of home. After all, I had a relationship with the children, and they did not do any wrong that I compromised on their studies by not taking their assessment. I was filled with remorse once I gained composure.

However, I was still furious with Anish and ignored him as he walked past me. Anish had to meet an architect who was doing the house of his friend Kamal. I pretended to not see him as he closed the gate. I was really brutal then. Once he left the house, I quietly went near the iron grill to see him from a distance. I was still in love with him—intense love—but my anger stopped me from expressing it to him. He went to the shop, located 600 metres away, and I continued to gaze at him, fully assured that he cannot see me looking at him. Yes, I was vulnerable in love and I wanted to protect my vulnerability so that I get my rights from him.

He came home by 7 pm and switched off all the lights of house. I was lying in the outer room as I saw the house engulfed in a veil of darkness. I got worried; the issue was spinning out of control and was becoming bitter with no end in sight. What was I to do? I started panicking and, in a moment, decided to drop my guard and talk to him. I actually hoped he would come to me, seek forgiveness and mend but nothing of that sort happened. I was left on my own to repair the damage. It was a gruelling effort as I was to face his wrath. I went inside the room where he was pretending to sleep. I had checked his status on Facebook a few minutes back and he was online. I gently nudged him but he kept on pretending to be asleep. I called him but he did not respond. I then said, 'I know you are awake. You were online just five minutes back.'

He then said that he is not my servant that he needs to reply any time I want him to. His silence was becoming unbearable and I insisted to talk with him. But he declined and said he is not in a position to speak. My fury and my hurt feeling were rising acutely and I alerted him—'If you don't listen to me, I am not going to stay in this house.'

He told me to leave and I stomped to my room, thinking about how all this love and all this effort were in vain when I cannot even get him to talk to me for two minutes. I booked my flight tickets to Jharkhand impulsively. That whole night, we slept in different rooms. I don't know about him, but I did not sleep the entire night. The next day, I woke up, dragged my suitcase in the living hall and started stacking my clothes. It was painful! I had never thought that I would have such an abrupt departure from a home I tended to like a mother. I was weeping inside but still doing the packing.

Anish woke up at 9 am and asked me if I had booked my tickets. I nodded. My heart was spilling with love for him, and I was torn inside as I realised that in some time, I will be thousands of miles away from my beloved. The frantic cries of separation scavenged my peace and yet I was trying to keep a calm exterior for he has not approached me. I thought of packing and then going back to my room but seeing the house untidy, I could not stop myself from doing the chores that I had been doing for the last three months. Yes, it is my house too and I cannot stop loving this house. I picked up the broom and went about my routine as usual. It was when I was cleaning the dishes that Anish came near me and asked if he could talk for some time. I was frozen with hurt and disbelief but followed him. We sat facing each other and then Anish folded his hands and apologised to me. I was stunned! 'I did wrong and I should not have done that in front of the children. I will take care of it next time.'

Hearing this, I burst in tears, crying inconsolably. I started repenting why I booked my tickets in such a hurry. How would I bear separation with this man I loved most in the world, even more than my child?! Anish hugged me and I wailed, so much that it moistened his t-shirt. He comforted me and said that is a temporary separation and it is also a moment of scrutiny for him if he can fulfil his promise. He said we will meet soon, and I left the place with a heavy heart.

But once I reached home, things took an ugly turn. Anish's father intervened to my surprise and said you are moving too fast in this relationship and that they had not been consulted and we solely decided our relationship. It was a jolt for me as I had always been on friendlier terms with his parents. I tried to assuage Anish but his father said its better if we stay in two separate homes. Anish, to my surprise, said this is the right thing to do. The sudden change in the status of our relationship usurped my peace. I fought back saying it is wrong and was not promised. But Anish, fixated on his philosophy of unending happiness, chided me at not been able to maintain a stable state of mind. How could I? I am just being human. I felt helpless; each time I tried to protest, he would bring up that I am being agitated, I am not in harmony and, thus, I am not a good addition to his life and to the project.

The emotional upheaval continued for different reasons—my longing to go back to meet him was dismissed by him as desperation (wrong feeling); my insistence to stay with him in the same house and being in a monogamous relationship. We mostly interacted on chats for he would not pick up my phone daily. The chats and the words often get misinterpreted and he would not even allow me to explain my stand. The man has changed.

The breaking point in our relationship came when he talked about inviting another female friend to his house in my absence. I was hurt, knowing fully well what might happen if a man and a woman stay in the same house alone for a week. I protested to which he said that he doesn't want any person to control his sexuality, be it following celibacy, monogamy or non-monogamy. I found it unable to discern. Just a month back, he advocated celibacy as a route to spiritual enlightenment. It was a double-edged sword, the more I failed to understand him, the more the mystery of this person allured me.

Anish is otherwise a nice man, his kindness, his detachment to material pleasure, his intellect, his mission to make the world a better place made me fall in love passionately with him. As my friend Joyee says, the concept of love is beautiful but to love 'love' is hard because it also means loving the other person's imperfections. But there is a difference between accepting someone's imperfections and accepting someone's abuse. I felt it at the time a documentary on my life is being released. I had shot this documentary before I met Anish.

This documentary chronicles the journey of my sexuality, my intimate tales with men, social judgements and ridicules of my profession of being a sex coach, covert offers from lusty, unhappily married men because they think a woman openly talking about sex can be easy to take to bed, my sexless marriage and my quest to claim my sexual pleasure and independence. In the documentary, I am shown doing a sensual dance where I am cupping my breasts, talking about my masturbation experience and my stand on infidelity as something natural that can happen in a monotonous marriage. Yes, it is true but is controversial by social norms which emphasise on status quo. The documentary is aesthetically shot, and I was delighted to see the initial rushes. I showed it to Anish thinking he will respect my courage, as he did in the beginning when he mailed me for the first time. 'Pallavi you are a warrior taking up an issue that very few people in the society have the courage to talk about.'

But ever since I entered into a relationship with him, he has changed his outlook on my profession. After watching this documentary, he warned me that it will dent my 'image'. People will see me as a slut, a pornographic actress, a woman who is easy to take to bed. His family and the villagers will be embarrassed that I shot bold scenes (I am only shown cupping my breasts while being fully clothed). He said that the best thing for me would be that the film flops so that no one watches it.

I knew I am right; that the objective of shooting this video intellectually uncensored is to bring out the inner voice of a woman who has been sexually objectified and used by men since centuries. It is no wonder that even in 2019, more than 60 per cent of Indian women do not get an orgasm. Their partners (men) are unaware of female sexual pleasure, female anatomy and simply ejaculate (that too within minutes), and then turn their backs and sleep leaving them high and dry.

But Anish did not listen and yes, his stereotyped thinking is a mirror of the larger society who treats woman in public like Sita (a central female character in the Hindu epic, Ramayana, known for her dedication, self-sacrifice, courage and purity) but wants her to be horny in their bedroom. I understand where he was coming from. Also, as my friend Joyee said, it is a way for patriarchal men to protect their women from public ridicule. I was afraid to lose Anish and despite my past bold self, getting into a relationship with the man and eventually his family made me think about the consequences of audacity I had shown in the documentary. I told him (under pressure to comply) that yes, certain scenes could have been changed. But then later, I shared it with Joyee and she was aghast on knowing the words Anish had used for me.

'Pallavi, you need to take a stand for yourself and your work. A person who respects you should respect your work as well. There are tons of movies—*Satyam Shivam Sundaram*, *Ram Teri Ganga Maili*, *Jism*, *Fire*, *Earth*, etc.— where protagonists are exposing. Hasn't he watched them? Damn! When he stayed with you for three months, slept with you, he knew about your work, right? Why did he not think of his family then? And now suddenly this family is coming in between? Pallavi think about it from a third person perspective? What advice would give you to a woman in this situation?'

Her words were a wake-up call for my dormant soul. How could I acquiesce to a man's irrational terms and conditions? I was enraged and wrote back to him fiercely—

Anish,

I need to share one thing. I don't care about what other people think of me. When I chose this subject, I knew it will ruffle feathers because most Indians are used to watch porn and molest women in their bedrooms. The same people who you say will call me slut, etc. Have they watched porn? And if yes, why?

Does someone who has watched porn even has a right to say that I talk about sex in the open? Isn't this hypocrisy? Tell me. Seventy per cent of Indian women do not get any orgasm, their husbands simply ejaculate and leave them high and dry.

When you first reached out to me, you understood the importance of this work and you respected me (as you said there are very few people in this country who have the courage to do this). Such people will always be under the scanner.

There will be trolling but the film will make an impact on the lives of women I have aimed to, who are suppressed and objectified. The film will give them their voice. I am sure the film will get raving reviews as an act of courage. Hope, at least after this, a rapist or a roadside assaulter will think twice before molesting a woman. This brazenness is the need of the hour for women.

About touching breasts, you know there is way more nudity in Indian films. Families watch them, why? Anish, I was agreeing all this time because you are important for me, but I shot this documentary with a very different purpose. Women have been subjugated and molested since centuries by men. They need to find their bold and fearless voice. This film is that voice.

There is no nudity in this documentary. And it will get critical acclaim and positive reviews because it is addressing the issue of female subjugation, Anish.

Rapes are manifestation of power exerted by man on a woman in a patriarchal society. Think about it. This is so unfortunate that the same men who watch porn sneakily in our society, who watch naked women, who might have entered this profession out of financial need and abduction, they will judge my film. I would say every man who has watched porn is the client of a SLUT!

After writing this, I took a deep breath. This is a rare time I dared to raise my voice against his oppressive mindset and I was all ready for a bash, a retaliation from his side, a threat of a breakup or a threat of not being allowed to come back to village. But surprisingly he was calm in his response.

'Okay! Let's just relax. :)' He used a smiley.

Although, he did not say it explicitly but it was an indication that he understood my reasons. Yes, our relationship is going through turbulent phases, especially in the pandemic when I could not go back and meet him. I had to persevere. Surprisingly, the children at the village are playing cupid between me and Anish, calling me often and asking me to come back. My love-hate relationship with Anish and life continues. I am yearning to have sex with Anish...

ABOUT THE AUTHOR

Pallavi Barnwal has always lived on the razorblade edge of life, from being born in a dysfunctional family to living through a series of failed relationships. Her unconventional life experiences have shaped and enriched her mission of bringing happiness and contentment in the intimate lives of people. Having worked for a decade in the corporate, she left it all after realising the futility of the rat race and instead chose a field that had many people drop their jaws the moment they heard it—sex education. She founded a sex-positive start-up, wrote in leading national dailies on sexual pleasure and gave a TEDx talk on the importance of having conversations around sex in families. Her work has been well received across sections of all age groups and genders.